THE AGING CONSUMER

Perspectives from Psychology and Economics

Edited by

Aimee Drolet

University of California, Los Angeles

Norbert Schwarz

University of Michigan

Carolyn Yoon

University of Michigan

Routledge
Taylor & Francis Group
New York   London

See. www.consumerpsychologyarena.com

Routledge
Taylor & Francis Group
270 Madison Avenue
New York, NY 10016

Routledge
Taylor & Francis Group
27 Church Road
Hove, East Sussex BN3 2FA

© 2010 by Taylor and Francis Group, LLC
Routledge is an imprint of Taylor & Francis Group, an Informa business

Printed in the United States of America on acid-free paper
10 9 8 7 6 5 4 3 2 1

International Standard Book Number: 978-1-84872-810-3 (Hardback) 978-1-84872-811-0 (Paperback)

Library of Congress Cataloging-in-Publication Data

The aging consumer : perspectives from psychology and economics / edited by
Aimee Drolet, Norbert Schwarz, Carolyn Yoon.
    p. cm.
Includes bibliographical references and index.
ISBN 978-1-84872-810-3 -- ISBN 978-1-84872-811-0
    1. Older consumers. 2. Consumer behavior. 3. Consumption (Economics)
4. Marketing. I. Drolet, Aimee Leigh. II. Schwarz, Norbert, Dr. phil. III. Yoon,
Carolyn, 1960-

HF5415.332.O43A385 2010
658.8'340846--dc22   2009045729

**Visit the Taylor & Francis Web site at
http://www.taylorandfrancis.com**

**and the Psychology Press Web site at
http://www.psypress.com**

THE
AGING
CONSUMER

Marketing and Consumer Psychology Series

Curtis P. Haugtvedt, Ohio State University
Series Editor

For Donna, Leon, Genevieve, and Peter

Aimee Drolet

Contents

Section 1   What Changes With Aging?

Section 2   Decision Making

Section 3   Older Consumers in the Marketplace

About the Editors

Aimee Drolet is Associate Professor of marketing at UCLA, Anderson School of Business. She is a psychologist who studies consumer decision making. In particular her research focuses on the mental processes that underlie consumers' judgments and choices. Much of her recent research is on elderly consumers.

Norbert Schwarz is Charles Horton Cooley Collegiate Professor of psychology at the University of Michigan, where he also holds positions as Professor of marketing and Research Professor in the Institute for Social Research. His research focuses on human cognition, communication and judgment, including its implications for consumer behavior. He has been elected to the American Academy of Arts and Sciences and the German National Academy of Science *Leopoldina*.

Carolyn Yoon is Associate Professor of marketing at the Ross School of Business, University of Michigan. She holds appointments as Associate Professor of psychology and as faculty associate in the Research Center for Group Dynamics of the Institute for Social Research. Her research centers on understanding memory, cognition and judgment processes across the life span in social and consumer related contexts. She is a leading expert in the field of consumer neuroscience.

Contributors

Eric J. Arnould   Department of Management and Marketing, College of Business, University of Wyoming

Carolyn M. Bonifield   Department of Marketing, School of Business Administration, University of Vermont

Gary Burtless   The Brookings Institution, Washington, DC

Michael Champion   Department of Psychology, College of Arts and Sciences, Florida State University

Neil Charness   Department of Psychology, College of Arts and Sciences, Florida State University

Catherine A. Cole   Department of Marketing, Henry B. Tippie College of Business, University of Iowa

Carolyn Folkman Curasi   Department of Marketing, Robinson College of Business, Georgia State University

Aimee Drolet   Department of Marketing, UCLA Anderson School of Management, Los Angeles

Fred Feinberg   Department of Marketing, Ross School of Business, University of Michigan

Angela H. Gutchess   Department of Psychology, College of Arts and Sciences, Brandeis University

Michael D. Hurd   Center for the Study of Aging, The RAND Corporation, Santa Monica, California

Hyewook Genevieve Jeong   Department of Marketing, UCLA Anderson School of Management, Los Angeles

Raphaëlle Lambert-Pandraud   Department of Marketing, ESCP Europe, Paris, France

Gilles Laurent Department of Marketing, HEC Paris, France

Loraine Lau-Gesk Department of Marketing, The Paul Merage School of Business, University of California, Irvine

Melayne M. McInnes Department of Economics, Moore School of Business, University of South Carolina

Harry R. Moody The Office of Academic Affairs, AARP, Washington, DC

Ellen Peters Decision Research, Eugene, Oregon

Linda L. Price Department of Marketing, Eller College of Management, University of Arizona

Susann Rohwedder Center for the Study of Aging, The RAND Corporation, Santa Monica, California

Norbert Schwarz Department of Psychology and Department of Marketing, Ross School of Business, University of Michigan

Judith A. Shinogle Maryland Institute for Policy Analysis and Research, University of Maryland, Baltimore County

Sanjay Sood Department of Marketing, Anderson School of Management, University of California, Los Angeles

Patti Williams Department of Marketing, The Wharton School, University of Pennsylvania

Stacy L. Wood Department of Marketing, Moore School of Business, University of South Carolina

Carolyn Yoon Department of Marketing, Ross School of Business, University of Michigan

Ryan Yordon Department of Psychology, College of Arts and Sciences, Florida State University

Series Foreword

One of the goals of the Marketing and Consumer Psychology Book series is to provide a forum for discussion of academic and practitioner views on issues important to consumers, consumer researchers, practitioners, and policy makers. *The Aging Consumer*, edited by Drolet, Schwarz, and Yoon, highlights critical dimensions of a topic important to all of us, personally, professionally, and socially. Accomplished researchers and practitioners discuss challenges and opportunities in addressing the fast growing and increasingly complex market segment of aging consumers. This book will be of great interest to policy makers and strategists in a wide range of public and private institutions with goals of enhancing the lives of consumers. Likewise, the authors of the book chapters challenge basic and applied researchers as to future studies needed to better understand and predict the behaviors of aging consumers. Finally, all of us, as "aging consumers," will find insights in this book that may help us make better decisions regarding our own futures and those of our loved ones.

Curtis P. Haugtvedt
Series Editor
Ohio State University

Preface

Population aging is a worldwide phenomenon. At present, about 45 million Americans are over the age of 65, and by 2020, one out of every six Americans will be 65 or older. Over the next several decades, the proportion of older adults (age 65 and over) in all major industrial countries will increase rapidly as the share of the total adult population declines. The ramifications of an aging population are serious and potentially enormous. As the median age of the world rises from 29 to 38 by 2050, the labor force will shrink and more people will become pensioners, leaving fewer younger workers to sustain growth and the strength of economies all over the world.* Indeed, according to many, the economic woes of population aging will be far greater than anything experienced at present or in the past. However, many researchers, appear unaware of the existence of the phenomenon.

Population aging originates from two sources. First, for the past 200 years, people everywhere have been living longer, healthier lives. At present, an average person in the developed world is expected to live to 78, and an average person from a developing country is expected to live to 67.† The rising number of older adults is more than the result of aging baby boomers. It is reflective of a worldwide phenomenon in developing and developed countries alike since the Industrial Revolution. Second, in addition to a longer lifespan, people are having fewer children. Because of the high cost of food, clothing, education, and entertainment, raising children has been becoming increasingly expensive. Currently, the birthrate in developed countries is 1.6 children per woman, and the worldwide average is expected to drop from 2.6 children to 2 by 2050.‡ As more people reach retirement age, there will be fewer younger workers left to replace them in the workforce.

Many developed countries are already on an inescapable path to population aging. Although not quite apparent now, developed countries with small families like Spain, Germany, and Italy will notice visible signs by 2020.§ For other countries, mostly those in the developing world, a younger population may ward off population aging for now, but they, too, will face the same set of problems eventually. Greater longevity and lower fertility

---

* United Nations. World Population Prospects: The 2008 Revision (p. 13). 8/22/09. [http://www.un.org/esa/population/publications/wpp2008/wpp2008_highlights.pdf]. 2009.

† United Nations. *World Population Prospects: The 2008 Revision* (p. 14).

‡ United Nations. *World Population Prospects: The 2008 Revision* (p. 64).

§ The Economist. *A slow-burning fuse.* 8/22/09. [http://www.economist.com/specialreports/displaystory.cfm?story_id=13888045]. 6/27/09

are universal trends. For some countries, the consequences of population aging are already a reality.

For example, since the end of World War II, the median age of Japan has doubled from the low 20s to mid 40s.* Once hailed for its innovation and industry, the age cohort that has brought the country enormous growth until the 1980s is now in retirement. In fact, the country's population of 127 million people is projected to drop below 100 million by 2046.† Although the Japanese government has been actively pursuing numerous initiatives to avert the graying of the country, efforts to encourage higher birth rates have met with little success. This is largely because like many women in other developed countries, Japanese women are increasingly postponing childbirth and marriage in favor of longer working hours. As of yet, there have been no signs of a reversal of fewer children and more elderly people.

Declining fertility rates at a time when a large portion of the population is nearing retirement age is a trend that is being experienced by most developed countries. One notable exception is the United States. An intersection of welcoming labor markets and flexible immigration policies has allowed the United States to keep the fertility rate close to the equilibrium point between birth rate and death rate.‡ Yet, just like developing countries where the population age is still young, population aging may only be a few decades away.

In addition to its overall effect on the economy, population aging may alter the consumer market in several ways. According to the life-cycle theory of saving and consumption, people will vary their consumption habits depending on their age, marital status, and economic resources. People will try to save during their middle years and spend more than their income (i.e., dis-save) in their old age. However, current research has painted a more nuanced portrait of life-cycle spending patterns. Rather than considering consumption of some (theoretical) composite good, it studies the consumption of total spending and how it changes as households age. For some goods like transportation services, vacations, and food, people tend to decrease the share of total spending as they age. For other goods like health care, donations, and gifts, people tend to increase their share of total spending as they reach old age. As population aging takes hold in countries everywhere, some goods more than others may be positioned to benefit from the changing consumption habits of older adults.

---

* National Institute of Population and Social Security Research, Tokyo. *Population Statistics of Japan 2008.* 8/22/09. [http://www.ipss.go.jp/p-info/e/psj2008/PSJ2008.html].
† Kaneko et al. *Population Projections for Japan: 2006–2055 Outline of Results, Methods, and Assumptions.* 8/22/09. [http://www.ipss.go.jp/webj-ad/WebJournal.files/population/2008 _4/05population.pdf]. 3/2008.
‡ The Economist. *A slow-burning fuse.* 8/22/09. [http://www.economist.com/specialreports/ displaystory.cfm?story_id=13888045]. 6/27/09.

In summary, population aging presents challenges never before seen. Despite the significant demographic shift, older consumers have received limited attention in consumer research. This is surprising given that the increasing population of older consumers corresponds to an increasingly economically powerful part of the population. Although there is much debate over the impact of and solutions to population aging, what we do know is that fertility rates are getting lower, people are living longer, and the world population is getting older. Based on the conference held at the University of Michigan sponsored by the University of Michigan's Ross School of Business, the UCLA Anderson School of Management, and Michigan's Institute of Social Research in May 2008, *The Aging Consumer* examines the economic and psychological research behind how aging consumers behave, make decisions, and choose in the marketplace.

This book is divided into three sections. In the first section, What Changes With Aging, three chapters consider the neurological and psychological changes in behavior and consumption that occur as people age. In particular, in Chapter 1, Angela Gutchess reviews the changes that aging has on working memory, long-term memory, knowledge-based memory, and speed of processing. Aging is shown to impair both working memory, which is the capacity to retain information for short durations, and long-term memory. These declines do not necessarily render our memories wholly useless in old age. Instead, our memories will be remembered in much less detail and will be more prone to memory errors, such as recalling a similar but different event. The cause of the decline can be traced to the physical changes in a number of neural structures in the cortical regions. However, memories come in different forms. For emotional memory, older adults are able to remember both negative and positive information better than neutral information. Moreover, their memory for specific details may improve only for negative relative to neutral information. In studying the aging consumer on a global level, some of the neurobiological processes like memory and attention that may appear to be universal may in fact differ based on culture. In Chapter 2, Michael Hurd and Susann Rohwedder deal with the concrete differences in consumption behavior across a person's life span. Although there is a pervasive belief that households reduce consumption at retirement, the interpretation that consumers adjust their spending after discovering they have fewer economic resources than they had anticipated prior to retirement is not wholly consistent with empirical evidence. The spending habits of older adults are determined by a variety of factors like age, marital status, and economic resources. Specifically, as the population ages, it will tend to spend less on transportation services, vacations, and food; and more on health care and charitable giving. In Chapter 3, Aimee Drolet, Lorraine Lau-Gesk, Patti Williams, and Hyewook Jeong explore the implications of socioemotional selectivity theory for older adults' behavior in consumer contexts. According to socioemotional selectivity theory, when time is viewed as limited, people tend to pursue satisfaction in the present and devote greater attention to social connectedness, feeling states, and deriving emotional meaning, all of which can be experienced and enjoyed now. Consequently, older adults are better able both to acknowledge and manage their emotions compared to young adults. Perceptions of the life span as limited lead older adults to shift their attention toward emotion regulation goals and away from knowledge acquisition goals.

The second section of the book, comprising four chapters, focuses on how age influences the decision making processes of older adults. Ellen Peters, in Chapter 4, provides a thorough overview of the age-related differences in cognition, affect, and goals that interact to influence the decision making of older adults as well as the differences in the decision processes and outcomes of older versus younger consumers. For the most part, older adults process information differently than younger adults. Although declines in deliberative processes suggest that older adults make worse decisions than younger adults, the implications may be oversimplified because older adults appear to selectively use their deliberative capacity. Moreover, accumulated experience can compensate for age-related declines, and emotional focus appears to increase with age. As a result, in some situations, older adults may be better decision makers than younger adults.

In Chapter 5, Gary Burtless considers the empirical evidence on whether workers are well informed, far sighted, and rational in making retirement decisions as economists predict, or whether they are myopic and irrational in making retirement choices. Stacy Wood, Judith Shinogle, and Melayne McInnes, in Chapter 6, examine the extent to which the abundance and complexity of choices in medical programs like Medicare contribute to the high observed rate of nonparticipation by seniors. Finally, in Chapter 7, Carolyn Curasi, Linda Price, and Eric Arnould consider the precipitating events, emotions, and decisions associated with older consumers' disposition of special possessions. Heirlooms hold special symbolic meanings for the previous owner and the recipients and differ from inalienable wealth. Using stories, older consumers act as conscientious and proactive guardians of special objects for potential heirs, and try to convey values and meanings of significance to their kin.

The third and final section of the book focuses on the marketing implications related to older consumers. In addition to insights about the types of advertisements that appeal to the senior segment, Carolyn Bonifield and Catherine Cole, in Chapter 8, examine the vulnerability of older consumers to deceptive advertising by considering reasons like deficits in the cognitive system due to aging. Although many advertisements are processed in the same manner by consumers of all ages, marketers may want to adapt the format, content, location, and timing of marketing communications, including warnings, to the comprehension abilities of older adults. Organizations concerned about comprehension of specific claims in a message or warnings need to take the target market's information processing skills into account. In Chapter 9, Raphaëlle Lambert-Pandraud and Gilles Laurent describe age-related differences in consumer choice and brand loyalty. More specifically, they consider the underlying psychological processes that cause older consumers to make their choice from a smaller consideration set, spend less time searching for product information, repeat their choices more often, and consider older brands. Older adults may be affected by a variety of mechanisms that include: cognitive decline, biological aging, aversion to change, innovativeness, attachment, expertise, habits, nostalgia, and cohort effects. In Chapter 10, Carolyn Yoon, Fred Feinberg, and Norbert Schwarz document the phenomenon that older consumers report being more satisfied with a range of products and services compared to their younger counterparts, and propose a number of explanations for the increases in customer satisfaction with age. In Chapter 11, Harry Moody and Sanjay Sood focus on age branding, which refers to the primary brand message underlying products or services targeted at older consumers. Using case studies on Botox, Sun City, luxury cruises, and more, the chapter discusses the four categories of age brands: age-denial, age-adaptive, age-irrelevant, and age-affirmative. Finally, in Chapter 12, Neil Charness, Michael Champion, and Ryan Yordon consider how products can be designed to help the growing number of older consumers maintain their independence.

A number of people deserve particular thanks for making this book a reality. First, we thank our editor at Routledge/Psychology Press, Anne Duffy, for all her support and encouragement. We also thank Curt Haugtvedt, series editor for the Marketing and Consumer Psychology Series, for motivating this project and cheering us on. We owe deep gratitude to Lynn Kujawa at the University of Michigan for helping to organize the conference that brought all the authors together to share knowledge and exchange ideas about the aging consumer. We thank the authors for their excellent and prompt chapters, and acknowledge generous support by the Harold Price Center for Entrepreneurial Studies at the UCLA Anderson School of Management, the Ross School of Business as well as the Institute for Social Research at the University of Michigan, and the Marketing Science Institute. Finally, completion of the book was facilitated by a fellowship from the Center for Advanced Study in the Behavioral Sciences to Norbert Schwarz.

Aimee Drolet
Norbert Schwarz
Carolyn Yoon

Section 1

What Changes With Aging?

1

Cognitive Psychology and Neuroscience of Aging

Angela H. Gutchess
Brandeis University

Overview

Aging is associated with pronounced impairments in a number of cognitive domains, including speed of processing, working memory, and long-term memory, whereas knowledge-based domains are relatively spared with age. Evidence from cognitive psychology and cognitive and affective neuroscience suggests that older adults can compensate for memory impairments under appropriate task conditions and through the recruitment of additional neural regions. This chapter reviews evidence for these age-related changes as well as evidence that changes to memory are malleable, particularly when information is emotionally, culturally, or personally relevant.

Effects of Aging on Cognition

A large body of evidence suggests that healthy aging affects a number of cognitive functions. At a basic level, speed of processing, the speed with which one conducts mental operations (often measured by perceptual comparisons; e.g., is one pattern the same or different from a second pattern?), is reduced with age (Salthouse, 1996). This fundamental difference, thought to represent the speed of neural transmission, can underlie a host of other age-related deficits. For example, the longer

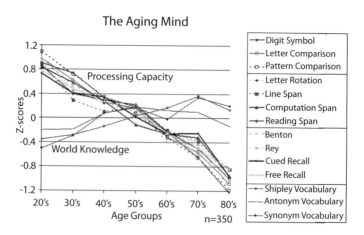

FIGURE 1.1
Declines with age occur in a number of cognitive domains, including speed of process-ing, working memory, and long-term memory. In contrast, world knowledge, assessed with vocabulary measures, is maintained or even improves with age. Copyright 2002 by the American Psychological Association (APA). Adapted with permission. Park et al. (2002). Models of visuospatial and verbal memory across the adult life span. *Psychology and Aging,* 17(2), 299–320. The use of APA information does not imply endorsement by APA.

it takes to transmit information, the more it can decay or the longer the products of mental operations must be maintained for use by other pro-cesses (Salthouse, 1996). Not surprisingly, age-related changes in the speed of processing are highly correlated with performance in other domains, such as working memory (Salthouse, 1996). Working memory is the ability to hold information in mind for brief periods of time. As seen in Figure 1.1, this ability declines gradually over the life span (Salthouse & Babcock, 1991), as assessed by cross-sectional study of individuals aged in their 20s to 80s (Park et al., 2002). This pattern of loss characterizes multi-ple domains of working memory for information, including letters, digits, and spatial positions. Although passive maintenance abilities are affected by aging, higher loads and active manipulation of information, requir-ing executive functions, undergo greater age-related decline (Babcock & Salthouse, 1990). Inhibiting, or suppressing, irrelevant information or inappropriate responses, which is often required in working memory or executive tasks, is also impaired in older adults (Hasher & Zacks, 1988; Zacks & Hasher, 1997).

As opposed to working memory, in which information is maintained in consciousness, long-term memory assesses memory for information that has passed from consciousness and must be retrieved. Long-term memory is also affected by aging (for a review, see Kausler, 1994) and, like working memory, appears to decline in a gradual manner from the 20s to the 80s (Park et al., 2002). This is true for a wide variety of information, although the deficits are greater when information must be recalled from memory when few or no cues are present (cued or free recall) as opposed to recognized on the basis of a re-presented item (Craik & McDowd, 1987; Kausler, 1994). Even when information is recognized, older adults tend to remember it in less detail and are particularly prone to memory errors, such as mistakenly remembering information that is similar or related to previously encountered items (Norman & Schacter, 1997; Schacter, Koutstaal, & Norman, 1997; Schacter, Norman, & Koutstaal, 1998; Tun, Wingfield, Rosen, & Blanchard, 1998).

While these studies of basic processes present a rather grim picture of cognitive aging, emerging evidence in several domains suggests some promising avenues. The remainder of the chapter reviews evidence for compensatory processes using neuroimaging measures, research on motivating conditions or domains of information, and identification of successful strategies based on the investigation of cross-cultural differences.

Effects of Aging on Neural Structure and Function

Changes in brain volume generally mirror the pattern of loss that characterizes behavioral performance with aging. A number of cortical regions decrease in volume with age, particularly in the prefrontal cortex, as well as in subcortical structures, such as the hippocampus (Raz, 2000). Although these findings have been substantiated using a number of different measures, including cross-sectional and longitudinal (albeit rather short time periods, such as 5 years) magnetic resonance imaging (MRI) studies, the different measures do not always converge (Raz, 2000; Salat et al., 2004). For example, shrinkage of the hippocampus has not been identified across all samples, but the general pattern of loss in the prefrontal cortex seems to be robust. Despite the overwhelming evidence for volumetric loss with age, some brain regions are less impacted than others, and normal aging appears to be distinct from pathological aging in a number of ways (Hedden & Gabrieli, 2005). Sensory cortices, such as the visual cortex, are relatively unaffected by aging, experiencing little age-related shrinkage (Raz, 2000).

Even though there is relative convergence between behavioral data indicating losses in cognitive function with age and measures of neural structural integrity, the measure of brain function via techniques such as functional MRI presents a more complex picture than one of simple decline with age. Although there is some evidence that older adults do not robustly activate regions to the same extent as young adults (e.g., Logan, Sanders, Snyder, Morris, & Buckner, 2002), older adults often evince a pattern of increased activity and recruitment of unique regions that are not engaged during task performance by young adults (Reuter-Lorenz & Lustig, 2005). In some cases, this additional activity has been interpreted as compensatory, enhancing or maintaining memory performance relative to cases in which the activity does not occur. For example, young adults and low-performing older adults activate a region in one hemisphere of prefrontal cortex, whereas high-performing older adults activate the same region of prefrontal cortex in both hemispheres (Cabeza, 2002; Reuter-Lorenz & Lustig, 2005). Although this pattern of increased bilaterality, that is, activation of a region in one hemisphere and its homologue in the other hemisphere, is pervasive across many studies of aging (Cabeza, Anderson, Locantore, & McIntosh, 2002; Cabeza, Dolcos, Graham, & Nyberg, 2002), other compensatory changes also occur with age. We identified a pattern of increased activation of frontal cortex in response to reduced engage-ment of medial temporal regions during memory encoding (Gutchess et al., 2005). Increased activity in prefrontal cortex occurred selectively on trials for which older adults successfully formed memory traces, as opposed to those items that were not encoded, suggesting that increased prefrontal activity contributed functionally to memory processes. Other studies have suggested that increased prefrontal activity may compen-sate for reduced sensory signals with age, perhaps helping to resolve the details of visual information or engaging top-down processes that can help to resolve noisy bottom-up signals (Davis, Dennis, Daselaar, Fleck, & Cabeza, 2008; Gazzaley, Cooney, Rissman, & D'Esposito, 2005).

The question of when increased activation contributes to better cogni-tive performance is a difficult one. In some cases, older adults who per-form better on memory tasks recruit additional neural regions compared to lower-performing older adults (e.g., Cabeza, Anderson, et al., 2002; Reuter-Lorenz et al., 2000). Moreover, temporarily inhibiting frontal regions in either hemisphere with repetitive transcranial magnetic stimulation (rTMS) impairs performance for older adults, but application of rTMS to only one hemisphere affects the performance of young adults (Rossi et al., 2004). These data suggest that recruiting both hemispheres does contrib-ute to performance in older adults. Despite these findings, there are other cases in which additional activation is associated with poorer performance (e.g., Logan et al., 2002). The seeming inconsistency in positive and nega-tive relationships between performance and brain activity can be recon-ciled with an analogy to a walking stick (Daselaar & Cabeza, 2005). Even though older adults with poorer mobility tend to use a walking stick, indi-cating that a walking stick is related to poor performance, using a walking stick nonetheless improves motor performance for populations in need of one compared to walking without one. Thus, additional activation could reflect improved performance relative to the level of performance that would be expected *without* the engagement of additional neural regions. Although the use of rTMS can address this question in part, this is a thorny issue because it suggests that different patterns of activation may have different meanings for different populations.

While there is considerable debate over the function and purpose of changes in neural activation with age, some evidence indicates that it can serve a compensatory function. Identifying precisely which processes are being compensated for and how the engagement of additional regions ameliorates losses with age requires further investigation. The biggest advance from the use of cognitive neuroscience methods may be the recognition that age-related changes in cognition reflect a complex interplay of gains, losses, and reorganization and reallocation of processes rather than a simple pattern of decline.

Motivated Cognition and Aging: Behavioral Effects

Behavioral studies converge with the findings of flexible neural responses with age by illustrating conditions under which older adults perform like young adults, thus identifying situations in which older adults successfully harness cognitive resources. Notably, research on differences in motivation has begun to garner widespread attention in the cognitive aging literature. This can be attributed, in part, to the development of the socioemotional selectivity theory of aging, which proposes that as the time remaining in one's life becomes limited, older adults become more attuned to maintaining intimate, personal relationships and are less interested in acquiring new knowledge compared to younger adults (Carstensen, Isaacowitz, & Charles, 1999; Carstensen & Mikels, 2005; Mather & Carstensen, 2005). These motivational shifts lead older adults to allocate their time differently from younger adults, regulate their emotional responses, and attend to positive information more than negative information. Motivation has been assessed through preference measures (Fung & Carstensen, 2003; Fung, Carstensen, & Lutz, 1999), as well as through attention and memory measures (Carstensen & Mikels, 2005; Charles, Mather, & Carstensen, 2003; Fung & Carstensen, 2003; Kennedy, Mather, & Carstensen, 2004; Mather & Carstensen, 2003, 2005).

Socioemotional selectivity theory is covered more extensively in the chapter by Drolet and colleagues; in the remainder of this section, I focus on intriguing evidence that motivating conditions, broadly construed, benefit older adults. Older adults may be able to perform equivalently to young adults when socioemotional information relevant to their well-being motivates them to flexibly deploy cognitive resources. For example, one ability that is particularly impaired with age is source memory, that is, the ability to recall from whom, or where, a fact was learned. When participants study a series of statements presented by Pat or Chris (for example), older adults are much poorer than young adults at remembering which of the speakers presented each statement. But when participants are told that Pat is honest and tells the truth and that Chris is a liar who makes false statements, older adults recall the source information just as well as young adults (Rahhal, May, & Hasher, 2002). Character (Rahhal et al., 2002) and safety information (May, Rahhal, Berry, & Leighton, 2005) also motivate older adults to remember information as well as young adults (but see Siedlecki, Salthouse, & Berish, 2005). These findings are important because they suggest that memory and resource limitations with age can be improved depending on the goals and motivations of the individual.

Socioemotional information does not seem to be the only type of information capable of motivating older adults. When older adults are asked to remember realistic price information for groceries, they perform as well as younger adults (Castel, 2005). This pattern is in contrast to the age impairment for remembering unrealistic prices, as well as the typical poor performance of older adults when they must recall information, that is, self-initiate retrieval in the absence of external cues (Craik & McDowd, 1987).

Although older adults can perform as well as younger adults when information is relevant and meaningful to one's life, as in the case for information regarding trustworthiness or safety, it may be the case that the effects operate at a general level and do not improve memory for specific information. This possibility has been explored previously for highly arousing emotional information (Kensinger, Garoff-Eaton, & Schacter, 2006). Kensinger and colleagues found that negative arousing information can improve memory for visual details in young adults. For example, young adults encode enough specific visual details to identify correctly which exemplar of a gun was studied previously, and they do so better for arousing negative images than neutral images. However, subsequent research with older adults identified some limits to the benefit. While older adults exhibited superior memory for the details of negative arousing items, positive information was not remembered in more detail than neutral information (Kensinger, Garoff-Eaton, & Schacter, 2007). This suggests that information must be highly arousing and negative for the precise details to be better remembered; future research is needed to investigate the specific situations and domains in which socioemotional information benefits memory for older adults.

Motivated Cognition and Aging: Neural Effects

Understanding the brain activity that supports improved cognition under personally motivating conditions is important for identifying the mechanisms that can be harnessed to support cognitive performance with age. The literature on aging is restricted, thus far, primarily to the response of the amygdala, a region implicated in emotion. While several studies note that the response of the amygdala is reduced in older adults (Gunning-Dixon et al., 2003; Iidaka et al., 2002; Tessitore et al., 2005), this finding is not universal. One study found no age difference across the age groups (Kensinger & Schacter, 2008), and another reported increased responsivity of the amygdala for positive compared to negative pictures relative to young adults (Mather et al., 2004). These studies focused on the response of the amygdala to arousing emotional stimuli under conditions in which participants were attending to the emotional nature of the stimuli and making judgments. One possibility is that both age groups may similarly activate the amygdala under passive viewing conditions (Wright, Wedig, Williams, Rauch, & Albert, 2006) consistent with findings of age-invariant habituation of the amygdala (Wedig, Rauch, Albert, & Wright, 2005). Thus, under conditions that do not reference emotion so explicitly, the response of the amygdala may be intact with age. Although Williams et al. (2006) note some changes in the response of the amygdala across the life span, the results do not reveal a consistent decline in middle and late adulthood and may reflect a decreased need to regulate emotional response with age rather than dysfunctional activation of the region.

Aside from the amygdala, there is little systematic research on regions implicated in socioemotional processing. The medial prefrontal cortex (mPFC) response is intact with age for the referencing of information to the self (Gutchess, Kensinger, & Schacter, 2007; see next section), and exhibits a larger role in emotion regulation for older adults (Williams et al., 2006). In one study, the insula activation increased in older adults when perceiving angry faces, and the authors interpreted this as evidence of a shift from subcortical (i.e., amygdala) to cortical (i.e., insula) areas with age (Fischer et al., 2005). The finding that the number of dopamine receptors decreases with age (Volkow et al., 2000) suggests that activation patterns in dopamine-sensitive regions, such as the striatum and ventromedial prefrontal cortex, may change with age. In terms of the response to rewards, there is some evidence for change with age. Older adults have an intact response for monetary gains in the striatum (a region rich in dopamine receptors) and the insula but show impaired activation in response to monetary losses in these same regions (Samanez-Larkin et al., 2007). This pattern of findings may be consistent with older adults' increased attention to positive information and decreased attention to negative information in other domains (Mather & Carstensen, 2005).

Motivated Cognition and Aging: Self-Referencing

One highly effective encoding strategy for young adults is that of *self-referencing*, relating information to oneself (Rogers, Kuiper, & Kirker, 1977; Symons & Johnson, 1997). Although some have argued that the self-reference effect represents a simple depth-of-processing effect (Craik & Lockhart, 1972; Craik & Tulving, 1975), others speculated that the self represented a "special" module in memory. That is, it has long been recognized that engaging "deep," or elaborative, encoding processes, such as thinking about the meaning of information, improves memory. Elaborative encoding engages the inferior frontal gyrus (Demb et al., 1995; Kapur et al., 1994; Poldrack et al., 1999; Wagner et al., 1998), whereas self-referenced information engages a distinct region of prefrontal cortex, the mPFC. Importantly, this dissociation indicates that depth-of-processing effects, which extend across social and nonsocial domains, do not solely account for the improvement of memory for these modalities or encoding strategies (Craik & Lockhart, 1972; Craik & Tulving, 1975). This dissociation between regions activated during elaborative encoding and regions activated during the encoding of social information suggests that the mechanisms that support superior memory for social information are distinct from those that support depth of encoding effects in other domains.

This claim is supported by neuroimaging data, with distinct neural regions, chiefly the mPFC, subserving self-relevant processes. These processes are distinct from those engaged when thinking about other people or semantic information (Craik et al., 1999; Kelley et al., 2002; Macrae, Moran, Heatherton, Banfield, & Kelley, 2004). Due to its unique neural signature, self-referential memory has been proposed to represent a distinct module in memory (Macrae et al., 2004), akin to other specific modules in memory, such as emotion (see Schacter, Gutchess, & Kensinger, 2009).

Research has begun to investigate the extent to which self-referencing strategies mitigate the effects of aging on memory. The strategy has been well characterized in young adults, and research (see Figure 1.2) establishes that older adults also benefit from a self-referencing strategy in the domains of recall (Mueller, Wonderlich, & Dugan, 1986) and recognition (Glisky & Marquine, 2009; Gutchess, Kensinger, Yoon, & Schacter, 2007). However, these results also reveal potential limitations to the

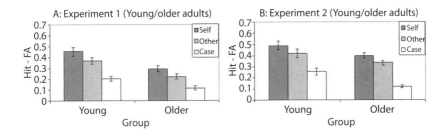

FIGURE 1.2
Young and older adults' memory performance for information that has been encoded using self-referencing, other referencing (Panel A, Albert Einstein; Panel B, a personally known close other), or perceptual judgments (i.e., uppercase font). Both young and older adults benefitted from self-referencing of information, even though overall young adults exhibited better memory than the older adults. Hit-FA represents a corrected recognition measure. Reproduced with permission of Taylor & Francis Informa UK Ltd.–Journals, from *Memory*, Gutchess, Kensinger, Yoon, et al., *15*(8), 2007; permission conveyed through Copyright Clearance Center Inc.

self-referencing effects with age, based on the availability of cognitive resources, age, and the flexibility required to apply the strategy (Glisky & Marquine, 2009; Gutchess, Kensinger, Yoon, et al., 2007).

In terms of the neural regions that support self-referencing, the medial prefrontal region engaged during self-referencing by young adults exhibits a different trajectory with aging. Whereas lateral prefrontal regions, such as the inferior frontal cortex, exhibit shrinkage and reduced activation with age (Logan et al., 2002; Raz, 2000), the mPFC may not lose volume with age, and older adults may activate the region more robustly than young (Salat et al., 2004; Williams et al., 2006). In the domain of self-referencing, young and older adults robustly engage the same medial prefrontal region when referencing the self, as shown in Figure 1.3 (Gutchess, Kensinger, & Schacter, 2007), in contrast to reports of dysfunctional activation during cognitive tasks (Buckner et al., 2005; Grady, Springer, Hongwanishkul, McIntosh, & Winocur, 2006; Lustig et al., 2003; Persson, Lustig, Nelson, & Reuter-Lorenz, 2007). In an examination of the *encoding* of self-referenced information, we identified age differences in the activation of additional prefrontal regions, suggesting that the intact activation of the mPFC may not extend to demanding task conditions or that a broader network of regions is recruited to support older adults' encoding processes (Gutchess, Kensinger, & Schacter, 2010).

Although self-referencing research thus far has investigated the effects of aging on memory for words and the basic neural responses of the mPFC, it remains to be tested whether the self-referential module of memory shares the general characteristics of aging memory. Memory deficits with

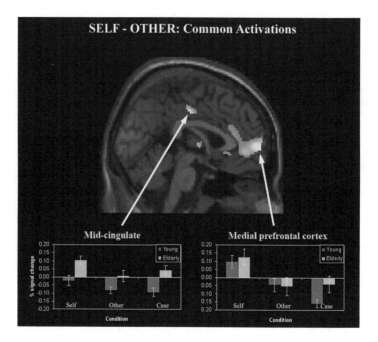

FIGURE 1.3

Regions activated by both young and older adults in the contrast of self minus other judgments. Notably, the medial prefrontal cortex is similarly engaged by both groups. Reproduced with permission of Taylor & Francis Informa UK Ltd.–Journals, from *Social Neuroscience*, Gutchess, Kensinger, and Schacter, 2(2), 2007; permission conveyed through Copyright Clearance Center Inc.

age initially were considered to be absolutes, reflecting limited cognitive resources with age (see reviews by Park & Gutchess, 2005; Zacks, Hasher, & Li, 2000). Indeed, initial work suggests that self-referencing seems to similarly affect item memory (e.g., memory for words) in younger and older adults. However, we have yet to assess whether the strategy has a similar impact on the specific *qualities* of the memories across both age groups (e.g., perceptual details or information about the source). In the domain of emotional memory, older adults better remember both negative and positive items in comparison to neutral information, but their memory for specific details is improved only for negative relative to neutral information (Kensinger et al., 2006; Kensinger, O'Brien, Swanberg, Garoff-Eaton, & Schacter, 2007). However, it is also possible that self-referencing confers advantages to older adults compared to other nonsocial strategies. For example, Kensinger and Schacter interpreted their finding of increased activity in the mPFC during the encoding of emotional information to indicate that older adults are more likely to spontaneously encode information in relation to oneself (Kensinger & Schacter, 2008).

Cognitive Aging Across Cultures

Another domain that is only beginning to be investigated is how cognitive aging unfolds across different cultures. Because most research to date has been conducted predominantly in Western cultures, our understanding of cognitive aging may be culturally bound. Research thus far has identified many domains that are impaired with age, including long-term memory and executive function. As reviewed in previous sections, some work suggests that particular strategies can reduce or, in some cases, eliminate age-related declines. This suggests that cognitive declines with age are not inevitable, providing a window through which culture could operate. For example, culturally prioritized strategies or details of information may be preserved with age for peoples of one culture while subject to decline in peoples of a different culture without the same priorities in information processing. Neurobiologically driven aspects of aging are expected to operate as universals, constant across cultures, whereas experience-dependent aspects of aging should diverge across cultures. However, some of the psychological processes and cognitive mechanisms that are often thought of as universals, such as attention and memory, may in fact be shaped by culture.

Evidence reveals dramatic differences in the ways that people from different cultures perceive the world around them. Individuals from Western cultures tend to focus on that which is object based, categorically related, or self-relevant, whereas people from Eastern cultures tend to focus more on contextual details, similarities, and group-relevant information (Nisbett & Masuda, 2003; Nisbett, Peng, Choi, & Norenzayan, 2001). For example, when asked to describe animated vignettes of underwater scenes, Americans' descriptions focused on the prominent fish in the scene, whereas Japanese incorporated many more contextual details, such as the color of the seaweed and water and the relationship of the fish to the other elements in the scene (Masuda & Nisbett, 2001). Consistent with Americans' object-focused attention, eye-tracking studies show that Americans fixate to objects earlier and for more time than East Asians (Chua, Boland, & Nisbett, 2005). These different ways of perceiving the world suggest that culture operates as a lens that directs attention and filters the processing of the environment. These cultural differences extend from perception to higher-order cognitive processes, such as memory and reasoning.

Comparison of cultural differences across the life span provides another window into the ways in which culture shapes cognition by comparing the effects of life experiences (e.g., culture) against a pattern of neurobiological decline (e.g., aging). Comparing the trajectory of aging across diverse cultures is an important test of the universality of the aging processes that to date have been primarily investigated in Western cultures. Those functions, guided largely by neurobiological aging, should exhibit universal decline with age, whereas experience-dependent aspects of aging should diverge across cultures (Park & Gutchess, 2002, 2006). Although pervasive cognitive changes occur with age, research suggests that some strategies or life experiences, such as exercise, cognitive training, and engaged lifestyles (Ball et al., 2002; Park, Gutchess, Meade, & Stine-Morrow, 2007), can reduce the magnitude of cognitive decline, allowing for potential contributions from culture (but see Salthouse, 2006). Substantial neural reorganization occurs throughout the life span in response to life experiences. For example, extensive experience with spatial navigation, as is the case with highly trained London taxi drivers, leads to growth in posterior hippocampal volume in adults (Maguire et al., 2000), and participation of older adults in an exercise intervention improves executive function and alters corresponding neural activations (Hillman, Erickson, & Kramer, 2008). Culture represents a proxy for a rich collection of life experiences that direct the lens through which one views the world and conveys certain strategies or preferred modes of information processing. Exploring cognitive aging across cultures can reveal how different information-processing styles or life experiences can improve outcomes in later life. If older adults diverge across cultures in the degree to which certain cognitive abilities are affected by the aging process, this pattern would indicate that certain strategies or orientations may better support memory and cognitive functions across the life span than others. The investigation of culture can illustrate the cognitive priorities and strategies associated with greater preservation of cognitive function with age, suggesting mechanisms to reduce age-related cognitive decline.

One way of conceptualizing the possible effects of culture on cognitive aging is by distinguishing between *mechanics* and *pragmatics*. Baltes (1987) contrasted basic information-processing "hardware" (mechanics) versus the context- and knowledge-specific "software" (pragmatics) and theorized that aging could differentially affect the two types of intelligence, with more decline in mechanics but relative maintenance, or even gains, for pragmatics. Park, Nisbett, and Hedden (1999) maintain that Baltes's distinction is important to consider in the study of culture. When initial cultural differences are present for young adults in basic information-processing abilities such as speed of processing or working memory (Park et al., 1999), the limitations to cognitive resources that occur with age would reduce or even eliminate cultural differences. For example, if young adults from one culture performed better on a speed-of-processing task than young adults from a second culture, reduced speed-of-processing ability with age would similarly impair speed-of-processing performance across cultures or perhaps even eliminate the advantage that one group initially had over the other group, operating to equalize performance across cultures with age. In contrast, cultural differences in the use of strategies or world knowledge, which rely on pragmatics, would be maintained or magnified with age (Park et al., 1999). In this case, the advantage present for young adults from one culture would be unaffected by declines in cognitive ability, and the successful strategy would continue to benefit older adults. Alternatively, the second culture would be affected by cognitive resource limitations or reduced mechanics, which would make them less likely to employ an unfamiliar or effortful strategy with age, thus magnifying cultural differences for older adults.

To date, few studies have investigated cross-cultural differences across the life span, but there is some evidence to support the distinction between the effects of culture on mechanics and pragmatics with age. Mechanics, such as speed of processing and working memory, undergo equivalent decline with age across American and Chinese cultures, a pattern that indicates that the effects of aging on some basic information-processing abilities are universal (Geary, Salthouse, Chen, & Fan, 1996; Hedden et al., 2002). When initial cultural differences were present for young adults, there was evidence that performance is more similar across cultures with age, particularly at higher processing loads (Geary et al., 1996; Hedden et al., 2002). Source memory ability also appears to be affected across the two cultures by the aging process. Relative to their young adult counterparts, older Chinese and Americans exhibit similar impairments in source memory, assessed in terms of their ability to remember which of four speakers had presented a trivia statement (Chua, Chen, & Park, 2006).

Investigation of higher-order cognitive processes draws on both mechanics and pragmatics, muddying the distinction between the two types of abilities. For example, East Asians and Westerners differ in their attention to and use of categories, with Americans organizing information by taxonomic categories and adopting rule-based categorization strategies more than East Asians (Chiu, 1972; Choi, Nisbett, & Smith, 1997; Ji, Zhang, & Nisbett, 2004; Norenzayan, Smith, Kim, & Nisbett, 2002). Category fluency tasks, which require subjects to generate the names of as many items as possible that belong to a category (e.g., vegetables) in a given amount of time, treat the use of categories as an indicator of executive function, a basic cognitive process. In a Hong Kong sample, Chan and Poon (1999) found age-related declines in category fluency that appeared to mimic the pattern in Western cultures, a finding consistent with predictions for the effects of aging on mechanics. However, older adults across cultures differed in their use of a categorization strategy on a long-term recall task (Gutchess, Yoon, et al., 2006). Interestingly, this study showed evidence for differences in the trajectory of aging across cultures for pragmatics as well as similarities in the effects of aging on mechanics. Whereas cultures diverged with age in the use of a strategy relying on semantic knowledge and experiences (categorization), there were culture-equivalent effects of aging on the amount of information recalled from long-term memory (Gutchess, Yoon, et al., 2006), consistent with the findings on speed of processing and source memory (Chua et al., 2006; Geary et al., 1996; Hedden et al., 2002).

Heightened attention to positive socioemotional information with age (Mather & Carstensen, 2005) may also be affected by cultural context. As assessed with eye-tracking measures, older adults from Western cultures tend to look toward happy faces and away from negative faces (Isaacowitz, Wadlinger, Goren, & Wilson, 2006). However, older, but not younger, Hong Kong Chinese participants tend to look *away* from happy faces (Fung et al., 2008). These findings indicate that the positivity bias may be a culture-specific phenomenon, and that social cognition may be an especially fertile area for cross-cultural investigation.

Cross-cultural research is beginning to incorporate a cognitive neuroscience approach to investigate cognitive aging. There could be substantial reorganization of functional networks based on culture-specific experiences, and this reorganization could support the flexible engagement of cognitive resources with age. Two neuroimaging studies with young adults converge with behavioral evidence to suggest that Americans tend to process objects in isolation, whereas East Asians are more context dependent. During the encoding of complex scenes, Americans engaged object-processing regions more than East Asians (Gutchess, Welsh, Boduroglu, & Park, 2006), and during a reasoning task, culture-inconsistent strategies (i.e., context dependent for Americans; context independent for East Asians) demanded executive functions more than culture-consistent strategies (i.e., context independent for Americans; context dependent for East Asians) (Hedden, Ketay, Aron, Markus, & Gabrieli, 2008). Another neuroimaging study explored the joint effects of age and culture on the neural activity during the viewing of complex scenes. Although aging was associated with reduced adaptation in the lateral occipital complex (an object-processing region) across both cultures, the reduced adaptation response was exaggerated for the East Asian elderly relative to the Western elderly (Goh et al., 2007). This pattern reflected the relative lack of object emphasis for East Asians compared to Westerners. Even though a reduced emphasis on objects in daily life might exacerbate age-related reductions in engaging the region, further investigations suggest that the response of the region is malleable. When older East Asians were instructed to attend to the object or presented with objects in isolation, the lateral occipital complex exhibited a robust response (Chee et al., 2006). Thus, although life experiences associated with culture may bias attention to certain aspects of information or guide the selection of cognitive strategies, these effects are malleable and depend on the task demands and immediate goals, even in old age.

Conclusions

While research has barely begun to identify the conditions and mechanisms through which culture and motivating conditions influence and improve cognition for older adults, these represent promising avenues for future research. Not only do these directions have the potential to unveil information-processing strategies that lead to better cognitive outcomes with age, but also they could suggest remediation strategies or methods to present information to older adults in meaningful ways that efficiently engage limited cognitive resources. Cognitive neuroscience methods suggested that plasticity exists in a number of domains with aging, supporting the flexible engagement of resources. These methods should be particularly potent when applied to the study of culture and motivating conditions with age.

Acknowledgments

I thank Carolyn Yoon for helpful feedback on an earlier version of the manuscript and Jennifer Coleman for her assistance preparing the chapter. This chapter was written while the author was an AFAR research grant recipient.

References

Babcock, R. L., & Salthouse, T. A. (1990). Effects of increased processing demands on age-differences in working memory. *Psychology and Aging, 5*, 421–428.

Ball, K., Berch, D. B., Helmers, K. F., Jobe, J. B., Leveck, M. D., Marsiske, M., et al. (2002). Effects of cognitive training interventions with older adults—A randomized controlled trial. *JAMA–Journal of the American Medical Association, 288*, 2271–2281.

Baltes, P. B. (1987). Theoretical propositions of life-span developmental-psychology—On the dynamics between growth and decline. *Developmental Psychology, 23*, 611–626.

Buckner, R. L., Snyder, A. Z., Shannon, B. J., LaRossa, G., Sachs, R., Fotenos, A. F., et al. (2005). Molecular, structural, and functional characterization of Alzheimer's disease: Evidence for a relationship between default activity, amyloid, and memory. *Journal of Neuroscience, 25*, 7709–7717.

Cabeza, R. (2002). Hemispheric asymmetry reduction in older adults: The HAROLD model. *Psychology and Aging, 17*, 85–100.

Cabeza, R., Anderson, N. D., Locantore, J. K., & McIntosh, A. R. (2002). Aging gracefully: Compensatory brain activity in high-performing older adults. *Neuroimage, 17*, 1394–1402.

Cabeza, R., Dolcos, F., Graham, R., & Nyberg, L. (2002). Similarities and differences in the neural correlates of episodic memory retrieval and working memory. *Neuroimage, 16*, 317–330.

Carstensen, L. L., Isaacowitz, D. M., & Charles, S. T. (1999). Taking time seriously— A theory of socioemotional selectivity. *American Psychologist, 54*, 165–181.

Carstensen, L. L., & Mikels, J. A. (2005). At the intersection of emotion and cognition—Aging and the positivity effect. *Current Directions in Psychological Science, 14*, 117–121.

Castel, A. D. (2005). Memory for grocery prices in younger and older adults: The role of schematic support. *Psychology and Aging, 20*, 718–721.

Chan, A. S., & Poon, M. W. (1999). Performance of 7-to 95-year-old individuals in a Chinese version of the category fluency test. *Journal of the International Neuropsychological Society, 5*, 525–533.

Charles, S. T., Mather, M., & Carstensen, L. L. (2003). Aging and emotional memory: The forgettable nature of negative images for older adults. *Journal of Experimental Psychology–General, 132*, 310–324.

Chee, M. W., Goh, J. O., Venkatraman, V., Tan, J. C., Gutchess, A., Sutton, B., et al. (2006). Age-related changes in object processing and contextual binding revealed using fMR adaptation. *Journal of Cognitive Neuroscience, 18*, 495–507.

Chiu, L. H. (1972). A cross-cultural comparison of cognitive styles in Chinese and American children. *International Journal of Psychology, 7*, 235–242.

Choi, I., Nisbett, R. E., & Smith, E. E. (1997). Culture, category salience, and inductive reasoning. *Cognition, 65*, 15–32.

Chua, H. F., Boland, J. E., & Nisbett, R. E. (2005). Cultural variation in eye movements during scene perception. *Proceedings of the National Academy of Sciences of the United States of America, 102*, 12629–12633.

Chua, H. F., Chen, W., & Park, D. C. (2006). Source memory, aging and culture. *Gerontology, 52*, 306–313.

Craik, F. I. M., & Lockhart, R. S. (1972). Levels of processing—Framework for memory research. *Journal of Verbal Learning and Verbal Behavior, 11*, 671–684.

Craik, F. I. M., & McDowd, J. M. (1987). Age differences in recall and recognition. *Journal of Experimental Psychology: Learning, Memory, & Cognition, 13*, 474–479.

Craik, F. I. M., Moroz, T. M., Moscovitch, M., Stuss, D. T., Winocur, G., Tulving, E., et al. (1999). In search of the self: A positron emission tomography study. *Psychological Science, 10*, 26–34.

Craik, F. I. M., & Tulving, E. (1975). Depth of processing and retention of words in episodic memory. *Journal of Experimental Psychology–General, 104*, 268–294.

Daselaar, S., & Cabeza, R. (2005). Age-related changes in hemispheric organization. In R. Cabeza, L. Nyberg, & D. Park (Eds.), *Cognitive neuroscience of aging: Linking cognitive and cerebral aging* (pp. 325–353). New York: Oxford University Press.

Davis, S. W., Dennis, N. A., Daselaar, S. M., Fleck, M. S., & Cabeza, R. (2008). Que PASA? The posterior-anterior shift in aging. *Cerebral Cortex, 18,* 1201–1209.

Demb, J. B., Desmond, J. E., Wagner, A. D., Vaidya, C. J., Glover, G. H., & Gabrieli, J. D. E. (1995). Semantic encoding and retrieval in the left inferior prefrontal cortex—A functional MRI study of task-difficulty and process specificity. *Journal of Neuroscience, 15,* 5870–5878.

Fischer, H., Sandblom, J., Gavazzeni, J., Fransson, P., Wright, C. I., & Backman, L. (2005). Age-differential patterns of brain activation during perception of angry faces. *Neuroscience Letters, 386,* 99–104.

Fung, H. H., & Carstensen, L. L. (2003). Sending memorable messages to the old: Age differences in preferences and memory for advertisements. *Journal of Personality and Social Psychology, 85,* 163–178.

Fung, H. H., Carstensen, L. L., & Lutz, A. M. (1999). Influence of time on social preferences: Implications for life-span development. *Psychology and Aging, 14,* 595–604.

Fung, H. H., Isaacowitz, D. M., Lu, A. Y., Wadlinger, H. A., Goren, D., & Wilson, H. R. (2008). Age-related positivity enhancement is not universal: Older Chinese look away from positive stimuli. *Psychology and Aging, 23,* 440–446.

Gazzaley, A., Cooney, J. W., Rissman, J., & D'Esposito, M. (2005). Top-down suppression deficit underlies working memory impairment in normal aging. *Nature Neuroscience, 8,* 1298–1300.

Geary, D. C., Salthouse, T. A., Chen, G. P., & Fan, L. (1996). Are East Asian versus American differences in arithmetical ability a recent phenomenon? *Developmental Psychology, 32,* 254–262.

Glisky, E. L., & Marquine, M. J. (2009). Semantic and self-referential processing of positive and negative trait adjectives in older adults. *Memory, 17,* 144–157.

Goh, J. O., Chee, M. W., Tan, J. C., Venkatraman, V., Hebrank, A., Leshikar, E. D., et al. (2007). Age and culture modulate object processing and object-scene binding in the ventral visual area. *Cognitive, Affective, and Behavioral Neuroscience, 7,* 44–52.

Grady, C. L., Springer, M. V., Hongwanishkul, D., McIntosh, A. R., & Winocur, G. (2006). Age-related changes in brain activity across the adult lifespan. *Journal of Cognitive Neuroscience, 18,* 227–241.

Gunning-Dixon, F. M., Gur, R. C., Perkins, A. C., Schroeder, L., Turner, T., Turetsky, B. I., et al. (2003). Age-related differences in brain activation during emotional face processing. *Neurobiology of Aging, 24,* 285–295.

Gutchess, A. H., Kensinger, E. A., & Schacter, D. L. (2007). Aging, self-referencing, and medial prefrontal cortex. *Social Neuroscience, 2,* 117–133.

Gutchess, A. H., Kensinger, E. A., & Schacter, D. L. (2010). Functional neuroimaging of self-referential encoding with age. *Neuropsychologia, 48,* 211–219.

Gutchess, A. H., Kensinger, E. A., Yoon, C., & Schacter, D. L. (2007). Ageing and the self-reference effect in memory. *Memory, 15,* 822–837.

Gutchess, A. H., Welsh, R. C., Boduroglu, A., & Park, D. C. (2006). Cultural differences in neural function associated with object processing. *Cognitive, Affective & Behavioral Neuroscience, 6,* 102–109.

Gutchess, A. H., Welsh, R. C., Hedden, T., Bangert, A., Minear, M., Liu, L. L., et al. (2005). Aging and the neural correlates of successful picture encoding: Frontal activations compensate for decreased medial-temporal activity. *Journal of Cognitive Neuroscience, 17*, 84–96.

Gutchess, A. H., Yoon, C., Luo, T., Feinberg, F., Hedden, T., Jing, Q., et al. (2006). Categorical organization in free recall across culture and age. *Gerontology, 52*, 314–323.

Hasher, L., & Zacks, R. T. (1988). Working memory, comprehension, and aging: A review and a new view. In G. H. Bower (Ed.), *The psychology of learning and motivation: Advances in research and theory* (Vol. 22, pp. 193–225). San Diego, CA: Academic Press.

Hedden, T., & Gabrieli, J. D. (2005). Healthy and pathological processes in adult development: New evidence from neuroimaging of the aging brain. *Current Opinion in Neurology, 18*, 740–747.

Hedden, T., Ketay, S., Aron, A., Markus, H. R., & Gabrieli, J. D. E. (2008). Cultural influences on neural substrates of attentional control. *Psychological Science, 19*, 12–17.

Hedden, T., Park, D. C., Nisbett, R., Ji, L. J., Jing, Q., & Jiao, S. (2002). Cultural variation in verbal versus spatial neuropsychological function across the life span. *Neuropsychology, 16*, 65–73.

Hillman, C. H., Erickson, K. I., & Kramer, A. F. (2008). Be smart, exercise your heart: Exercise effects on brain and cognition. *Nature Reviews Neuroscience, 9*, 58–65.

Iidaka, T., Okada, T., Murata, T., Omori, M., Kosaka, H., Sadato, N., et al. (2002). Age-related differences in the medial temporal lobe responses to emotional faces as revealed by fMRI. *Hippocampus, 12*, 352–362.

Isaacowitz, D. M., Wadlinger, H. A., Goren, D., & Wilson, H. R. (2006). Selective preference in visual fixation away from negative images in old age? An eye-tracking study. *Psychology and Aging, 21*, 40–48.

Ji, L. J., Zhang, Z., & Nisbett, R. E. (2004). Is it culture or is it language? Examination of language effects in cross-cultural research on categorization. *Journal of Personality and Social Psychology, 87*, 57–65.

Kapur, S., Craik, F. I. M., Tulving, E., Wilson, A. A., Houle, S., & Brown, G. M. (1994). Neuroantomical correlates of encoding in episodic memory—levels of processing effect. *Proceedings of the National Academy of Sciences of the United States of America, 91*, 2008–2011.

Kausler, D. H. (1994). *Learning and memory in normal aging*. San Diego, CA: Academic Press.

Kelley, W. M., Macrae, C. N., Wyland, C. L., Caglar, S., Inati, S., & Heatherton, T. F. (2002). Finding the self? An event-related fMRI study. *Journal of Cognitive Neuroscience, 14*, 785–794.

Kennedy, Q., Mather, M., & Carstensen, L. L. (2004). The role of motivation in the age-related positivity effect in autobiographical memory. *Psychological Science, 15*, 208–214.

Kensinger, E. A., Garoff-Eaton, R. J., & Schacter, D. L. (2006). Memory for specific visual details can be enhanced by negative arousing content. *Journal of Memory and Language, 54*, 99–112.

Kensinger, E. A., Garoff-Eaton, R. J., & Schacter, D. L. (2007). Effects of emotion on memory specificity in young and older adults. *The Journals of Gerontology Series B–Psychological Sciences and Social Sciences, 62,* P208–P215.

Kensinger, E. A., O'Brien, J. L., Swanberg, K., Garoff-Eaton, R. J., & Schacter, D. L. (2007). The effects of emotional content on reality-monitoring performance in young and older adults. *Psychology and Aging, 22,* 752–764.

Kensinger, E. A., & Schacter, D. L. (2008). Neural processes supporting young and older adults' emotional memories. *Journal of Cognitive Neuroscience, 20,* 1161–1173.

Logan, J. M., Sanders, A. L., Snyder, A. Z., Morris, J. C., & Buckner, R. L. (2002). Under-recruitment and nonselective recruitment: dissociable neural mechanisms associated with aging. *Neuron, 33,* 827–840.

Lustig, C., Snyder, A. Z., Bhakta, M., O'Brien, K. C., McAvoy, M., Raichle, M. E., et al. (2003). Functional deactivations: Change with age and dementia of the Alzheimer type. *Proceedings of the National Academy of Sciences of the United States of America, 100,* 14504–14509.

Macrae, C. N., Moran, J. M., Heatherton, T. F., Banfield, J. F., & Kelley, W. M. (2004). Medial prefrontal activity predicts memory for self. *Cerebral Cortex, 14,* 647–654.

Maguire, E. A., Gadian, D. G., Johnsrude, I. S., Good, C. D., Ashburner, J., Frackowiak, R. S. J., et al. (2000). Navigation-related structural change in the hippocampi of taxi drivers. *Proceedings of the National Academy of Sciences of the United States of America, 97,* 4398–4403.

Masuda, T., & Nisbett, R. E. (2001). Attending holistically versus analytically: Comparing the context sensitivity of Japanese and Americans. *Journal of Personality and Social Psychology, 81,* 922–934.

Mather, M., Canli, T., English, T., Whitfield, S., Wais, P., Ochsner, K., et al. (2004). Amygdala responses to emotionally valenced stimuli in older and younger adults. *Psychological Science, 15,* 259–263.

Mather, M., & Carstensen, L. L. (2003). Aging and attentional biases for emotional faces. *Psychological Science, 14,* 409–415.

Mather, M., & Carstensen, L. L. (2005). Aging and motivated cognition: The positivity effect in attention and memory. *Trends in Cognitive Sciences, 9,* 496–502.

May, C. P., Rahhal, T., Berry, E. M., & Leighton, E. A. (2005). Aging, source memory, and emotion. *Psychology and Aging, 20,* 571–578.

Mueller, J. H., Wonderlich, S., & Dugan, K. (1986). Self-referent processing of age-specific material. *Psychology and Aging, 1,* 293–299.

Nisbett, R. E., & Masuda, T. (2003). Culture and point of view. *Proceedings of the National Academy of Sciences of the United States of America, 100,* 11163–11170.

Nisbett, R. E., Peng, K., Choi, I., & Norenzayan, A. (2001). Culture and systems of thought: Holistic versus analytic cognition. *Psychological Review, 108,* 291–310.

Norenzayan, A., Smith, E. E., Kim, B. J., & Nisbett, R. E. (2002). Cultural preferences for formal versus intuitive reasoning. *Cognitive Science, 26,* 653–684.

Norman, K. A., & Schacter, D. L. (1997). False recognition in younger and older adults: Exploring the characteristics of illusory memories. *Memory & Cognition, 25,* 838–848.

Park, D. C., & Gutchess, A. H. (2002). Aging, cognition, and culture: A neuroscientific perspective. *Neuroscience and Biobehavioral Review, 26,* 859–867.

Park, D. C., & Gutchess, A. H. (2005). Long-term memory and aging: A cognitive neuroscience perspective. In R. Cabeza, L. Nyberg, & D. C. Park (Eds.), *Cognitive neuroscience of aging: Linking cognitive and cerebral aging* (pp. 218–245). New York: Oxford University Press.

Park, D. C., & Gutchess, A. H. (2006). The cognitive neuroscience of aging and culture. *Current Directions in Psychological Science, 15*, 105–108.

Park, D. C., Gutchess, A. H., Meade, M. L., & Stine-Morrow, E. A. (2007). Improving cognitive function in older adults: Nontraditional approaches. *The Journals of Gerontology. Series B, Psychological Sciences and Social Sciences, 62* (Special Issue 1), 45–52.

Park, D. C., Lautenschlager, G., Hedden, T., Davidson, N. S., Smith, A. D., & Smith, P. K. (2002). Models of visuospatial and verbal memory across the adult life span. *Psychology and Aging, 17*, 299–320.

Park, D. C., Nisbett, R., & Hedden, T. (1999). Aging, culture, and cognition. *The Journals of Gerontology. Series B, Psychological Sciences and Social Sciences, 54*, P75–P84.

Persson, J., Lustig, C., Nelson, J. K., & Reuter-Lorenz, P. A. (2007). Age differences in deactivation: A link to cognitive control? *Journal of Cognitive Neuroscience, 19*, 1021–1032.

Poldrack, R. A., Wagner, A. D., Prull, M. W., Desmond, J. E., Glover, G. H., & Gabrieli, J. D. E. (1999). Functional specialization for semantic and phonological processing in the left inferior prefrontal cortex. *Neuroimage, 10*, 15–35.

Rahhal, T. A., May, C. P., & Hasher, L. (2002). Truth and character: Sources that older adults can remember. *Psychological Science, 13*, 101–105.

Raz, N. (2000). Aging of the brain and its impact on cognitive performance: Integration of structural and functional findings. In F. I. M. Craik & T. A. Salthouse (Eds.), *The handbook of aging and cognition* (2nd ed., pp. 1–90). Mahwah, NJ: Erlbaum.

Reuter-Lorenz, P. A., Jonides, J., Smith, E. E., Hartley, A., Miller, A., Marshuetz, C., et al. (2000). Age differences in the frontal lateralization of verbal and spatial working memory revealed by PET. *Journal of Cognitive Neuroscience, 12*, 174–187.

Reuter-Lorenz, P. A., & Lustig, C. (2005). Brain aging: Reorganizing discoveries about the aging mind. *Current Opinion in Neurobiology, 15*, 245–251.

Rogers, T. B., Kuiper, N. A., & Kirker, W. S. (1977). Self-reference and the encoding of personal information. *Journal of Personality and Social Psychology, 35*, 677–688.

Rossi, S., Miniussi, C., Pasqualetti, P., Babiloni, C., Rossini, P. M., & Cappa, S. F. (2004). Age-related functional changes of prefrontal cortex in long-term memory: A repetitive transcranial magnetic stimulation study. *Journal of Neuroscience, 24*, 7939–7944.

Salat, D. H., Buckner, R. L., Snyder, A. Z., Greve, D. N., Desikan, R. S. R., Busa, E., et al. (2004). Thinning of the cerebral cortex in aging. *Cerebral Cortex, 14*, 721–730.

Salthouse, T. A. (1996). The processing-speed theory of adult age differences in cognition. *Psychological Review, 103*, 403–428.

Salthouse, T. A. (2006). Mental exercise and mental aging. *Perspectives on Psychological Science, 1*, 68–87.

Salthouse, T. A., & Babcock, R. L. (1991). Decomposing adult age-differences in working memory. *Developmental Psychology, 27,* 763–776.

Samanez-Larkin, G. R., Gibbs, S. E. B., Khanna, K., Nielsen, L., Carstensen, L. L., & Knutson, B. (2007). Anticipation of monetary gain but not loss in healthy older adults. *Nature Neuroscience, 10,* 787–791.

Schacter, D. L., Gutchess, A. H., & Kensinger, E. A. (2009). Specificity of memory: Implications for individual and collective remembering. In P. Boyer & J. Wertsch (Eds.), *Memory in mind and culture* (pp. 83–111). Cambridge, UK: Cambridge University Press.

Schacter, D. L., Koutstaal, W., & Norman, K. A. (1997). False memories and aging. *Trends in Cognitive Sciences, 1,* 229–236.

Schacter, D. L., Norman, K. A., & Koutstaal, W. (1998). The cognitive neuroscience of constructive memory. *Annual Review of Psychology, 49,* 289–318.

Siedlecki, K. L., Salthouse, T. A., & Berish, D. E. (2005). Is there anything special about the aging of source memory? *Psychology and Aging, 20,* 19–32.

Symons, C. S., & Johnson, B. T. (1997). The self-reference effect in memory: A meta-analysis. *Psychological Bulletin, 121,* 371–394.

Tessitore, A., Hariri, A. R., Fera, F., Smith, W. G., Das, S., Weinberger, D. R., et al. (2005). Functional changes in the activity of brain regions underlying emotion processing in the elderly. *Psychiatry Research, 139,* 9–18.

Tun, P. A., Wingfield, A., Rosen, M. J., & Blanchard, L. (1998). Response latencies for false memories: Gist-based processes in normal aging. *Psychology and Aging, 13,* 230–241.

Volkow, N. D., Logan, J., Fowler, J. S., Wang, G.-J., Gur, R. C., Wong, C., et al. (2000). Association between age-related decline in brain dopamine activity and impairment in frontal and cingulate metabolism. *American Journal of Psychiatry, 157,* 75–80.

Wagner, A. D., Schacter, D. L., Rotte, M., Koutstaal, W., Maril, A., Dale, A. M., et al. (1998). Building memories: Remembering and forgetting of verbal experiences as predicted by brain activity. *Science, 281*(5380), 1188–1191.

Wedig, M. M., Rauch, S. L., Albert, M. S., & Wright, C. I. (2005). Differential amygdala habituation to neutral faces in young and elderly adults. *Neuroscience Letters, 385,* 114–119.

Williams, L. M., Brown, K. J., Palmer, D., Liddell, B. J., Kemp, A. H., Olivieri, G., et al. (2006). The mellow years? Neural basis of improving emotional stability over age. *Journal of Neuroscience, 26,* 6422–6430.

Wright, C. I., Wedig, M. M., Williams, D., Rauch, S. L., & Albert, M. S. (2006). Novel fearful faces activate the amygdala in healthy young and elderly adults. *Neurobiology of Aging, 27,* 361–374.

Zacks, R., & Hasher, L. (1997). Cognitive gerontology and attentional inhibition: A reply to Burke and McDowd. *The Journals of Gerontology Series B–Psychological Sciences and Social Sciences, 52,* P274-P283.

Zacks, R. T., Hasher, L., & Li, K. Z. H. (2000). Human memory. In F. I. M. Craik & T. A. Salthouse (Eds.), *The handbook of aging and cognition* (2nd ed., pp. 293–357). Mahwah, NJ: Erlbaum.

2

Spending Patterns in the Older Population

Michael D. Hurd
RAND, NBER, MEA, and NETSPAR

and

Susann Rohwedder
RAND and NETSPAR

Introduction

As people age from middle to old age, the composition of their spending changes. For example, they spend relatively more on health care services, donations, and gifts and relatively less on automobiles, trips, and vacations. Furthermore, the level of spending declines. These patterns of spending are of interest to economists because the patterns convey information about how people choose to allocate their resources over the life cycle and about how changing physical capacities with age alter the benefit from different types of spending. The patterns are also of interest to researchers of consumer behavior because they can be used to understand how the changing demographic structure of the population will cause changes in the demand for different types of goods and services. In this chapter, we present results on spending by the U.S. population aged 51 or older. We show how the composition and level of spending vary with age and with income and wealth.

Age and Consumption

The leading model for understanding consumption by the older population is the life-cycle model of consumption. Its main emphasis has been the intertemporal allocation of the consumption of just one consumption good (Attanasio, 1999; Deaton, 1992; Gourinchas & Parker, 2002; Modigliani, 1986; Modigliani & Brumberg, 1954; Yaari, 1965). One important strand of this literature has made extensive use of household expenditure survey data to test whether or to what extent hypothesized economic models of intertemporal decision making are supported by the data. With its focus on one composite consumption good, this literature has shown little interest in the *composition* of consumption and how this might change over time.

Another extensive literature is concerned with the estimation of the determinants of the consumption of different types of goods within a single time period rather than across time periods, that is, the share of total spending or budget shares (Deaton & Muellbauer, 1980). An objective in this literature is to find the effects of prices on budget shares and to estimate demand elasticities with respect to income, so-called Engel curves.

There are some few studies that have combined these literatures to investigate the composition of household spending over the life cycle. Blundell, Browning, and Meghir (1994) showed that the allocation of spending across various types of goods within a period can be separated from the choice about how much to spend in each period. Their model estimation was limited to those younger than age 60, so the study is not empirically relevant to the older population. Fernández-Villaverde and Krueger (2002, 2007) developed a theoretical model that incorporates spending on durables, and they presented evidence based on the U.S. Consumer Expenditure Survey (CEX) providing empirical support for their model. Aguiar and Hurst (2008) used the CEX to study consumption categories by age, illustrating important variation in the age patterns across categories. One limitation of the CEX, however, is its rough data on income and its complete lack of data on assets. Both income and assets are important variables in determining both the levels of consumption and the composition of consumption.

To understand the consequences of an aging population, it is useful to combine a life-cycle model and a within-period choice model. The life-cycle model can help us understand the likely evolution of total spending as the population ages. A budget share model can help us understand shifts in demand for the various goods that will accompany both aging and the economic status of those approaching retirement.

In this chapter, we present age profiles of total consumption and its components for the U.S. population over the age of 50. Separately for singles and couples, we present how these vary not only by age but also by income and wealth. There is little comparable empirical evidence to the results we present. This is largely due to lack of adequate data. Collecting high-quality spending data is a survey time-intensive task, and it has largely been thought that to obtain good-quality data on total household spending would require asking about a very large number of spending categories, too many to be included in a general-purpose household survey. For example, the U.S. CEX collects information on spending on hundreds of different items, leaving limited room for other survey content. While it also elicits information on household income, it does not have any information on household assets. The data we use in this study stand out in this regard, combining good-quality information on household spending with high-quality income and wealth data as well as other covariates in the same survey. The data come from the Consumption and Activities Mail Survey (CAMS), which elicits spending over 12 months in more than 30 categories of spending. It is an ongoing supplement to the Health and Retirement Study (HRS), which is a longitudinal survey representative of the U.S. population over the age of 50.

Theoretical Considerations

In traditional economic analysis, goods and services are categorized as having a demand that is income elastic or a demand that is income inelastic. An income-elastic good has an income elasticity greater than 1, which means that if income increases by 1%, the amount spent on that good will increase by more than 1%. Such goods are called *superior goods*. An income-inelastic good has an income elasticity less than 1, so that if income increases by 1%, spending on that good will increase by less than 1%. Such goods are called *normal goods* or *necessities*. If all income is spent on consumption, which is the assumption in static economic analysis, the share of total spending on a superior good (the budget share) will increase with income, whereas the share spent on a necessity will decrease with income. In an intertemporal setting in which households may spend less than their income (save) or more than their income (dissave out of wealth), it is misleading to speak of the income elasticity of consumption of a good: Consumption is partially financed out of assets and partially out of income.

In multiperiod utility maximization, a household will decide how much to spend in a particular time period and how much to carry forward to the next time period. Once that decision has been made, it must decide how much of the budget allocated to the current time period to spend on each good. Thus, the within-period decision is the same as in the traditional static model, in which now income is replaced by the current period budget. The current period budget will depend on a number of factors, but the most important components will be income and wealth. Increases in income or wealth will increase the budget allocated for each time period. The share of spending on a superior good will increase as the allocated budget increases. If goods have differing elasticities of demand, their share of spending within a time period will differ across households because of differing within-period spending of the households, reflecting the differing levels of income and wealth of the households. The factors influencing these decisions will vary for singles and couples.

Singles

According to the life-cycle model, which is the leading model of inter-temporal economic decision making, the wealth of single persons will decline at advanced ages because spending will be greater than income. (Hurd and Rohwedder, 2009, reported that spending is greater than after-tax income by single persons age 65 and older, and that wealth declines in panel data.) As wealth declines, the fraction of total spending devoted to different categories of goods will change: Some goods are superior goods, and some are necessities. Thus, as a single person ages we would expect that the amounts spent on different categories of goods would not decline evenly, but some declines would be greater than others.

In addition to changes in the composition of consumption caused by changes in the overall level of consumption with age, it is likely that the composition will change because of a pure age effect. The effect on utility of the consumption of some types of goods is likely to change with age because of changes in physical and cognitive capacities. For example, the rate of automobile accidents increases with age, which makes the expected utility from driving an automobile decrease with age. Thus, we would expect that all else held equal (including total spending), spending on private transportation would decline with age, and the rate of decline would be greater than for many other categories of goods. The budget share devoted to private transportation would decline with age.

Couples

According to the life-cycle model, economic decision making by couples is much more complex than it is for single persons. The couple will want to make economic provisions for the surviving spouse, which means that its spending level will depend in a complicated way on the ages of both spouses, the economic circumstances of the couples, and the economic circumstances of the surviving spouse. Because all of these determinants change as the couple ages and because death is a stochastic event, the model makes no simple predictions about any wealth decline with age. Therefore, knowing that some particular good has inelastic demand does not mean that the budget share of that good will decline with age because total spending may not decline with age.

An additional complicating factor is related to returns-to-scale in consumption. For some types of consumption, each spouse requires as much spending to achieve a given level of utility as a single person. An example would be clothing, for which, all else held equal, a couple would spend twice as much as a single person. For other types of spending, however, a couple requires less than twice as much spending as a single person. Examples are housing, for which a considerable amount of the space in a house can be shared, or private transportation, for which a couple may share a car. If there are no returns-to-scale in consumption, a couple would need to spend twice as much as a single person to achieve the same utility level. This would happen if all goods were like clothing. If there are complete returns-to-scale, a couple could spend the same amount as a single person to achieve the same utility level: Two could live as cheaply as one. Actual returns-to-scale vary between the two extremes, and for any particular household, it will depend on the combination of goods the household consumed. Because the wealth elasticities of consumption of different goods are different, some wealthy couples may consume a bundle of goods for which returns-to-scale in consumption is high because of the particular mix of goods they have chosen, whereas other couples may consume a bundle of goods for which returns-to-scale in consumption is low because of the bundle of goods they have chosen to consume. The implication is that returns-to-scale is not fixed, but it will depend on the mix of goods actually chosen, which in turn will partially depend on wealth and age.

Because returns-to-scale depends on many factors, in our discussion of budget shares we will speak of some goods that exhibit greater returns-to-scale and some goods that exhibit lesser returns-to-scale rather than trying to classify goods according to their absolute level of returns-to-scale.

The implication is that even holding income and wealth constant, the budget shares of couples are likely to differ from the budget shares of single persons. Thus, to find interpretable age patterns we need to study the budget shares of the two groups separately.

Data

The data for this analysis come from the HRS, a multipurpose, longitudinal household survey providing extraordinarily rich data that is representative of the U.S. population over the age of 50.

At baseline, respondents were selected from the community-dwelling population (including retirement homes but not nursing homes). In subsequent waves, respondents were followed even if they entered an institution. The initial HRS wave took place in 1992 and had a unit response rate of 81%. The sample consisted of individuals born in 1931–1941 (age 51–61 in 1992), plus their spouses (of any age). They have since been interviewed every 2 years. The HRS oversamples Mexican Americans, African Americans, and Floridians. Over time, additional cohorts were added so that since 1998 the HRS has been representative of the U.S. population over the age of 50. Refresher cohorts of those 51–56 years old are added every 6 years. Newly married spouses of original respondents are included as new respondents. As a result, the HRS has interviewed about 30,000 individuals; some of them have been followed as long as 14 years. The most recent available data collection in 2006 (Wave 8) included 18,500 respondents in just over 12,500 households.

Consumption and Activities Mail Survey: A Supplement to the HRS

Our measure of consumption comes from the CAMS, which is administered to a random subsample of respondents to the HRS. The CAMS is a paper-and-pencil survey that is collected biennially in odd-numbered years. Its objective is to measure (among other things) total household spending over the previous 12 months. In this study, we use the first four waves of CAMS spanning the period from 2001 to 2007.

A random sample of 5,000 households (38.2% of all households interviewed in HRS 2000) was asked to participate in the initial wave of CAMS. The questionnaire was sent to one of the spouses, chosen at random, in each HRS household. The response rate to the first two waves was about 78% and in the next two waves about 72%. CAMS Wave 3 added 850 households representing the new cohort of 51- to 56-year-olds who were inducted into HRS in 2004.

In Wave 1, the respondent was asked about spending in 26 categories of nondurables and 6 categories of durables. The categories were chosen to match published CEX aggregates and cover all but a small percentage of spending as reported in the CEX. The rate of item nonresponse was very low, in the single digits for most categories. Waves 2 and 3 added a few more categories, amounting to about 7% of total spending for households aged 55 and above according to the CEX. We used imputations to deal with missing values in specific categories. If possible, we used additional background information from the HRS core. For example, when rent was missing, we checked home ownership status in adjacent HRS core waves, which resolved the vast majority of missing values for this category because these households typically report that they own their home. Because item nonresponse is so low, total imputed spending was a small fraction of total estimated spending (just 6.0% in Wave 1 and even lower in subsequent waves of CAMS).

TABLE 2.1

Spending in CAMS and CEX (2003$), Averaging Annual
Spending for 2001, 2003, and 2005, Weighted

Age Band	CAMS	CEX
55–64	38970	39677
65–74	34276	32436
75+	28761	24066
All	34472	33096

Source: CEX—publications on annual expenditures. CAMS—authors'
calculations based on a consistent list of spending categories
as elicited in CAMS 2001. CE Annual Reports: Consumer
Expenditures in 2001, 2003, 2005. Available online http://
www.bls.gov/cex/csxann01.pdf; http://www.bls.gov/cex/
csxann03.pdf; http://www.bls.gov/cex/csxann05.pdf

Note that for the purpose of measuring consumption, a mail survey is
highly advantageous because respondents can consult a spouse, examine
records, and answer at their convenience. The information collected in
CAMS can be linked to the rich information collected in the HRS core
survey. Another important feature of the CAMS is that it overlaps with
the measure of total income for the last calendar year in the HRS core. For
example, HRS 2006 collected total income for the calendar year of 2005,
which coincides with the CAMS 2005 spending measure. This allows
direct comparisons of spending with income for the same calendar year.

The validity of consumption measures is always a concern because of
inherent difficulties in their measurement. We have compared spending as
measured in CAMS with spending as measured in the CEX. Table 2.1 shows
averages from three waves of CAMS and from 3 years of the CEX in constant dollars (years 2001, 2003, and 2005). Averaged over all ages 55 or over,
CAMS and CEX spending were very close. The only notable difference was
at the oldest age, for which CAMS has higher spending. We have compared
"active saving," the difference between spending and after-tax income, with
wealth changes observed over long time periods and have concluded that
for the HRS population, the CAMS measure at older ages is more accurate
(Hurd & Rohwedder, 2009). Active saving implied by CAMS spending and
HRS after-tax income approximately predicts the wealth change, whereas
CEX spending would produce too much active saving at older ages.

Definition of Total Consumption and Categories of Consumption

CAMS collects information on spending, but the measure of interest for
this study is consumption. The difference between these two concepts
stems from durable goods that are paid for in one period (year) but whose
consumption services are enjoyed over several periods (years). We used

the data on spending on durables to estimate their consumption value for each household. For housing and transportation, we used additional data from the HRS core. Appendix 2.1 provides the details of our method.

Total consumption is the sum of the consumption of all measured nondurables, the consumption of services from five durables, the consumption of services from transportation (mainly automobiles), and the consumption of services from owner-occupied housing. (In CAMS Wave 2, the number of nondurable categories was increased to cover a small additional number of items. We adjusted the Wave 1 measure proportionally to account for this difference.)

We present evidence not only on total consumption but also on its components. To that end, we divided total consumption into the following subcategories:

Housing	Leisure
Health	Household supplies and services
Transportation	Clothing
Utilities	Durables
Donations and gifts	Personal care
Food	

Appendix 2.2 lists the detailed categories elicited in CAMS that were included in each of these consumption categories.

Income, Wealth, and Total Consumption

To put our results about budget shares in context, we first present averages of income, wealth, and total consumption. Income and wealth were measured in the HRS core preceding the CAMS survey. Thus, we used pooled data from HRS 2000, 2002, 2004, and 2006 and converted to 2003 dollars using the Consumer Price Index.

Figure 2.1 has the results. Income begins to decline at typical retirement ages (60–64) and declines steadily to advanced old age. (We have deleted the observation for couples 90 or older because of small sample size; there were just 28 couples aged 90 or older in the CAMS.) Couples have more than twice the income of single persons at almost all ages. The age pattern of wealth is much more complex because of four effects. (*Wealth* is the net value of all assets, including housing wealth. It does not include capitalized pension or Social Security income, which are included in the income flows.) The first is that individuals in the different age bands come from different cohorts that had different levels of lifetime wealth and different

Income in 2003$

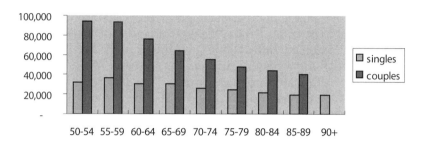

Wealth in 2003$

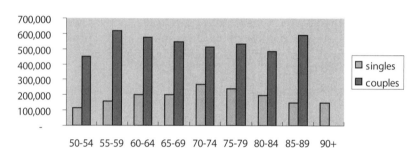

Total consumption in 2003$

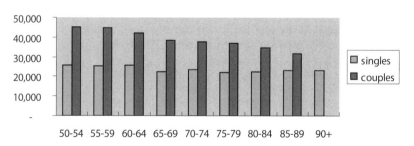

FIGURE 2.1
Patterns of income, wealth, and consumption by age.

rates of return on their savings. Thus, they would have had different levels of wealth at retirement. Second, the poor die sooner than the well-to-do, so that the average wealth of a cohort will tend to increase over time. Third, as predicted by the life-cycle model, single persons consume more than their income, so that their wealth declines as they age. Fourth, and most importantly for singles, couples have much more wealth than singles, so that at widowing a relatively wealthy widow(er) joins a group of relatively poor prior single persons, increasing the average wealth of all singles. Because there are a large number of couples whose ages are 70 to 80 and the rate of widowing is fairly high, the flow of new widow(er)s is high in the 70s. When combined with declining wealth as single persons age, the average wealth of single persons peaks in the age band 70–74.

As shown in the last panel of Figure 2.1, consumption by couples is less than twice consumption by singles, even though economic resources are more than twice as great. The relatively low level of consumption by couples partially reflects returns-to-scale in consumption. Consumption by single persons is greater than income at advanced ages, which would lead to wealth declines with age. In fact, the decline is greater than suggested by this comparison because income is measured prior to taxes: Particularly for couples and for younger single persons, taxes reduce income by a substantial amount. As with wealth, these cross-section patterns reflect cohort differences, differential mortality, life-cycle declines in consumption, and widowing effects.

Composition of Consumption

We present evidence about the composition of consumption based on budget shares. A *budget share* is the ratio of spending on a particular category of spending to total spending. To reduce any effect of observation error, we calculated budget shares at the group level. For example, the budget share in food of single persons aged 50–54 was total spending on food by people in that age group divided by total spending by the same people.

We pooled the four waves of CAMS data, expressing all consumption items in constant 2003 dollars. Stratifying by marital status and age, we computed average consumption in each of 11 categories of consumption and divided by average total consumption for that group. Figure 2.2 shows the resulting patterns for singles and couples by age.

Housing

Housing is the largest consumption item for both single and couple households. It amounts to between 20% and 30% of total consumption. Holding age constant, the budget share for single persons is about 5 percentage points greater than for couples. To see the effect of returns-to-scale in housing services, it is useful to compare housing with consumption of health care services. The budget shares of singles and couples in health care services are almost the same, suggesting that housing provides substantial returns-to-scale relative to health care. This is, of course, quite reasonable as health care services are delivered to an individual rather than to a household, whereas two people only need one kitchen, one heating system, and

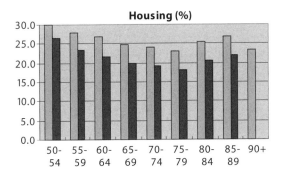

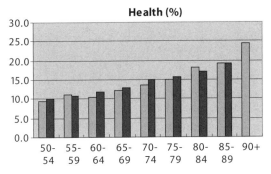

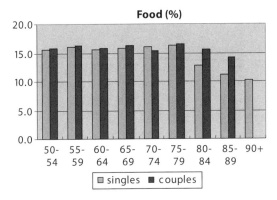

FIGURE 2.2
Budget shares in percent of total consumption.

so on. The age pattern of housing services is U-shaped, most likely a reflection of downsizing with age, differential mortality, and widowing.

Health

Among the younger age groups in our sample, the fraction of total consumption dedicated to health-related goods and services is of moderate

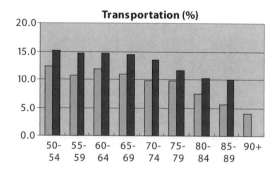

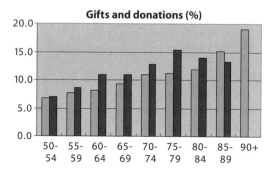

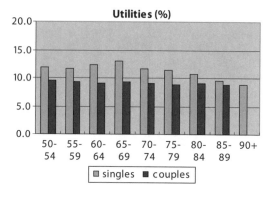

FIGURE 2.2 (continued)

size, around 10% of total consumption. (Our measure of health care spending is only out-of-pocket spending, which is just a fraction of total spending. The larger portion is paid by insurance, especially Medicare after the age of 65.) However, this fraction is substantially higher at more advanced ages (20% or more for those aged 85+). As individuals' health status declines with age, the marginal utility of consumption of health-related goods and services increases, which is consistent with our observation of a higher fraction of total spending being allocated to this cause.

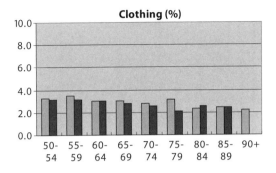

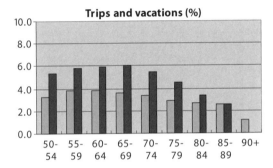

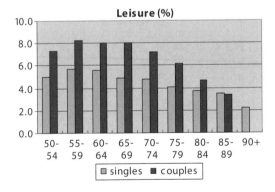

FIGURE 2.2 (continued)

Food

Singles and couples devoted about the same share (about 16%) of their consumption to food, and this share is constant across all age groups, except for those aged 80 and older, for whom the budget share of food is smaller. This suggests no returns-to-scale in food consumption. Of course, this is not true for the *time* spent on food preparation: One person can fix the same meal for two persons in roughly the same time that it takes for one person. However, home production is not accounted for in our measure

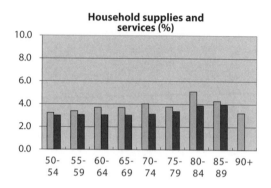

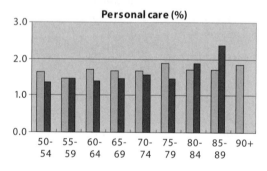

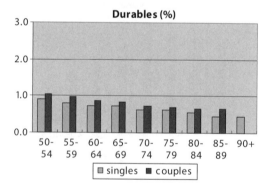

FIGURE 2.2 (continued)

of consumption. At older ages, the physical demands of meal preparation may be responsible for smaller budget shares. In addition, some meals may be included in rent in group living situations.

Transportation

Couples devote a higher share of their total consumption to transportation than single persons, whereas considerations of returns-to-scale would suggest just the opposite. Apparently, the greater wealth of couples more than offsets any returns-to-scale. The strongly declining age pattern is in line with reduced use and reduced replacement of cars at older ages. Limited physical mobility and declines in cognitive ability at higher ages lead individuals to use their car less.

Gifts and Donations

The age variation in the budget shares of gifts and donations is distinctly different from that of most other consumption categories. It is strongly increasing in age, in particular for singles: Among 50- to 54-year-olds, gifts and donations make up about 7% of total consumption, and the share steadily increases until it reaches about 19% for singles aged 90 or older. This increase suggests a substitution between intervivos giving and bequests: At advanced age, when mortality risk is high, money that would be given as a bequest can safely be given as an intervivos transfer because the risk for outliving resources is low. Couples in their early 50s devote about the same fraction of total spending to this consumption category as their single peers at that age (about 7%). However, at almost any older ages the budget share is higher among couples than among singles. This higher level is likely a reflection of the greater fraction of couples who are parents (97%) compared with single persons (88%).

Utilities

The observed patterns in the budget share committed to utilities show close resemblance to those observed for housing, albeit at lower levels. It is quite natural to think of some proportionality between house size and utilities such as heating and electricity. The age profile is largely flat, and the share of couples (just under 10%) is lower than that of singles (around 12%) except at advanced old age (85 and older), when the budget share of utilities for singles is about the same as that for couples. This is suggestive of returns-to-scale in the consumption of utility services at most ages.

Clothing

The budget shares for clothing are virtually identical between singles and couples because there are no returns-to-scale in this category. Age patterns are somewhat difficult to detect as clothing makes up such a small fraction of total consumption, ranging between 2 and 3.5%. Closer inspection reveals higher budget shares at younger ages than at older ages in our sample. This is likely due to work-related expenses incurred by a large fraction of people in their early 50s and much reduced replacement of clothes by those at advanced old ages.

Trips and Vacations

Spending on trips and vacations is part of spending on leisure, but it is of interest in its own right. The age patterns of spending by couples and singles are approximately the same: higher levels during the years of retirement and shortly following retirement as people use some of the time previously spent working in travel. But spending on travel decreases at older ages. Reduced mobility and cognitive capacity make trips and vacations harder to undertake. Couples spend more of their budgets than single persons, mostly likely because the availability of a traveling companion increases the utility from traveling.

Leisure

Trips and vacations make up about three fourths of spending on leisure activities, so naturally the pattern is very similar.

Household Supplies and Services

The budget share of single persons allocated to this consumption category is slightly higher than that of couples. This is the case for all age groups we considered. This implies that there are returns-to-scale in household supplies and services, as there are with anything housing related. Note that overall the size of budget shares devoted to this category (and the scale in the graph) are substantially smaller than the ones we have discussed so far. Households in their early 50s—singles as well as couples—commit about 3% of total consumption to this category. At older ages, this fraction is slightly higher (4% for couples, 5% for singles), reflecting the need for additional help in the household as individuals' mobility declines.

Personal Care

Personal care spending is a small fraction of total spending. Any age pattern is not quantitatively important.

Durables

Durables comprise a very small share of total budget, and the fraction declines with age. Apparently, older people replace durables less frequently than younger people.

Income and Wealth Effects

We found income and wealth effects on budget shares by marital status from the regression at the individual level of the budget share (as percent of total spending) on indicator variables for age band and indicator variables for income and wealth quartiles. We defined the quartiles separately by marital status. An example of such a regression is in Table 2.2. It shows estimated age, income, and wealth effects for single persons for the share of donations and gifts in the budget. The age pattern is the same as in Figure 2.2, which did not control for income or wealth, but the pattern was attenuated. In the figure, the difference in budget shares between the youngest and oldest groups is 12 percentage points, whereas the difference in the regression is about 5 percentage points (3.5 – (−1.4)). The differences arise because the regression was at the individual level, whereas the figure is based on grouped shares and because the regression controls for income and wealth.

Table 2.2 shows that income and wealth affect the budget share on donations and gifts in approximately the same manner: Those in the highest quartile of either income or wealth spend about 4 percentage points more of their budgets on donations than those in the lowest quartile. This variation is a substantial fraction of the average budget share, which is 7.4%.

The pattern of age effects in Figure 2.2 carries over to the regressions of many of the other budget shares, but with attenuation, so we do not present more of them.

TABLE 2.2

Singles: Regression of Percentage of Total
Spending for Donations and Gifts

	Coefficient	P-value
Age band		
50–54	−1.4	0.01
55–59	−0.5	0.37
60–64	−0.4	0.29
65–69	—	—
70–74	0.7	0.15
75–79	1.9	0.00
80–84	2.1	0.00
85–89	3.7	0.00
90+	3.5	0.00
Wealth lowest quartile	—	—
2	0.5	0.18
3	2.5	0.00
Highest	4.5	0.00
Income lowest quartile	—	—
2	0.4	0.25
3	2.1	0.00
Highest	3.8	0.00
Constant	3.3	0.00

Of more interest are the income and wealth elasticities. To simplify the presentation and to show maximal variation in budget shares as economic resources vary, we added together the income and wealth effects, and Figure 2.3 shows the sum of the two.

The consumption of housing services by single persons averages about 25% of total spending. Relative to that high level, the fraction of total spending on housing services shows no strong, consistent pattern across the quartiles. However, over the three bottom quartiles, the budget share declines with increases in economic resources, indicating that for most of the income/wealth distribution, housing is a normal good or necessity. Among couples, average spending on housing is about 20% of the budget. There is no variation except at the top quartile, for which the share increases by about 2 percentage points.

Near the bottom of the income/wealth distribution, transportation is a superior good among single persons; otherwise, there is little variation in budget shares. The implication is that as economic resources decline to a low level, spending on transportation would be reduced at a high rate. Among couples, there is little variation in budget shares on transportation. One possible explanation is that couples have substantially greater economic resources than singles (see Figure 2.1), so that even couples in the lowest wealth quartile have resources equivalent to singles in the second or third quartile.

The fraction of the budget spent on utilities declines consistently for both singles and couples. The average budget share is 11–14%, so that the decline is a substantial fraction of the average. The implication is that utilities are a necessity.

With the exception of the lowest quartile for singles, budget shares for health decline systematically, indicating health care spending is a necessity. The anomaly at the lowest quartile can be explained by Medicaid, which covers all spending by those who qualify. A substantial fraction of single persons in the lowest income/wealth quartile would be covered by Medicaid, whereas very few couples would be covered because of their higher economic status even in the lowest quartile for couples. (In the 2004 HRS, 13.4% of single persons were covered by Medicaid, but just 3.1% of couples were covered.)

The average budget share for gifts and donations is 7–8%. As shown in Figure 2.3, the variation with the income/wealth quartiles is 8–9 percentage points. Gifts and donations are a strongly superior good.

The budget share of food declines consistent with economic resources. The comparison with donations shows why it is meaningful to call food a necessity: Whereas the budget share allocated to donations falls sharply as economic resources decline, the budget share allocated to food increases sharply.

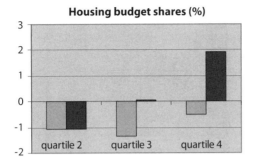

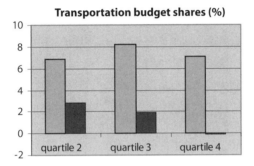

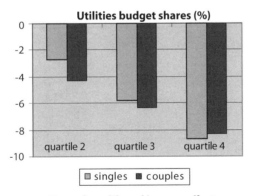

Sum of wealth and income effects

FIGURE 2.3
Income and wealth effects on budget shares, expressed as percentage point deviations from the first income and wealth quartile.

Note: The figures show the difference in the percentage spent on a category by households in the upper income and wealth quartiles relative to households in the lowest quartile.

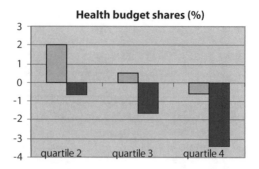

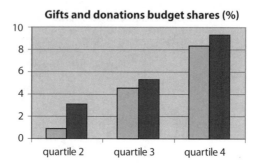

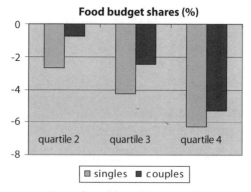

Sum of wealth and income effects

FIGURE 2.3 (continued)

Among single persons, clothing is a necessity at the lowest level of economic resources; at higher levels, it is neutral. Among couples, with their higher levels of economic resources, clothing is always neutral.

The average budget share for leisure activities, which includes trips and vacations, is 4–7%. As shown in Figure 2.3, it is a strongly superior

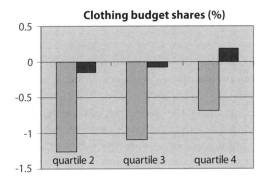

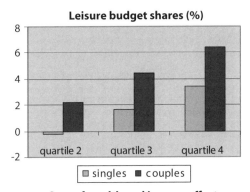

Sum of wealth and income effects

FIGURE 2.3 (continued)

good, particularly among couples, for whom the variation is as large as the average.

The other categories of spending, household supplies and services, personal care, and durables have small budget shares, and the variation across the quartiles is less than 1 percentage point. Therefore, we do not show them.

We summarize the income and wealth effects on budget shares as follows: For some categories, whether the good is necessary or superior depends on the position of the household in the income/wealth distribution. For example, among single persons, the budget share on transportation is approximately constant except at the lowest quartile. Thus, transportation is a superior good at the lower end of the income/wealth distribution and a neutral one at the upper end of the distribution. Clothing is a necessity at the lower end and a neutral good at the upper end of the income/wealth distribution. Donations and leisure spending are consistently superior goods; food, utilities, and health care spending are consistently necessities. Housing is approximately a neutral good.

Conclusions

We have shown that there are economically important patterns in the budget shares of many goods and services consumed by the older population. The patterns are a function of age, marital status, and economic resources. The results imply that as the population ages it will tend to consume fewer transportation services and spend less on trips and vacations and food. It will spend more on health care services and make more gifts and donations. However, these predictions need to be modified by the trend in economic resources of the older population. If the older population continues to become more wealthy (as it has in the past), it will spend relatively less on health care and food and more on leisure activities, primarily travel.

Acknowledgment

Financial support from the National Institute on Aging under grant P01AG008291 and P01AG022481 is gratefully acknowledged. Thanks to Joanna Carroll for excellent programming assistance.

Appendix 2.1: Estimating Consumption Services Derived From Durables

For five of our big-ticket items (excluding automobile purchases), our general strategy was to estimate in CAMS the probability of a purchase and the expected value conditional on a purchase as functions of important covariates such as income, wealth, age, and marital status. Then, we imputed an annual purchase amount that, in equilibrium, would be equal to the annual consumption with straight-line depreciation. In particular, we made the following assumptions and calculations: We assumed straight-line depreciation and that average annual consumption is equal to average annual depreciation. We estimated logistic functions for the probability of annual purchase. Covariates were age, income, marital status, and number of household residents. We estimated spending conditional on purchase using the same covariates as for purchase. Then, predicted average annual consumption on five big-ticket items was calculated as

$$\text{Average annual consumption on five big-ticket items} = \sum_{i=1}^{5}$$

(Probability of purchasing item *i*) (Expected amount given purchase of item *i*)

To give an example of the resulting consumption services from durables that we obtained in this manner, the mean consumption in 2001 of the five big-ticket items was estimated to be $282 per year with a range of $70 to $2,682.

Because we had the value of automobiles and other vehicles used for transportation in the HRS in 2000 and 2002, we calculated the flow of services from the actual values. This calculation more accurately estimated the flow of services for low-income households. We made these assumptions and calculations: The value of transportation (almost all automobiles) was measured in the HRS core; user cost is the sum of interest on the value, depreciation on a 12-year schedule, and observed maintenance costs from CAMS. We found that the mean flow of services was $2,912 per year with a range of $0 to $41,040.

We followed a similar strategy to estimate the flow of consumption services from owner-occupied housing by estimating a rental equivalent: the amount the housing unit would rent for in a competitive market in equilibrium. In particular, we made the following assumptions and calculations: (a) The interest cost is the value of housing multiplied by the prevailing interest rate. We used the observed house value from the HRS core and assumed an interest rate of 7.16%, which was the average 30-year mortgage interest rate in 2001. (b) We estimated depreciation from maintenance costs, which were observed in CAMS and from the observed house value: We assumed depreciation of 2.14% per year, which is equivalent to a depreciation period of 47 years. The flow of housing services is the sum of these items, amounting to $13,500 dollars at the mean among home owners and $10,000 dollars at the median.

Appendix 2.2: Detailed Composition of Consumption Categories

Consumption categories were derived directly from the spending items collected in the CAMS questionnaires. The questionnaires are available onlineathttp://hrsonline.isr.umich.edu/meta/sho_meta.php?hfyle=qnaires #online2, see "Off-Year Questionnaires."

Housing
- Estimated consumption services from housing as detailed in Appendix 2.1. Conceptually, it accounts for the interest cost on the value of the house, depreciation, and maintenance.

Health (out-of-pocket cost only, not what is covered by insurance)
- Health insurance premiums
- Prescription and nonprescription medications
- Health care services
- Medical supplies

Transportation
- Estimated consumption services from owned vehicles as detailed in Appendix 2.1. Conceptually, it accounts for the interest cost on the value of any owned vehicles, depreciation, and maintenance.

Utilities
- Electricity
- Water
- Heating fuel for the home
- Telephone, cable, Internet

Gifts and donations
- Contributions to religious, educational, charitable, or political organizations
- Cash or gifts to family and friends outside the household

Food
- Food and beverages
- Dining or drinking out

Leisure
- Trips and vacations
- Hobbies and leisure equipment
- Sports
- Tickets to movies, sporting events, and performing arts

Household supplies and services
- Housekeeping supplies
- Housekeeping, dry cleaning, and laundry services
- Gardening and yard supplies
- Gardening and yard services

Clothing
- Clothing and apparel

Durables
- Refrigerator
- Washing machine and dryer
- Dishwasher
- TV
- Computer

Personal care
- No further subcategories

References

Aguiar, M., & Hurst, E. (2008). *Deconstructing lifecycle expenditure.* Michigan Retirement Research Center Working Paper WP 2008-173. University of Michigan, Ann Arbor.

Attanasio, O. P. (1999). Consumption demand. In J. Taylor and M. Woodford (Eds.), *Handbook of macroeconomics* (Vol. 1, pp. 741–812). Amsterdam: Elsevier Science.

Blundell, R., Browning, M., & Meghir, C. (1994). Consumer demand and the life-cycle allocation of household expenditures. *The Review of Economic Studies, 61,* 57–80

Deaton, A. (1992). *Understanding consumption.* New York: Oxford University Press.

Deaton, A. S., & Muellbauer, J. (1980). An almost ideal demand system. *American Economic Review, 70,* 312–326.

Fernández-Villaverde, J., & Krueger, D. (2002). Consumption and saving over the life cycle: How important are consumer durables. Stanford Institute for Economic Policy Research Discussion Paper 01-34, August 2002.

Fernández-Villaverde, J., & Krueger, D. (2007) Consumption over the life cycle: Facts from Consumer Expenditure Survey data. *Review of Economics and Statistics, 89,* 552–565.

Gourinchas, P., & Parker, J. (2002). Consumption over the life cycle. *Econometrica, 70,* 47–89.

Hurd, M. D., & Rohwedder, S. (2009). Wealth change and active saving at older ages. Paper presented at the American Economic Association annual meetings, San Francisco, January 2009.

Modigliani, F. (1986). Life cycle, individual thrift, and the wealth of nations. *American Economic Review, 76,* 297–313.

Modigliani, F., & Brumberg, R. (1954). Utility analysis and the consumption function: An interpretation of the cross section data. In K. Kurihara (Ed.), *Post-Keynesian economics* (pp. 388–436). New Brunswick, NJ: Rutgers University Press.

Yaari, M. E. (1965). Uncertain lifetime, life insurance and the theory of the consumer. *Review of Economic Studies, 32,* 137–150.

3

Socioemotional Selectivity Theory: Implications for Consumer Research

Aimee Drolet
University of California, Los Angeles

Loraine Lau-Gesk
University of California, Irvine

Patti Williams
University of Pennsylvania

and

Hyewook Genevieve Jeong
University of California, Los Angeles

Introduction

Older consumers are an increasingly important market segment. Understanding the goals of their consumption activities is critical for marketers who seek to create products and services that are relevant to them. Past research has revealed substantial differences in how older versus young adult consumers respond to marketplace factors (for reviews, see Cole et al., 2008; Yoon et al., 2005; Yoon, Cole, & Lee, 2009). Until relatively recently, most of this research has attributed these differences to age-related short-falls in the cognitive system. Previous studies have shown that, compared to young adults, older adults have decreased attentional ability and memory (including sensory, working, short-term, long-term, and remote memory; for a review, see Poon, 1985). Older adults also have a relatively decreased capacity to process data deeply and elaborately. These cognitive deficits influence how older consumers process information (e.g., John & Cole, 1986; Yoon, 1997) and in turn how they respond to marketing variables, such as product information (e.g., Cole & Balasubramanian, 1993; Cole & Gaeth, 1990); advertising (e.g., Drolet, Williams, & Lau-Gesk, 2007; Gaeth & Heath, 1987; Skurnik, Yoon, Park, & Schwarz, 2005); and retail channels (e.g., Lambert-Pandraud, Laurent, & Lapersonne, 2005).

However, cognitive performance is not the only thing that changes with age. Studies have demonstrated significant age-related motivational differences that, in addition to changes in cognition, influence how older versus young adult consumers process information (e.g., Hashtroudi, Johnson, Vnek, & Ferguson, 1994; Isaacowitz, Charles, & Carstensen, 2000). For example, research has attributed differences in preferences and memory for different kinds of marketing communications to motivational developments due to aging (e.g., Fung & Carstensen, 2003; Williams & Drolet, 2005).

Specifically, research shows that aging is associated with an increase in people's motivation to attend to more emotional versus nonemotional information, such as factual information (e.g., Labouvie-Vief & Blanchard-Fields, 1982). Undirected, older adults tend to adopt a more subjective and evaluative processing style, whereas young adults tend to adopt a more objective and factual processing style (Isaacowitz et al., 2000). Some researchers have attributed this difference in style to the fact that older adults place a heavier emphasis on personal values and experiences (Labouvie-Vief & Blanchard-Fields, 1982). This heavier emphasis affects attentional processes, leading them to focus more on emotional information (for a review, see Mather, 2004). This increased focus is associated with a decrease in memory for factual information (e.g., Hashtroudi et al., 1994) and can have an impact on older adults' decision-making performance in certain tasks (e.g., Peters, Finucane, MacGregor, & Slovic, 2000).

What explains older adults' increased focus on emotion? Research has offered several distinct perspectives. A familiar one is cognitive decline, with an emphasis on how factual information is processed and which suggests that older adults somehow become sidetracked by emotion. Age-related declines, for example, in attentional ability have been implicated. Declining attentional ability has been linked to an increase in the activation of nongoal paths (Hasher & Zacks, 1988). This results in greater competition for target ideas at retrieval (Isaacowitz et al., 2000) and, correspondingly, more intrusions of irrelevant and peripheral information. Past research (e.g., in persuasion and decision making) has often treated emotional information as peripheral to decision tasks (e.g., Eagly & Chaiken, 1993). In contrast, another perspective suggests that older adults' increased focus on emotion is the result of maturation and acknowledges that, in real life, facts and emotions are inextricably entwined. As people mature, they develop a more complex understanding of emotions and, as part of wisdom development, try to integrate their emotions with their cognitions (i.e., thoughts and beliefs) (Labouvie-Vief, 1998). As a result, older adults are better able both to acknowledge and to manage their emotions (i.e., accept them, integrate them with factual information, and regulate them) compared to young adults (Blanchard-Fields, 1986; Gross et al., 1997; Labouvie-Vief, DeVoe, & Bulka, 1989).

In addition to both cognitive decline and maturation, the perception of the shortness of the life span is a key reason why older adults are more motivated to focus on emotion (Carstensen, 1992). According to socioemotional selectivity theory (SST), a view that time is limited—that people do not have all the time left in the world—versus expansive leads people to shift their attention toward emotion and emotion regulation goals and away from knowledge acquisition goals.

The implications of SST are far reaching, and a large body of research supports the predictions of SST. Despite both the breadth and the depth of this research, thus far, relatively little research has considered the implications of SST within consumer contexts. The goal of this chapter is to consider how SST fits with research on older consumers.

This chapter is organized as follows: We first provide a review of SST and of the psychology literature on SST. We then discuss literature that has considered SST within consumer contexts. Next, we present an experiment whose aim was to add to both the psychological and consumer literatures and, importantly, our understanding of the implications of SST for consumer behavior. Finally, we consider several issues relating to the application of SST to consumer contexts. We propose several suggestions for future consumer research based on SST.

Socioemotional Selectivity Theory

Socioemotional selectivity theory addresses the impact of time in predicting the goals that people pursue, especially social goals. The fundamental tenet of SST is that individuals naturally tend to assess time as either limited or expansive (Carstensen, 1992). This time horizon perspective has implications for which goals are salient and, in turn, which goals people choose to pursue.

In particular, when time is viewed as limited, people tend to be more present oriented. They tend to seek satisfaction in the moment and are focused on what can be experienced and enjoyed now (Carstensen, Isaacowitz, & Charles, 1999). People with a limited time horizon view devote more effort to deriving emotional meaning and more attention to social connectedness. Perceiving time as limited has consequences for the selection of social partners. People with a limited time horizon view are generally more focused on intimacy and affective gain in their social interactions. As a result, they tend to limit their interactions to people with whom they are familiar and care most about, thereby garnering emotional experiences that are generally more predictable and more likely to be positive (Carstensen & Charles, 1998). When people with a limited time horizon view do consider new social partners, they tend to be more focused on their emotional potential rather than, for example, on their potential for supplying new information.

In contrast, according to SST, when people view time as expansive, they tend to be more future oriented. They seek future rather than present satisfaction. They focus more on what can be experienced and enjoyed later. Accordingly, they devote more effort to pursuing knowledge and to planning to be prepared for the future. In general, people with an expansive time horizon tend to be more acquisitive and more likely to seek novelty (e.g., Fung, Carstensen, & Lutz, 1999).

There are several important assumptions underlying SST. One assumption has to do with the monitoring of time. SST maintains that the monitoring of time (i.e., to be more limited vs. expansive) is a nonconscious, ongoing, regular process. It is this process, and not aging per se, that is responsible for the motivational changes seen in information-processing and emotion regulation goals (Carstensen et al., 1999). In addition, SST assumes that people simultaneously hold multiple goals. As a precursor to action, a selection of goals occurs. Specifically, according to SST, the time horizon perspective, whether limited or expansive, influences the appraisal process that precedes goal selection (Carstensen et al., 1999). Next, we discuss these two assumptions in more detail, as they have important implications for our understanding of the goal-setting and behavior of older consumers.

Effects of Time Horizon Perspective Versus Aging

The majority of research related to SST has centered on age as a determinant of people's time horizon perceptions. According to SST, age is essentially a proxy for the time horizon perspective, with the time horizon perspective naturally becoming more limited as people age. Indeed, the perception of time as limited is more likely to occur in later versus earlier adulthood (Carstensen & Charles, 1998). Older adults typically have a more limited time horizon view (Carstensen & Lang, 1997). This is not surprising given that, chronologically speaking, they are closer to the end of their lives.

Researchers have looked at other naturally occurring determinants of the length of people's time horizon view. For example, Fredrickson (1995) compared college seniors to college freshmen and found that the former, who were faced with a social ending (graduation), tended to prefer intimate and familiar others versus new social partners (see also Pruzan & Isaacowitz, 2006). Carstensen and Fredrickson (1998) showed that HIV status, whether positive or negative and symptomatic or asymptomatic, was related to time horizon perspective and the degree to which individuals pursued emotional closeness with others. Fung and Carstensen (2006) examined people's interpersonal goal pursuits before and after the September 11 attacks and during the SARS (severe acute respiratory syndrome) epidemic in Hong Kong. Their findings likewise suggested that, apart from aging, events that prime the shortness of the life span shift social goal pursuit from acquiring knowledge to deriving emotional meaning.

Notwithstanding, without prompting, the default mode appears to be for young adults to view time as expansive and for older adults to view time as limited (Fung et al., 1999). Far more than young adults, older adults describe their futures as limited. In contrast, far more than young adults, older adults recognize they may be nearing the end of life (Carstensen & Lang, 1997).

Importantly—perhaps especially so for marketers—the time horizon perspective can also be created situationally. Young adults can be made to adopt a limited time horizon view and as a result prefer to interact with familiar versus unfamiliar others (Fredrickson & Carstensen, 1990). Correspondingly, older adults can be made to adopt an expansive time horizon view and as a result prefer to interact with unfamiliar versus familiar others, mimicking the preferences typically found for young adults when undirected (e.g., Fung et al., 1999). That the time horizon perspective can be manipulated has important implications for consumer research, as we discuss in this chapter.

In summary, SST supports the notion that, regardless of age, social preferences hinge on time horizon perspective. In this way, SST stands out as a theory that identifies situational rather than dispositional factors as the cause of changes in the goal setting and behavior of older adults (for discussion, see Sneed & Whitbourne, 2005). Indeed, consistent with SST, older adults tend to have more limited social networks that consist of people who are already well known. When older or young adults perceive time as limited, their social goals tend to be more present oriented and take the form of maximizing emotionally positive and meaningful interactions with close others. Accordingly, the size of their social networks is smaller (compared to people who do not perceive time as limited). Over the life span, people gradually interact with fewer people, as they withdraw from peripheral relationships and become more involved in their central relationships (i.e., relationships with family and close friends).

In this chapter, we consider the implications of this for consumer research. Consumer research has not, for example, directly examined the influence of time horizon perceptions on the size of relevant consumer networks (e.g., a network of retailers or products). Some research indicated that consumers become more loyal as they age. For example, Lambert-Pandraud and colleagues (2005) found that older consumers shopping for a new car visited fewer dealerships. This finding may be due to older consumers having a more limited time horizon perspective, and as a result, they may seek to interact with familiar sales and maintenance people. However, in addition to having a limited time horizon perspective, there are many other factors (e.g., decreased mobility, differences in brand knowledge, etc.) that underlie this shopping behavior. These age-related factors converge. Accordingly, the degree to which having a limited time horizon perspective is responsible for this and other older consumer shopping behaviors is unclear and may be difficult to ascertain.

Implications of SST for Emotion-Related Versus Knowledge-Related Goal Pursuit

According to SST, as time passes and people's time horizon perspectives become more limited, goals focusing on knowledge acquisition become less salient and goals focusing on emotional well-being become more so. This change in goal pursuit serves an adaptive function, with people seeking to maximize gains and minimize risks in social and emotional domains.

The perception of time as limited has important implications for emotion regulation processes. The increased attention to emotion due to a limited time horizon view results in increased attempts to manage emotions, especially negative emotions. People with a limited time horizon view try to avoid negative events and information (i.e., stimuli that can detract from their current emotional experience).

Consistent with SST, emotion regulation does appear to be a more central goal for older adults than for young adults. Older adults appear more likely than young adults to engage in emotion regulation, particularly in antecedent-focused emotion regulation, which involves attempts to prevent negative emotions from occurring in the first place, by selecting situations or people in order to avoid negative emotional triggers (Gross et al., 1997; but see Blanchard-Fields, Stein, & Watson, 2004). For example, people may avoid encounters with others (antecedents of emotional outcomes) known to provoke feelings of anger, fear, or sadness.

Older adults appear better able than young adults to manage their emotions. Studies have shown that older adults recall fewer negative (vs. positive) images (Charles, Mather, & Carstensen, 2003). Indeed, findings of functional magnetic resonance imaging (fMRI) studies implied that older adults have reduced encoding of negative emotional experiences. Older adults showed less activation in the amygdala for negative (vs. positive) images; this pattern of activation does not occur among young adults (Mather & Carstensen, 2003). In summary, both cross-sectional and longitudinal studies have found that older adults reported experiencing less negative affect (e.g., anxiety) compared to young adults (Charles, Reynolds, & Gatz, 2001; Gross et al., 1997). Some research has shown, however, that this "positivity effect" holds only for relatively nonarousing material (Kensinger, 2008). Young and older adults may remember negative and positive arousing words equally well. Notably, older adults appeared to experience positive affect as often as (Charles et al., 2001) or more often than (Mroczek & Kolarz, 1998) young adults (see also, Lawton, Kleban, Rajagopal, & Dean, 1992; Ryff, 1989).

Time horizon perspective may also be associated with the tendency to experience simultaneous mixtures of positive and negative emotions or poignancy (Ersner-Hershfield, Mikels, Sullivan, & Carstensen, 2008). Limited time horizons, when coupled with the loss of something emotionally meaningful, can produce feelings of both happiness and sadness. Both older and younger participants asked to envision endings have been found to experience an increase in mixed emotions, such that a component of sadness can be added to an already happy experience. Thus, graduating college seniors who are reminded that today will be their last day at their alma mater experience not only substantial happiness at the prospect of their graduations but also greater sadness than similar graduates in a control time horizon condition.

Accordingly, some issues relevant for consumer researchers are (a) the degree to which time horizon perspective affects how consumers make trade-offs between emotion-related and knowledge-related goals and (b) the degree to which older (vs. young adult) consumers engage in emotion regulation processes. In most consumer contexts, people seek to regulate their emotions and emotional experiences. Marketers help people do this by devising consumption activities that provide people with positive emotional outcomes and forestall negative ones. SST focuses on how people trade off between two kinds of goals, emotion-related goals and knowledge-related goals. In consumer contexts, these two goals can compete. However, frequently they do not. Marketers generally seek to provide consumers with sufficient knowledge about an upcoming consumption experience, namely, the knowledge that the experience will be emotionally rewarding. In what consumer contexts, then, is SST relevant? This question is considered next.

Socioemotional Selectivity Theory and Consumer Behavior

Socioemotional selectivity theory predicts that, to regulate their emotions efficiently, people who view their time as limited are motivated to focus on emotional content in all contexts, including consumer information-processing contexts (Isaacowitz et al., 2000). As evidenced by the increasing influence of SST in psychological research, the expectation is that SST will be increasingly influential in consumer research. We review prior work that has studied the effects of time horizon perspective and aging on consumer responses. Thus far, this research has been limited. This chapter supplements this research with new consumer study, which is described in the next section.

Fung and Carstensen (2003) studied the effects of aging and time horizon perspective on responses to advertising. Specifically, they investigated the effects of aging and of an expansive versus a control (no) time horizon perspective on preferences for ads that emphasized either emotion-related goals (how the product is related to love and caring) or knowledge-related goals (how the product is related to gaining new knowledge or achieving success in the future). The ads consisted of a slogan ("Capture the unexplored world" or "Stay healthy for your bright future" for the knowledge-focused ad vs. "Capture those special moments" or "Stay healthy for the ones you love" for the emotion-focused ad), a brand name, and a picture of the product.

In two experiments, Fung and Carstensen (2003) found qualified support for some predictions made by SST. In one, they tested for age-related differences in preference and memory for emotion-related versus knowledge-related ads. Older consumers evaluated both types of ads more favorably compared to their younger counterparts. They did not find significantly higher liking for the emotion-related ad among older consumers or that younger consumers preferred the knowledge-related ads. They did find enhanced recognition memory for the emotion-related ad among older consumers. However, there were no differences in memory for the emotion-related versus knowledge-related ads among young participants. In a second experiment, they found increased preference for emotion-related versus knowledge-related ads among older consumers forced to make a choice between two versions of the same ad. In addition, when perceived time was experimentally expanded, older adults' preferences for the emotionally relevant ads decreased to the same level shown by young adults. However, they found no evidence that young adults' preferences for the different ad types differed due to time horizon perceptions.

Williams and Drolet (2005) found strong support for the predictions of SST. Similar to Fung and Carstensen (2003), they examined the effects of aging and time horizon perspective on consumers' liking of and memory for advertising. Their ad stimuli were different from Fung and Carstensen's in that they did not manipulate emotion-related versus knowledge-related goals directly. Rather, they manipulated the language used to describe product information. The language used in an ad was either more emotional (i.e., hedonic) versus rational (i.e., utilitarian). For example, in the emotional ad condition for the coffee product, the ad read:

> If your passion is coffee, then your pleasure will be Coffea. Join in the joyous celebration of this magic bean by savoring each sip of our rich brew. Coffea has a smooth, velvety flavor that evokes its exotic journey from the tree in its country of origin to the cup in your hand. With a deep, enticing aroma that draws people to the coffee and to one another. Specially blended for complexity and balance. Try it and delight in our extraordinary coffee.

In the rational ad condition, the ad read:

> For your next cup of coffee, choose Coffea. A gourmet blend at grocery store prices, Coffea provides an excellent value. In ground, whole bean and flavored varieties, Coffea is carefully blended and roasted to have moderate acidity. With 10 gourmet varieties available in both caffeinated and decaf. Each foil package is vacuum-sealed for freshness. Try it for its non-bitter taste.

This content was constant across time horizon conditions. However, in the time horizon limited condition, the ad began with "Life is short" and ended with "Savor the moment." In the time horizon expansive condition, the ad began with "Life is long" and ended with "Enjoy it forever." Last, in the time horizon control condition, the ad began with "Enjoy life" and "Savor Coffea."

Williams and Drolet (2005) found significant differences in attitudinal and memory responses to emotional versus rational ads due to time horizon perspective and age. Consumers manipulated to have a limited time horizon view and older consumers in the no time horizon view control condition had higher liking and recall of emotional ads. In contrast, consumers manipulated to have an expansive time horizon view and young adult consumers in the no time horizon view control condition had higher liking and recall of rational ads. In summary, the results of this experiment were consistent with SST. Time horizon perspective moderated responses not only to emotional ads but also to rational ads, and among not only older adults but also young adults. Figure 3.1 shows their results.

Williams and Drolet (2005) presented a second experiment that provides more direct evidence regarding the role of time horizon perceptions in emotion regulation rather than just on emotion focus. They examined the

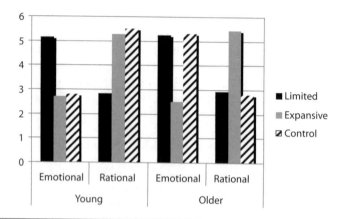

	Aad					
	Young Adult			**Older Adult**		
Time Horizon	**Limited**	**Expansive**	**Control**	**Limited**	**Expansive**	**Control**
Ad type						
Rational	2.85	5.27	5.50	2.93	5.46	2.79
Emotional	5.14	2.70	2.79	5.26	2.52	5.30

FIGURE 3.1

Aad (attitude towards the advertisement) by age group by time horizon condition by ad type (Study 1, Williams & Drolet, 2005).

influence of time horizon view and age on preferences for different types of emotional ads. In the time horizon control conditions, older consumers had a chronically higher preference for the ad that highlighted avoiding negative emotions, whereas the young adult consumers had a chronically higher preference for the ad that highlighted attaining positive emotions. Older and young consumers with a limited time horizon perspective found emotional ads that focused on avoiding negative emotions more likable and memorable. In contrast, young and older consumers with an expansive time horizon perspective found ads that focused on achieving positive emotions more likable and memorable. These results are interesting and may appear somewhat inconsistent with SST in that participants in both the limited and expansive time horizon conditions can be seen as engaging in emotion regulation. In the case of a limited time horizon perspective, there appeared to be more concern with avoiding negative outcomes, whereas in the case of an expansive time horizon perspective, there appeared to be more concern with seeking positive emotional outcomes. Figure 3.2 shows their results.

Although there is no published work in consumer behavior that has directly investigated the impact of time horizon perceptions on mixed

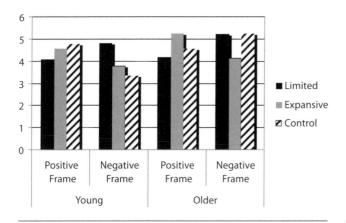

	Aad			
	Young Adult		**Older Adult**	
Message Frame	**Positive**	**Negative**	**Positive**	**Negative**
Time horizon				
Control	4.78	3.33	4.58	5.23
Limited	4.07	4.83	4.16	5.21
Expansive	4.58	3.77	5.26	4.13

FIGURE 3.2
Aad by age group by time horizon condition by frame (Study 2, Williams & Drolet, 2005).

emotions, Williams and Aaker (2002) did find that older adults preferred mixed emotional advertising appeals compared to younger adults and felt less emotional discomfort in response to such mixed emotions than did their young counterparts. They argued that these effects were driven by an increased tendency among older adults to accept contradiction, especially in the domain of emotions. While this explanation does not explicitly refer to SST, it does not conflict with the explanation according to SST for why individuals experience greater emotional poignancy when their time horizon is limited. It is possible that, as limited time horizons make the simultaneous experience of positive and negative emotions more likely, individuals become more adept at processing and coping with such dialectic relationships (Ersner-Hershfield et al., 2008). Further, this ability to integrate positive and negative emotions, similar to the ability to integrate affect and cognition, may reflect a maturation process, or wisdom, that occurs with age. Williams and Aaker (2008) directly manipulated time horizon perspectives and found that, when faced with meaningful endings (limited time horizons), young adults had more positive attitudes toward mixed emotional appeals. While young adults continued to feel discomfort in response to mixed emotional appeals, those feelings no longer drove their attitudes toward the mixed emotional appeals. Rather, under conditions of limited time horizons, mixed emotions were seen as possessing verisimilitude, or reflecting reality, and mixed emotional appeals prompted more positive attitudes.

Further Implications of Socioemotional Selectivity Theory for Consumer Research

The application of SST to the context of advertising has provided some important new insights into drivers of certain consumer attitude and memory responses. To add to consumer research relating to SST, we conducted a new experiment. Elderly participants (age 65–90; n = 91; nearly 60% female) were recruited from a Midwestern library, and completed the experimental materials in exchange for a $15 donation to the library. Young adult participants (age 18–25; n = 64; approximately 50% female) were undergraduates from two West Coast universities who were paid $7 for their participation. We sought to control for participants' level of education. All young adult participants were college students, and all older participants reported having at least graduated from high school. We also sought to control for "time-of-day" effects on cognitive functioning (Yoon, 1997). With few exceptions, the elderly participants completed their surveys at noon or earlier in the day, when they were typically at their peak cognitive capacity and so most like young participants in terms of cognitive ability. We excluded any participant who reported having any major illness or medical condition that might affect intellectual functioning.

According to SST, time horizon perspective affects emotion regulation processes, such as antecedent-focused regulation. Specifically, people with a limited time horizon perspective should be more likely to order events in such a way that they maximize the positive emotional potential of the overall experience and minimize its negative potential. All participants were asked to order a hypothetical sequence of three emotional events: one positive, one neutral, and one negative. Specifically, participants were asked to imagine the following:

> Imagine that you and a friend are dining at a "tapas" restaurant, a restaurant that serves appetizer-like dishes. You order three dishes. If you know that one of the dishes is going to taste excellent, the other so-so, and the other not very good at all, *to maximize your overall dining experience, in what order do you want to taste the dishes?*

Participants were then asked to order the three events (first, second, and third) such that they were maximizing their pleasure with the overall dining experience. Participants were assigned to one of two time horizon conditions: limited versus control. In the limited time horizon condition, participants were asked to imagine that they were leaving the area, moving to a new place (Australia) for a new job, and that they would be unlikely to see the friend again for a very long time. In the second control condition (no time horizon), participants were not presented with time horizon information.

Past research on how people make retrospective hedonic judgments suggests that people tend to neglect the duration of an overall experience (e.g., Redelmeier & Kahneman, 1996) and instead follow a "peak-and-end" rule (Fredrickson & Kahneman, 1993). That is, the most intense hedonic moment ("peak") and the last hedonic moment ("end") have disproportionate influence on people's overall evaluations of the sequence of events.

Indeed, research shows that people generally prefer sequences with improving versus declining final trends (Ariely, 1998; Ariely & Carmon, 2000). For example, when faced with hypothetical choices between sequences that end with a loss versus a gain, people tend to prefer the latter sequence to the former (Simonson, 1990). Succinctly, people prefer to "save the best for last." Researchers have documented these preferences for sequential orders across a variety of affective experiences, including those that are positive (e.g., Ratner, Kahn, & Kahneman, 1999), negative (e.g., Ariely, 1998), as well as mixed (e.g., Lau-Gesk, 2005). In the present experiment, the general expectation was that all participants, old and young, would tend to prefer consuming the "excellent" dish last.

Past researchers have also suggested that, for mixed hedonic events (i.e., events in which there are both positive and negative events in the sequence), the "temporal proximity" between the positive and negative events also affects retrospective evaluations of the overall experience. According to Linville and Fischer (1991), negative hedonic events can drain the affective resources people gain from positive hedonic events when both events occur close in temporal proximity. Depending on a person's ability to cope with negative events, temporal proximity between positive and negative affective events, closer or farther, can lead to differentially favorable responses regardless of their sequential ordering. Put briefly, whether a positive event and a negative event are separated by a neutral event influences people's evaluations of the overall experience. In the present case, consumers who sought to maximize their overall satisfaction (or minimize their overall dissatisfaction) would choose to consume the "so-so" dish in between the "excellent" and "not very good at all" dishes.

Interestingly, most of the studies in this research area have used young adults as participants. Given differences due to aging in emotion regulation abilities, one might expect that consumers' ordering of affective

Time Horizon Condition	Age Group			
	Young		Older	
	Control	Limited	Control	Limited
Sequence order				
+, 0, −	31.4	15.6	34.2	51.0
+, −, 0	5.7	3.1	9.8	9.8
0, +, −	2.9	9.4	2.4	0
−, +, 0	5.7	6.3	0	0
−, 0, +	37.1	43.8	56.6	37.3
0, −, +	17.1	21.9	2.4	2.0

+, "excellent" dish; 0, "so-so" dish; −, "not very good at all" dish.

FIGURE 3.3
Mean percentage of each sequence pattern by order by age group by time horizon condition.

events would differ depending on age. Further, in view of SST, one would expect that the same pattern of results—with the pattern of participants' choices in a limited time horizon perspective condition corresponding more closely to that of older adults and the pattern of participants' choices in the control time horizon perspective condition corresponding more closely to that of younger adults.

Given the three dishes, there were six prospective sequences that participants could choose to arrange. Figure 3.3 shows the share of each sequence pattern by age group and by time horizon perspective condition; Figure 3.4 shows the share of each type of dish (excellent, so-so, and not very good at all) by age group and by time horizon perspective condition. Considering only the time horizon control conditions, there was clear evidence of increased antecedent-focused regulation among older adults. In terms of sequence patterns, young participants favored ordering the dishes such that the not very good at all dish came first, the so-so dish second, and the excellent dish last (37.1%). Also, as one would predict, older participants were significantly more likely to order the dishes according to this pattern (56.6%; $\chi^2 = 3.83$, degrees of freedom [df] 5, $p < .05$). In summary, we found that older participants had an increased preference for improving sequences that end positively. In terms of the choice of which particular dish to experience in which particular order (Figure 3.4), the only significant age-related difference (at the $p < .05$ level) was that older (vs. young) participants were significantly more likely to order the so-so dish second (88.7% vs. 68.6%; $\chi^2 = 5.47$, df 1, $p < .01$). We discuss this particular result in more detail in the general discussion.

An examination of the influence of the time horizon manipulation revealed results only partly consistent with SST. In terms of sequence

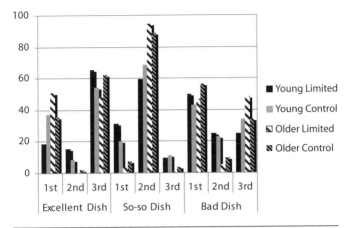

Time Horizon	Young		Older	
	Control	Limited	Control	Limited
Excellent dish				
First	37.1	18.8	35.9	50.9
Second	8.6	15.6	1.9	0
Third	54.3	65.6	62.2	49.1
So-so dish				
First	20.0	31.3	7.6	3.5
Second	68.6	59.4	88.6	94.8
Third	11.4	9.3	3.8	1.7
Not very good at all dish				
First	42.9	50.0	56.6	46.6
Second	22.9	25.0	9.4	5.2
Third	34.3	25.0	34.0	48.3

FIGURE 3.4
Choice by sequential order by age group by time horizon condition.

patterns, the time horizon manipulation did not have a significant effect on young participants' preference for ordering the dishes such that the not very good at all dish came first, the so-so dish second, and the excellent dish last (43.8% time horizon limited vs. 37.1% control; not significant [*ns*]) (see Figure 3.3). However, the effect was directional. Further, correspondingly, young participants' preference for ordering the dishes such that the excellent dish came first, the so-so dish second, and the not very good at all dish correspondingly decreased in the limited time horizon condition from 31.4% to 15.6%. This effect was only directional, perhaps due to sample size. An examination of the mean shares of each dish being consumed across sequence patterns (Figure 3.4) found results consistent with what SST would predict, namely, that both young participants' choice of consuming the excellent dish last and the not very good at all dish first increased from the control to the limited time horizon condition.

Whereas young participants' ordering choices aligned with the predictions of SST, older participants' ordering choices did not. Results for older participants were opposite those for younger participants. In terms of sequence patterns, a limited time horizon caused older participants to prefer ordering the dishes such that the excellent dish was first, the so-so dish second, and the not very good at all dish last (38.5% vs. 61.5%; $\chi^2 = 2.77$, $df\, 1, p < .09$). This effect was marginal. Moreover, the mean shares of when each dish was to be consumed (across sequence patterns; Figure 3.4) were entirely consistent with the data for the sequence patterns.

One (perhaps morbid) interpretation is that the time horizon perspective becomes so limited that the need to have the excellent dish first becomes overwhelmingly strong, as if participants might not make it through the meal. Such a strategy makes good sense in terms of emotion regulation— eat the excellent dish now and avoid the rest later if you can (and you might be full). Consistent with what SST would predict, there was a directional increase in the number of participants choosing to have the so-so dish between the first and last dishes in the time horizon-limited condition. Overall, however, the manipulation of time horizon did not result in all the predicted effects.

Limitations of Applying SST to Consumer Research and Suggestions for Future Research

Although the implications of SST are far reaching, there may be limitations to the application of SST in consumer contexts. These limitations might best be understood as boundary conditions for the predictions of SST.

Although SST represents an improvement over other models in that it proposes a universal process based on time perception and not age (Sneed & Whitbourne, 2005), it does not fully explain the effects of aging on consumer decision making. For example, as mentioned, the impact of differences in older versus young adult consumers' motivation to process emotional versus nonemotional information and to regulate emotion also depends on other factors, such as maturation. Indeed, Fung and Carstensen (2003), Williams and Drolet (2005), and the study presented in this chapter showed effects of age that were separable from the effects of time horizon perspective.

Past consumer research has studied the implications of SST mainly in the consumer context of advertising. Prior studies have shown that time horizon perspective moderates age-related differences in consumers' attitudes and memory for ads. Indeed, the present study investigated the effects of time horizon perspective on young versus older adult consumers' hypothetical orderings of mixed affective experiences, and its results were decadently mixed. It may be that the implications of SST are more straightforward in the context of advertising than in other consumer contexts.

In psychological research, SST has primarily been tested in the context of interpersonal goals. Future consumer research might apply SST to more similar contexts, such as service situations. Because SST deals specifically with social goals (e.g., choice of social partners), its application to service relationships appears particularly well suited. Consumers frequently make choices between familiar service providers who provide known benefits versus less-familiar service providers who might also provide new benefits. In general, research on service situations has been limited. In our view, tests of SST in service situations would be a good fit. For example, one could test whether older consumers' increased loyalty to retailers can be explained at least in part by changes over the life span in time horizon perspective.

In general, the application of SST to consumer contexts may prove more complicated because such contexts activate other goals that compete with the goals affected by time horizon perspective (i.e., knowledge acquisition and emotion regulation). For example, consumers often seek to self-express through their preferences and choices (e.g., Kim & Drolet, 2003; Kim & Markus, 1999). Self-expression goals may interact with knowledge-related and other emotion-related goals.

In addition, as mentioned briefly, in many consumer contexts, goals related to knowledge acquisition and emotion regulation do not conflict. In general, most consumer experiences are constructed to be positive (or at least not negative), and consumers are choosing among a set of experiences that are all positive. Further, marketers try to make the task of knowledge acquisition as easy as possible for consumers to accomplish. Accordingly, the effects of time horizon perspective may not be present in many consumer contexts.

Finally, consumers are not just passive recipients of time horizon view information. The consumer context is dynamic, with consumers bringing their own goals to consumption situations. Indeed, consumer contexts may represent ones in which people consciously seek to change their time horizon perspective. By consuming certain products and brands, consumers can push against the "prevailing" (chronic) time horizon view. Consumers can delay the physical signs of aging by buying the latest fashions and undergoing plastic surgery, thereby changing time perceptions (at least temporarily). Indeed, in general, marketers encourage consumers to think young and act young (e.g., "50 is the new 40"). A youthful appearance and outlook on life can be a source of self-esteem and social status. To convert consumers to customers, marketers teach consumers that they can alter their time horizon through the consumption of particular products and brands. A consumer culture that is geared toward having people glorify and idolize youth encourages people to adopt a more expansive time horizon perspective. Places like Disneyland are popular honeymoon destinations, perhaps because they offer adults the opportunity to shed their limited time horizon view. They revert to their childhood. Their whole life is now ahead of them.

Sometimes, marketers try to make consumers' time horizons shorter so that they will purchase a product or service that is beneficial only because they do not have all the time left in the world. Life insurance companies remind consumers that life is fragile. For peace of mind, they should plan today for the future of their loved ones. Similarly, saving for retirement today is motivated by a sense that tomorrow will arrive sooner than one thinks. Acts such as that of preparing a will or buying a burial plot require a sense that the end is close enough to merit planning for it. Nonetheless, it is important to note that people frequently act on their own time horizon perceptions. The fact that large numbers of people resist preparing for their retirement and death is itself evidence that they are trying to avoid viewing time as limited, at least when it comes to certain types of consumption categories.

More broadly, SST relies on a clear a priori distinction between emotions and rationality. However, this distinction is not nearly as clean as SST implies. Thoughts and emotions are often intertwined. A person's emotional reactions can be part of the "facts" of the situation, and emotional reactions can make certain thoughts more likely (Pham, Cohen, Pracejus, & Hughes, 2001). Many emotion regulation strategies at which older adults have been shown to be particularly adept depend on cognitive processing (e.g., reappraisal) to reduce negative emotion or increase positive emotion (Gross, 1999; Gross et al. 1997). Thus, the straightforward juxtaposition of preferences for emotionally relevant versus knowledge-relevant materials that is at the core of SST may be overly simplistic. Future research would benefit from a closer examination of when and how the two are related and how time horizon perspectives might influence their relationships.

Looking at consumers through the lens of SST, we understand that consumers, although having some chronic perspective about time, may move back and forth between limited and expansive time horizon perspectives. These psychological processes are dynamic and can be affected by the consumers' situations as well as by other consumer goals (e.g., social status). In summary, consumer research provides evidence regarding the predictive power of SST by revealing some of the boundary conditions of the theory. Every day, consumers face choices that elicit different time horizon perceptions. Consequently, the time horizon perspectives of consumers may shift much more so than psychological research on SST has suggested.

References

Ariely, D. (1998). Combining experiences over time: The effects of duration, intensity changes and on-line measurements on retrospective pain evaluations. *Journal of Behavioral Decision Making, 11,* 19–45.

Ariely, D., & Carmon, Z. (2000). Gestalt characteristics of experiences: The defining features of summarized events. *Journal of Behavioral Decision Making, 13,* 191–201.

Blanchard-Fields, F. (1986). Reasoning on social dilemmas varying in emotional saliency: An adult developmental perspective. *Psychology and Aging, 1,* 325–333.

Blanchard-Fields, F., Stein, R., & Watson, T. (2004). Age differences in emotion regulation strategies in handling everyday problems. *The Journals of Gerontology: Psychological Science, 59,* 261–269.

Carstensen, L. L. (1992). Social and emotional patterns in adulthood: Support for socioemotional selectivity theory. *Psychology and Aging, 7,* 331–338.

Carstensen, L. L., & Charles, S. T. (1998). Emotion in the second half of life. *Current Directions in Psychological Science, 7,* 144–149.

Carstensen, L. L., & Fredrickson, B. L. (1998). Socioemotional selectivity in healthy older people and younger people living with the human immunodeficiency virus: The centrality of emotion when the future is constrained. *Health Psychology, 17,* 1–10.

Carstensen, L. L., Isaacowitz, D. M., & Charles, S. T. (1999). Taking time seriously: A theory of socioemotional selectivity. *American Psychologist, 54,* 165–181.

Carstensen, L. L., & Lang, F. (1997). [Measurement of time orientation in diverse population]. Unpublished raw data. Stanford University, Stanford, CA.

Charles, S. T., Mather, M., & Carstensen, L. L. (2003). Aging and emotional memory: The forgettable nature of negative images for older adults. *Journal of Experimental Psychology: General, 132,* 310–324.

Charles, S. T., Reynolds, C. A., & Gatz, M. (2001). Age-related differences and change in positive and negative affect over 23 years. *Journal of Personality and Social Psychology, 80,* 136–151.

Cole, C. A., & Balasubramanian, S. K. (1993). Age differences in consumers' search for information: Public policy implications. *Journal of Consumer Research, 20,* 157–169.

Cole, C. A., & Gaeth, G. J. (1990). Cognitive and age-related differences in the ability to use nutritional information in a complex environment. *Journal of Marketing Research, 27,* 175–184.

Cole, C. A., Laurent, G., Drolet, A., Ebert, J., Gutchess, A. H., Lambert-Pandraud, R., et al. (2008). Decision making and brand choice by older consumers. *Marketing Letters, 19,* 355–365.

Drolet, A., Williams, P., & Lau-Gesk, L. (2007). Age-related differences in responses to emotional vs. rational ads for hedonic vs. utilitarian products. *Marketing Letters, 18,* 211–221.

Eagly, A. H., & Chaiken, S. (1993). *The psychology of attitudes.* Orlando, FL: Harcourt Brace Jovanovich.

Ersner-Hershfield, H., Mikels, J. A., Sullivan, S. J., & Carstensen, L. L. (2008). Poignancy: Mixed emotional experience in the face of meaningful endings. *Journal of Personality and Social Psychology, 94,* 158–167.

Fredrickson, B. L. (1995). Socioemotional behavior at the end of college life. *Journal of Social and Personal Relationships, 12,* 261–276.

Fredrickson, B. L., & Carstensen, C. L. (1990). Choosing social partners: How old age and anticipated endings make people more selective. *Psychology and Aging, 5,* 335–347.

Fredrickson, B. L., & Kahneman, D. (1993). Duration neglect in retrospective evaluations of affective episodes. *Journal of Personality and Social Psychology, 65,* 45–55.

Fung, H. H., & Carstensen, L. L. (2003). Sending memorable messages to the old: Age differences in preferences and memory for advertisements. *Journal of Personality and Social Psychology, 85,* 163–178.

Fung, H. H., & Carstensen, L. L. (2006). Goals change when life's fragility is primed: Lessons learned from older adults, the September 11th attacks and SARS. *Social Cognition, 24,* 248–278.

Fung, H. H., Carstensen, L. L., & Lutz, A. M. (1999). Influence of time on social preferences: Implications for life-span development. *Psychology and Aging, 14,* 595–604.

Gaeth, G. J., & Heath, T. B. (1987). The cognitive processing of misleading advertising in young and old adults: Assessment and training. *Journal of Consumer Research, 14,* 43–54.

Gross, J. J. (1999). Emotion regulation: Past, present, future. *Cognition and Emotion, 13,* 551–573

Gross, J. J., Carstensen, L. L., Pasupathi, M., Tsai, J., Skorpen, C. G., & Hsu, A. Y. C. (1997). Emotion and aging: Experience, expression, and control. *Psychology and Aging, 12,* 590–599.

Hasher, L., & Zacks, R. T. (1988). Working memory, comprehension, and aging: A review and a new view. In G. H. Bower (Ed.), *The psychology of learning and motivation: Advances in research and theory* (Vol. 22, pp. 193–225). San Diego, CA: Academic Press.

Hashtroudi, S., Johnson, M. K., Vnek, N., & Ferguson, S. A. (1994). Aging and the effects of affective and factual focus on source monitoring and recall. *Psychology and Aging, 9,* 160–170.

Isaacowitz, D. M., Charles, S. T., & Carstensen, L. L. (2000). Emotion and cognition. In F. Craik & T. Salthouse (Eds.), *Handbook of aging and cognition* (2nd ed., pp. 593–631). Mahwah, NJ: Erlbaum.

John, D. R., & Cole, C. A. (1986). Age differences in information processing: Understanding deficits in young and elderly consumers. *Journal of Consumer Research, 13,* 297–315.

Kensinger, E. A. (2008). Age differences in memory for arousing and nonarousing emotional words. *Journal of Gerontology: Psychological Sciences, 63B,* 13–18.

Kim, H.S., & Drolet, A. (2003). Choice and self-expression: A cultural analysis of variety-seeking. *Journal of Personality and Social Psychology, 85,* 373–382.

Kim, H.S., & Markus, H.R. (1999). Deviance or uniqueness, harmony or conformity? A cultural analysis. *Journal of Personality and Social Psychology, 77,* 785–800.

Labouvie-Vief, G. (1998). Cognitive-emotional integration in adulthood. In K. W. Schaie & M. P. Lawton (Eds.), *Annual review of gerontology and geriatrics: Focus on emotion and adult development* (Vol. 17, pp. 206–237). New York: Springer.

Labouvie-Vief, G., & Blanchard-Fields, F. (1982). Cognitive ageing and psychological growth. *Ageing and Society, 2,* 183–209.

Labouvie-Vief, G., DeVoe, M., & Bulka, D. (1989). Speaking about feelings: Conceptions of emotion across the life span. *Psychology and Aging, 4,* 425–437.

Lambert-Pandraud, R., Laurent, G., Lapersonne, E. (2005). Repeat purchasing of new automobiles by older consumers: Empirical evidence and interpretations. *Journal of Marketing, 69,* 97–113.

Lau-Gesk, L. (2005). Understanding consumer evaluations of mixed affective experiences. *Journal of Consumer Research, 32,* 23–28.

Lawton, M. P., Kleban, M. H., Rajagopal, D., & Dean, J. (1992). Dimensions of affective experience in three age groups. *Psychology and Aging, 7,* 171–184.

Linville, P., & Fischer, G. (1991). Preferences for separating or combining events. *Journal of Personality and Social Psychology, 60,* 5–23.

Mather, M. (2004). Aging and emotional memory. In D. Reisberg & P. Hertel (Eds.), *Memory and emotion* (pp. 272–307). New York: Oxford University Press.

Mather, M., & Carstensen, L. L. (2003). Aging and attentional biases for emotional faces. *Psychological Science, 14,* 409–415.

Mroczek, D. K., & Kolarz, C. M. (1998). The effect of age on positive and negative affect: A developmental perspective on happiness. *Journal of Personality and Social Psychology, 75,* 1333–1349.

Peters, E., Finucane, M. L., MacGregor, D. G., & Slovic, P. (2000). The bearable lightness of aging: Judgment and decision processes in older adults. In P. C. Stern & L. L. Carstensen (Eds.), *The aging mind: Opportunities in cognitive research* (pp. 144–165). Washington, DC: National Academy Press.

Pham, M. T., Cohen, J. B., Pracejus, J.W., & Hughes, G. D. (2001). Affect monitoring and the primacy of feelings in judgment. *Journal of Consumer Research, 28,* 167–188.

Poon, L. (1985). Differences in human memory with aging: Nature, causes, and clinical implications. In J. E. Birren & K. W. Schaie (Eds.), *Handbook of the psychology of aging* (pp. 427–462). New York: Van Nostrand Reinhold.

Pruzan, K., & Isaacowitz, D. M. (2006). An attentional application of socioemotional selectivity theory in college students. *Social Development, 15,* 326–338.

Ratner, R. K., Kahn, B. E., & Kahneman, D. (1999). Choosing less-preferred experiences for the sake of variety. *Journal of Consumer Research, 26,* 1–15.

Redelmeier, D., & Kahneman, D. (1996). Patients' memories of painful medical treatments: Real-time and retrospective evaluations of two minimally invasive procedures. *Pain, 66,* 3–8.

Ryff, C. D. (1989). Happiness is everything, or is it? Explorations on the meaning of psychological well-being. *Journal of Personality and Social Psychology, 57*, 1069–1081.

Simonson, I. (1990). The effect of purchase quantity and timing on variety seeking behavior. *Journal of Marketing Research, 27*, 150–162.

Skurnik, I., Yoon, C., Park, D. C., & Schwarz, N. (2005). How warnings about false claims become recommendations. *Journal of Consumer Research, 31*, 713–724.

Sneed, J. R., & Whitbourne, S. K. (2005). Models of the aging self. *Journal of Social Issues, 61*, 375–388.

Williams, P., & Aaker, J. L. (2002). Can mixed emotions peacefully co-exist? *Journal of Consumer Research, 28*, 636–649.

Williams, P., & Aaker, J. L. (2008). *Reflections of reality: Mixed emotional appeals and perceptions of verisimilitude.* Working paper. The Wharton School, University of Pennsylvania, Philadelphia, PA.

Williams, P., & Drolet, A. (2005). Age-related differences in responses to emotional advertisements. *Journal of Consumer Research, 32*, 343–354.

Yoon, C. (1997). Age differences in consumers' processing strategies: An investigation of moderating influences. *Journal of Consumer Research, 24*, 329–342.

Yoon, C., Cole, C. A., & Lee, M. (2009). Consumer decision making and aging: Current knowledge and future directions. *Journal of Consumer Psychology, 19*, 2–16.

Yoon, C., Laurent, G., Fung, H. H., Gonzalez, R., Gutchess, A. H., Hedden, T., et al., & (2005). Cognition, persuasion and decision making in older consumers. *Marketing Letters, 16*, 429–441.

Section 2

Decision Making

4

Aging-Related Changes in Decision Making

Ellen Peters

Decision Research

Introduction

In the movie *Shrek*, the lead character attempts to explain the complexity of ogres to his friend, the donkey. "Ogres are like onions. Onions have layers. Ogres have layers." Blanchard-Fields, Brannan, and Camp (1987) used a similar onion-peeling analogy when discussing the wisdom that develops with age and experience. They argued that wise reasoning and decision making concern the ability to integrate the multiple layers of thoughts and feelings that individuals have. In other words, dual modes of knowing—one that is based on more experiential and affective processing and another based on more deliberative and logical processing of information—are thought important to being wise. This dual-process approach can be fruitfully extended to our understanding of adult age differences in judgment and decision making. Understanding how decision making may change as we age entails more complicated (and interesting) layers than a cursory glance would suggest.

Across the adult life span, aging is associated with robust declines in deliberative processing, examples of which include memory performance, the speed with which information is processed, and comprehension and use of numeric information. Such declines are predictive of a general decline in the quality of decisions as we age. However, people over 65 make many of our nation's most important decisions (think about the White House, the Supreme Court, leading national corporations), implying that deliberative decline does not and cannot fully explain adult age differences in decision making. And, in fact, research demonstrates that at least three additional processes exist that compensate for age-related declines in deliberative ability: selective use of deliberative capacity, accumulated experience, and an increased focus on emotional information. After reviewing evidence for age-related changes in these processes, I briefly introduce methods based in these lower-level processes that may improve older adult decision making.

Good Decision Making Is Fundamental to Maintenance of Independent Functioning

By the year 2050, the number of people in the world over 60 years of age will surpass the number of children under age 15. As the potential demands of this growing population place increasing strain on already limited supports and resources, understanding the effects of aging on maintenance of independent functioning and facilitating such independent functioning becomes critical. Quality decision making is one key process. For example, because health problems increase with aging, older adults are the nation's biggest users of (and decision makers about) health care. They make decisions about when to go to the doctor, whether to pay for a medication (because out-of-pocket expenditures rise rapidly with age, health care could be considered a luxury good, especially for the oldest-old; De Nardi, French, & Jones, 2006), which preventive measures to take, what to eat, and whether to exercise. The elderly also make many consequential financial decisions in terms of Social Security and other sources of wealth and retirement income. They have to decide when to stop driving, whether to continue living independently, whether to trust an individual asking for money, and so on. The quality of the decisions they make will determine in part the quality of lives they and their loved ones lead.

Maintenance of independent functioning requires that the individual make good decisions. To make good decisions, Hibbard and Peters (2003) suggested that a number of processes have to take place. First, the decision maker must have appropriate information; it has to be available, accurate, and timely. Policy makers sometimes think that this is all that is needed for good decisions (i.e., provide all of the necessary information and an informed public will always make the choices that are right for them). However, decision makers also have to be able to comprehend the given information and its meaning. They have to be able to determine meaningful differences between options and to weight factors to match their own needs and values. Decision makers also have to be able to make trade-offs that might be big (Would I prefer to pay my electricity bill or fill my prescription for my heart medicine?) or might be small (Do I eat spaghetti or beef for dinner?). Finally, the decision maker has to choose.

Barriers to using provided information to make good decisions exist, however, and some of these barriers are related to age. For example, information may be available primarily on the Internet, and the elderly may have less access to Internet-based information. The information may not be understood, and such comprehension problems may be larger for older adults than for younger adults, particularly if the information is unfamiliar and numeric (Hibbard, Slovic, Peters, Finucane, & Tusler, 2001). Older adults may also have more difficulty making trade-offs that are emotionally uncomfortable (Mather, 2006).

A small but growing body of research exists on age differences in decision making (see Peters, Hess, Vastfjall, & Auman, 2007, for a review). The literature on the impact of dual information processes on judgments and decisions is much larger and provides a framework to understand and predict possible age differences in decision making.

Dual Modes of Thinking and Their Impact on Decision Making

The results of judgment and decision experiments lead us to believe that information in decision making is processed using two different modes of thinking: an experiential/affective system and a deliberative system (Epstein, 1994; Loewenstein, Weber, Hsee, & Welch, 2001; Reyna, 2004; Sloman, 1996; these modes are also called Systems 1 and 2, respectively— see Kahneman, 2003; Stanovich & West, 2002). Both modes of thought are important to forming decisions.

The experiential mode produces thoughts and feelings in a relatively effortless and spontaneous manner. The operations of this mode are implicit, intuitive, automatic, associative, and fast. This system is based on affective (emotional) feelings. As shown in a number of studies, affect provides information about the goodness or badness of an option that might warrant further consideration and can directly motivate a behavioral tendency in choice processes (Damasio, 1994; Osgood, Suci, & Tannenbaum, 1957). Marketers, who well understand the power of affect, typically aim their ads to evoke an experiential mode of information processing.

The deliberative mode, in contrast, is conscious, analytical, reason based, verbal, and relatively slow. It is the deliberative mode of thinking that is more flexible and provides effortful control over more spontaneous experiential processes. Kahneman (2003) suggested that one of the functions of the deliberative system is to monitor the quality of the information processing emerging from the affective/experiential system and its impact on behavior. Both modes of thinking are important. Some researchers claimed that good choices are most likely to emerge when affective and deliberative modes work in concert, and decision makers think as well as feel their way through judgments and decisions (e.g., Damasio, 1994; Peters & Slovic, 2000).

Affective and deliberative processes in decision making are interdependent—our thoughts and our feelings influence each other. The two systems also appear to be somewhat separable (e.g., Epstein, 1994; Petty & Wegener, 1999; Zajonc, 1980). The implicit assumption that good decision making is a conscious, deliberative process has been one of the field's most enduring themes, but in some contexts deliberation about reasons for choice appears to distract decision makers from fully considering their feelings and to have a negative effect on decision processes (e.g., Wilson, Dunn, Kraft, & Lisle, 1989). Research has also demonstrated that affect may have a relatively greater influence when deliberative capacity is lower, suggesting that, at least in some cases, these two modes are not separate but instead exist on a single continuum (Hammond, 1996; Kruglanski et al., 2003; Peters & Slovic, 2007). Shiv and Fedorikhin (1999), for example, demonstrated that decision makers were more likely to choose an affect-rich option (and make a decision of the heart) when deliberative capacity was diminished by cognitive load. Finucane, Alhakami, Slovic, and Johnson (2000) also found that the inverse relation between risks and benefits (linked to affect by Alhakami & Slovic, 1994) was enhanced under time pressure. Reducing the time for deliberation appeared to increase the use of affect and the affect heuristic. In subsequent sections, we link this balance between affect and deliberation to age differences in information processing and decision making.

Age Declines in Deliberative Processes, Including Numeracy

Traditional decision research relies on the assumption that we deliberate in order to make our best decisions. Decision research developed from economic theory and, as a result of this rationalistic origin, has concentrated mostly on consequentialist explanations for how people make decisions and form judgments. The problem with this view, however, is that we have limited capacity to represent information, process it, and manipulate it; we are boundedly rational (Simon, 1955). In addition, aging is accompanied by declines in the efficiency of controlled processing mechanisms associated with deliberation (e.g., explicit learning and memory; Salthouse,

2006). Park et al. (2002), for example, demonstrated that beginning in the 20s a decline occurs in processes related to deliberation (e.g., speed of processing, working memory, and long-term memory).

Many choices also involve numeric information that generally requires deliberative capacity to process; comprehension and use of such information appears to decline with age. For example, results from health plan choice studies support these age declines in comprehension of numeric information and suggest that elderly decision makers do not always comprehend even fairly simple information. Hibbard, Peters, Slovic, Finucane, and Tusler (2001) presented employed-aged adults (18–64 years old; n = 239) and older adults (65–94 years old; n = 253) with 33 decision tasks that involved interpretation of numbers from tables and graphs. For example, participants were asked to identify the health insurance plan with the lowest copayment from a table that included four plans with information about monthly premiums and copayments. A comprehension index reflected the total number of errors made across the 33 tasks. The youngest participants (aged 18–35) averaged 8% errors; the oldest participants (aged 85–94) averaged 40% errors; the correlation between age and the number of errors was .31 (p < .001). Higher education was somewhat protective of these age declines.

Numeracy refers to the ability to understand and use mathematical and probabilistic concepts. Based on the National Adult Literacy Survey, almost half of the general population has difficulty with relatively simple numeric tasks such as calculating the difference between a regular price and sales price using a calculator or estimating the cost per ounce of a grocery item; scores on these tasks decline with age (Kirsch, Jungeblut, Jenkins, & Kolstad, 2002). Lipkus, Samsa, and Rimer (2001) found that 16% of highly educated individuals incorrectly answered straightforward questions about risk magnitudes (e.g., Which represents the larger risk: 1%, 5%, or 10%?). In our studies, people varied considerably in their scores on the simple 11-item numeracy test from Lipkus et al. (2001), and scores decreased significantly with age and education (Peters, 2008). Age declines in numeric ability have also been demonstrated longitudinally (Schaie & Zanjani, 2006). Controlling for age and education, women also tend to score lower than men (see also Frederick, 2005, and Peters, Slovic, Västfjäll, & Mertz, 2008).

Less-numerate individuals, whether young or old, do not necessarily perceive themselves as "at risk" in their lives due to limited skills; however, research showed that having inadequate numeric skills is associated with lower comprehension and use of numeric information. In particular, inadequate numeracy may be an important barrier to individuals' understanding and use of health, financial, and other risks. Peters, Borberg, and Slovic (2007), for example, examined evidence for theorized age differences in the processing of numeric versus nonnumeric information about prescription drugs. Using a convenience sample of 301 adults (aged 18–88 years), participants were asked to imagine that they were prescribed a drug for high cholesterol, were provided information about drug risks in either numeric or nonnumeric terms, and were asked their likelihood of taking the drug. The results revealed that individuals higher in numeracy were more likely to use the drug when given numeric rather than non-numeric risk information, whereas those low in numeracy showed the opposite results. In addition, however, less-numerate older adults were significantly less likely than any other group to take the drug when given numeric rather than nonnumeric information. These results are potentially consistent with age-related declines in deliberative ability and suggest that less-numerate older adults, in particular, may have difficulty using numeric information about drugs, at least in the formats in which it was provided. Further study is required, however, to discover formats to provide numeric information that will facilitate processing even in less-numerate elderly adults (Peters, Hibbard, Slovic, & Dieckmann, 2007).

Because the elderly, as a cohort, tend to be less numerate, they are likely to understand and use numeric information less well in health, financial, and other consumer products. In the United States and other developed nations, low numeracy has been associated with a host of undesirable health outcomes, including self-reported poor health, health disparities, poor health knowledge and disease self-management skills, and choosing lower-quality health options (Baker, Parker, Williams, Clark, & Nurss, 1997; DeWalt, Berkman, Sheridan, Lohr, & Pignone, 2004; Hibbard, Peters, Dixon, & Tusler, 2007; Sentell & Halpin, 2006; Williams, Baker, Parker, & Nurss, 1998). For example, in a prospective cohort study of patients taking warfarin, low numeracy was significantly associated with poorer anticoagulation control (Estrada, Martin-Hryniewicz, Peek, Collins, & Byrd, 2004). In a study of asthma patients prescribed inhaled steroids, low numeracy was linked with a history of hospitalizations and emergency room visits for asthma (Apter et al., 2006). Rothman and colleagues (Rothman et al., 2006) found that lower comprehension of nutrition labels (thought to be important for health and health management) was significantly associated with lower numeracy skills, even after adjusting for education and income. The lower numeracy associated with older adulthood may exacerbate health and wealth disparities and potentially reduce the quality of older adults' lives.

Innumeracy also appears to have an effect on decisions beyond simple comprehension of numbers. Research has begun to examine numeracy's role in risk perception and decision processes. For example, Peters, Västfjäll, et al. (2006) pitted intuition against rational analysis by making an objectively worse choice more tempting. Subjects were offered a prize if they drew a colored jellybean from a bowl. Bowl A contained 9 colored and 91 white beans, and Bowl B contained 1 colored and 9 white beans.

Consequently, the chance of picking a colored jellybean was objectively better if the subject picked from Bowl B (10% chance of winning) than if he or she picked from Bowl A (9% chance of winning). Despite this, 33% of low-numerate subjects and 5% of high-numerate subjects picked from Bowl A, which was clearly not the rational choice if one wanted to win a prize. Whereas highly numerate subjects appeared to perceive the probability of winning more clearly and selected Bowl B, the less numerate were drawn more to the number of winning beans than by the objective probability. These results combined with those of other studies imply that, compared to high-numerate decision makers, the preferences expressed by the less numerate are likely to be more labile and influenced by extraneous cues, such as irrelevant sources of affect and emotion, and to be less influenced by objective numbers like probabilities.

Because of its link with risk perceptions and decision processes, numeracy may aid our understanding of the oft-cited link between greater educational attainment and improved health and wealth (Goesling & Baker, 2008; Goldman & Smith, 2002). A pilot study was conducted in four remote villages in the eastern region of Ghana with a high prevalence of HIV infection (Peters, Baker, Dieckmann, Leon, & Collins, 2010). The villages ranged in size from 200 inhabitants to 4,000 inhabitants, and all interviews were conducted in Twi, the local language. In a sample of 190 adults aged 30–65 whose highest education ranged from no schooling to completion of secondary school, we tested numeracy abilities (measured with the Woodcock-Johnson III test of calculation; McGrew, Wood, & Mather, 2001), executive-functioning capacities, decision-making tasks, health knowledge and attitudes, and healthy behaviors. Participants also reported levels of schooling, reasons for discontinuing or failing to attend school, socioeconomic status (SES; as measured by type of house, available amenities such as electricity and running water, and agricultural assets), religion, occupation, and access to information.

Numeracy and executive functioning were studied as mechanisms by which schooling may affect development of decision-making skills and thus facilitation of good decisions about one's health (we call this the Schooling–Decision-Making model). We modified the jellybean task into a stickman task in which participants were presented with a series of scenarios. In each scenario, participants chose between two images. The participant was informed that each image represented a different family or group; the red stickmen were individuals with HIV, and the black stickmen were individuals who did not have HIV. In each image, the number of red and black stickmen varied. The participant was asked if they were to visit each family or group, in which option, A or B, would it be most likely that the first person they met had HIV. Four of the scenarios provided congruent information in which the higher probability had numerically more (a greater frequency of) red stickmen. The other four scenarios presented incongruent information in which the option with a larger numerical number of red stickmen was actually a lower probability of the total group. The Ghana pilot data revealed robust and statistically significant correlations between accurate decision making in the incongruent choices and schooling, numeracy, and executive functioning. Further, regressing this indicator of decision-making skill on either numeracy or executive functioning demonstrated that each has a significant mediating effect of the schooling effects controlling for age, gender, SES, and general intelligence. Finally, more accurate decisions in the incongruent choices were associated with a greater likelihood of behaviors protective of HIV in this African nation with high rates of HIV infection. Greater education as a child or adolescent may lead to greater numeracy and executive functioning, improved decision skills in situations that involve an understanding of numbers, and ultimately better choices about health and financial risks (see also Bruine de Bruin, Parker, & Fischhoff, 2007; Goldman & Smith, 2002). It is not clear whether continued adult education may have similar effects among middle-aged and older adults to those hypothesized here.

If good decisions depend on deliberation, the robust age-related declines in executive functioning and numeracy suggest that the quality of judgments and decisions will suffer inevitably as we age. Several studies have identified biases in judgment processes that increase with age and were linked with deliberative processes such as working memory. For example, Mutter (2000) and Mutter and Pliske (1994) examined the impact of illusory correlation on performance. (In an illusory correlation, people perceive that two variables covary consistently with their prior expectations even though no actual relation exists.) They found that older adults' judgments were more influenced by prior expectancies than were those of younger adults, particularly under distraction conditions. Older adults were also less likely to correct their judgments when accurate information regarding the co-occurrence of events was made salient. Interestingly, Mutter found that age differences were more evident for memory-based judgments than for online judgments, suggesting that age differences in illusory-correlation biases may be based in part on the declining ability to encode and retrieve veridical information from episodic memory.

Such a conclusion was bolstered by other research (Mutter & Pliske, 1996; Mutter & Williams, 2004) that examined age differences in the ability to detect covariation between two events when there were no strong prior expectancies regarding contingencies between the events. In this research, aging-related declines in the ability to accurately judge covariation were eliminated when performance was adjusted to take into account memory errors. The researchers also found that older adults tended to use simpler strategies in constructing judgments than did younger adults, and that younger adults used simpler strategies when the task demands were increased relative to situations with fewer cognitive demands. In another example, Chasseigne and colleagues found that older adults performed as well as young adults in probability-learning tasks when the cues had a direct relation with the criterion but performed less well when the cues had a more complex inverse or multiplicative relation with the criterion (Chasseigne, Grau, Mullet, & Cama, 1999; Chasseigne, Lafon, & Mullet, 2002; Chasseigne, Mullet, & Stewart, 1997). Such findings suggest that some declines in judgments and decisions in later adulthood may be tied to reductions in cognitive resources.

Research by Chen (2002, 2004; Chen & Blanchard-Fields, 2000) has also suggested that aging-related declines in deliberative processes have a negative impact on judgment processes. In these studies, participants were presented with information about an individual, some of which was identified as true and some as false (and thus to be ignored); then they were asked to make judgments based on this information. Chen found that the judgments of older adults were more likely to be influenced by the false information than were those of younger adults. In addition, younger adults in a divided-attention condition performed similarly to older adults under full attention. These findings suggested that older adults may have more difficulty controlling attention and monitoring the accuracy of information in memory, which in turn makes judgments more prone to error based on irrelevant information. In a related study, Skurnik, Yoon, Park, and Schwarz (2005) found that repeatedly identifying a (false) consumer claim as false assisted older adults short term in remembering that it was false. Longer term, however, the repetition caused them to misremember it as true. A pragmatic implication of these studies is that information providers need to take care not to provide older adults with a "fact" and then state that it is a myth. This and similar tactics are surprisingly common (e.g., the U.S. Food and Drug Administration's (2009) "Facts About Generic Drugs" poses a question such as "Are brand-name drugs made in better factories than generic drugs?" and then answers "No.").

In general, evidence exists that, when making decisions, older adults use less-complex strategies and consider fewer pieces of information than younger adults do. For example, Johnson and her colleagues (Johnson, 1990, 1993; Johnson & Drungle, 2000; Riggle & Johnson, 1996) examined decision-making strategies by different-aged adults using an information matrix that contained specific features (shown in rows) for different product choices (shown in columns). Participants were allowed to view only one cell of the matrix at a time, but they could view as many cells as they wished for as long as necessary before making a product decision. A relatively consistent finding in this research, across different types of products (e.g., cars, apartments, over-the-counter drugs), was that older adults spent a longer time studying each cell but sampled fewer pieces of information than did younger adults before making their decisions.

Similar results were obtained by Streufert, Pogash, Piasecki, and Post (1990) in a study of decision making in managers and by Hershey, Walsh, Read, and Chulef (1990) in a financial-planning task.

In sum, the pattern of observed performance in these studies appears to be consistent with what might be expected with a decline in deliberative processes with aging. In fact, research has demonstrated that younger adults adopt a strategy similar to that observed in older adults when task demands are increased. It may be that information load interacting with limited cognitive resources in later adulthood results in the adoption of strategies that minimize demands on deliberative processes. For example, to conserve resources, older adults may adopt a strategy of eliminating alternatives as soon as possible (Riggle & Johnson, 1996). Thus, as soon as an undesirable piece of information about a product is encountered, the alternative is eliminated from further consideration. Alternatively, a satisficing strategy, in which information about a specific product is examined until a sufficient amount of information has been deemed acceptable, might be employed. Consistent with such an explanation, Chen and Sun (2003) found that both older and younger adults adopted satisficing strategies in a simulated real-world task (i.e., maximizing profit at a yard sale), but the strategy adopted by older adults was less memory demanding than that adopted by younger adults. Sorce (1995) recommended that marketing strategies should attempt to segment older consumers to customize products and information to compensate for their cognitive decline.

Age-Related Compensatory Processes, Including Selectivity, Increased Experience, and Affective Processes

The vast majority of older adults appear to function effectively and independently in everyday life, however, and many of the most influential and demanding positions in our society are held by late-middle-aged and older adults, suggesting that their ability to make decisions remains intact despite other declines (Carstensen, 2001; Salthouse, 1990). Deliberative decline appears to be too simple an explanation of age differences in decision making.

At least three reasons exist for why deliberative decline is too simple an explanation these age differences. First, older adults appear to use their deliberative capacity selectively. Older adults appear to adapt to real or perceived declines in cognitive resources by becoming increasingly selective about where they spend effort (Hess, 2000). That is, the costs associated with resource-demanding deliberative processing result in older adults being more judicious than younger adults in their allocation of resources. Hess has further hypothesized that this aging-related resource conservation should be most apparent in situations of low relevance or meaningfulness to the individual, with fewer age differences as relevance and meaningfulness increase. The impact of this heightened selectivity on the involvement of deliberative and affective processes can be seen, for example, in a study that examined the extent to which attitudes toward proposed legislation were influenced by irrelevant affective information (i.e., the likeability of the lawmaker proposing the legislation; Hess, Germain, Rosenberg, Leclerc, & Hodges, 2005). When the personal relevance of the legislation was low, older adults exhibited attitudes that were consistent with how much they liked the lawmaker, whereas younger adults' attitudes were unaffected by this information. In contrast, when the legislation was rated high in personal relevance, neither the younger nor older adults were influenced by the irrelevant affective information. Related findings were reported by Chen (2004), who observed that increasing personal accountability benefited older adults' source memory relatively more than it did that of younger adults.

A second reason for why deliberative decline is too simple an explanation is that the experience individuals gain in life can compensate for some of the age-related declines in deliberative processes. One way of operationalizing experience is through measures of crystallized knowledge. Simultaneous to finding age declines in processes associated with deliberation, Park et al. (2002) demonstrated robust increases across the adult life span for scores on vocabulary tests, a measure of crystallized intelligence, suggesting a role for increased experience. In that vein, Meyer, Russo, and Talbot (1995) found that older women behaved more like experts by seeking out less information, making decisions faster, and arriving at decision outcomes equivalent to younger women. Compared to the younger women, older individuals appeared to compensate for reductions in information seeking and bottom-up processing with a greater reliance on top-down processing, arriving at equivalent decisions.

A third reason for why deliberative decline cannot fully account for age differences in decision making concerns the role of affect and emotion in decisions. In research with brain-damaged patients, Bechara, Damasio, and colleagues (Bechara, Damasio, Damasio, & Anderson, 1994; Bechara, Damasio, Tranel, & Damasio, 1997; Bechara, Tranel, Damasio, & Damasio, 1996; Damasio, 1994) linked the learning of integral affect* to better

---

* Integral affect is defined as positive and negative feelings toward an external stimulus (e.g., a consumer product). Integral affect may become associated with an object not only through careful thought but also through experiential processes such as conditioning (Staats & Staats, 1958), familiarity (Zajonc, 1980), priming (Murphy & Zajonc, 1993), and mood misattribution (Schwarz & Clore, 1983). It is generally relevant to the decisions at hand. Affect can also be irrelevant to a decision but influence the decision nonetheless (e.g., the effect of a temporary mood state or the likeability of a lawmaker on a decision about a proposed law); this affect is termed incidental affect.

decision making. Patients with bilateral damage to the ventromedial prefrontal cortices experienced normal affective reactions to gains and losses they received from decks of cards in a task called the Iowa gambling task. In this task, subjects choose among decks of cards about which they initially know nothing; the decks vary in the amounts and frequencies of gains and losses and in overall expected value, and subjects learn about the decks as they choose cards and receive feedback after each choice. Unlike normal controls, however, patients with ventromedial prefrontal cortex damage were unable to use their otherwise normal affective reactions to learn an integral affective response linked to each deck (Bechara and colleagues called such an integral affective response a "somatic marker"). Among non-brain-damaged control subjects, affective reactions to actual gains and losses in each deck appeared to drive the learning of an anticipatory affective response (an integral affective response or somatic marker) that subsequently guided choices. Bechara and colleagues concluded that this anticipatory affective response must drive choice because the patients had abnormal anticipatory affective capabilities but normal cognitive capabilities. Peters and Slovic (2000) demonstrated, using a modified Iowa gambling task, that college students high in negative reactivity learned to choose fewer high-loss options, whereas those high in positive reactivity learned to choose more high-gain options—supporting the idea that affective reactions are used in the decision-making process.

Decision makers rely on affective meaning to guide judgments and decisions in everyday life (Slovic, Finucane, Peters, & MacGregor, 2002). According to the "affect heuristic," all of the images in a person's mind are tagged or marked to varying degrees with affect. The "affect pool" contains all positive and negative markers that are consciously or unconsciously associated with the images. Using this overall, readily available affective impression can be easier and more efficient than weighing the pros and cons of a situation or retrieving relevant examples from memory. This may be especially true when the required judgment or decision is complex or when mental resources are limited, as in conditions of time pressure (Finucane et al., 2000). Decision makers rely on affect in at least four ways in the decision-making process (Peters, 2006; Peters, Lipkus, & Diefenbach, 2006). First, affect can act as information (as a substitute for other, sometimes more relevant, information; Kahneman, 2003) in judgments such as life satisfaction (Schwarz & Clore, 1983). Second, it can act as a common currency that allows people to integrate multiple pieces of information more effectively than when it is absent. Third, it can act as a spotlight to focus people's attention on different information (e.g., numerical cues), which may then be used in judgments instead of the affect itself. Fourth, affect can motivate people to take some action or process information.

This reliance on affect may be learned over the life span as a particularly effective means of making decisions. Reyna (2004), for example, argued that information processing in this system is more advanced relative to the deliberative system. In support of this idea, she provided evidence that people process less information and process it more qualitatively as development progresses both from childhood to adulthood and from less expertise to more.

The examination of aging and affective influences on performance in a variety of cognitive domains (e.g., memory, judgment processes, decision making) is still in its infancy. But, two dominant perspectives on this relationship, each focusing on different types of mechanisms, can be identified in this literature. The first is a motivational perspective from socioemotional selectivity theory (SST; Carstensen, 1993, 2006). It focuses on aging-related chronic activation of emotion regulation goals and an associated motivation to process affective information. The most influential perspective regarding aging, affect, and motivation is SST (Carstensen, 2006). This theory posits that changes in time perspective result in emotional goals becoming increasingly important as the end of life nears, which in turn results in greater monitoring of affective information. Because older adults are, by virtue of age, closer to the end of life, age should be associated with an increased importance of emotional goals; increased attention to emotional content; and either an increased focus on positive information or a decreased focus on negative information to optimize emotional experience. These last predictions have potentially great relevance to the impact of affect and emotions in judgment and decision making. In one study, for example, Fung and Carstensen (2003) found that, relative to younger adults, older adults exhibited greater preference and superior memory for emotional advertisements than for nonemotional ones.

However, SST also predicts a specific focus on positive information in later life as older adults seek to optimize emotional experience. For example, Charles, Mather, and Carstensen (2003) found that overall picture recall declined with age but that older adults recalled a greater proportion of positive images than negative images, whereas young and middle-aged adults recalled similar amounts of each. The motivational basis for SST (and the need to have resources available to attain one's goals) has received support from a study by Mather and Knight (2005), who found that older adults who had more cognitive resources (due to better performance on tasks requiring cognitive control in one study and due to not being distracted by a divided attention task in a second study) remembered relatively more positive than negative pictures compared to those with fewer cognitive resources; younger adults showed no such effect. This positivity effect in memory may be driven by effortful, resource-demanding regulatory functions and thus may be shown primarily by high-functioning older adults (Mather & Knight, 2005).

The second perspective on the relation between aging and affect in cognitive domains is more cognitive in nature and focuses on the impact

of changing cognitive skills on the relative influence of affective processes on performance. This perspective is typified by theories such as
Labouvie-Vief's (2003, 2005) dynamic integration theory and by neuropsychological approaches that focus on the differential impact of aging on
normative changes in cortical systems underlying affective and deliberative processes. In this alternative perspective on aging, affective processes
take on increased importance as deliberative functions decline in later life.
One basis for this perspective is research suggesting that cortical structures associated with processing affect (e.g., the amygdala, the ventromedial prefrontal cortex) undergo less normative change with aging than
those areas underlying executive or deliberative functions (e.g., the dorsolateral prefrontal cortex; Bechara, 2005; Chow & Cummings, 2000; Good
et al., 2001). This relative preservation view is supported by neuropsychological data demonstrating that adult age differences in performance were
minimal on those tasks thought to be supported by affective-processing
systems (e.g., Kensinger, Brierley, Medford, Growdon, & Corkin, 2002;
MacPherson, Phillips, & Della Sala, 2002). These data contrast with the
normative decline consistently observed on tasks associated with executive functions (for a review, see West, 1996).

This relative preservation view would suggest that maintenance of
basic mechanisms associated with processing affect should not lead to
qualitative age differences (e.g., positivity effects). Thus, for example,
researchers have shown that when participants are required to actively
attend to emotional and neutral stimuli, younger and older adults exhibit
similar patterns of memory for positive, negative, and neutral stimuli
(Denburg, Buchanan, Tranel, & Adolphs, 2003; Kensinger et al., 2002). The
relative preservation view would not necessarily preclude the possibility
of qualitative differences arising in cognitively later stages of processing.

In sum, research suggested that aging is associated with a greater
focus on emotional content and on positive over negative information,
although the latter effect appears to be moderated by situational goals
and available cognitive resources. These processes are consistent with
the model of selective optimization with compensation proposed by
Baltes and colleagues (e.g., Baltes & Baltes, 1990), which postulates that
the developmentally relevant goal of efficient use of processing resources
results in older adults optimizing their best skills, in this case the processing of emotional information. A reasonable hypothesis at this point is
that basic mechanisms underlying the processing of affect are relatively
unchanged with age, but that variations may emerge at later stages of processing as goal-based factors (e.g., time perspective) or availability of cognitive resources influence the manner in which positive versus negative
information is handled.

Implications for Judgment and Decision Making

The study of adult age differences in decision making is still in its infancy. Deliberative declines predict that older adults will demonstrate lower comprehension and use of numeric information, less information seeking, and decision avoidance and delegation (to avoid negative emotions; see Mather, 2006).

An increased focus on affect and emotion (whether a relative preference for positive information or increased use of affective information), however, suggests different age-related changes. Older adults who focus relatively more on positive information may process gain-versus-loss information in decisions differently from their younger counterparts who do not share this same focus. As a result, losses may not loom as large for older adults as they have been demonstrated to do for younger adults (Kahneman & Tversky, 1979). Older adults may be more likely to request and process information presented in a positive frame rather than a negative frame, so older adults may not demonstrate the well-known negativity bias shown by younger adults. Some evidence exists already that is consistent with this expectation (Wood, Busemeyer, Koling, Cox, & Davis, 2005). Strough, Mehta, McFall, and Schuller (2008), for example, demonstrated that older adults were less susceptible to the sunk-cast fallacy, an effect thought to be motivated by negativity biases in younger adults. The age difference remained after controlling for cognitive ability, providing support for the difference being due to emotional changes. Older adults also appear more likely to be in positive moods, states that have been associated with greater engagement in schema-based processing and less-specific, bottom-up processing (e.g., Fiedler, 2001). These age differences in the experience of incidental affect may be misattributed to aging-related deficits in deliberative processes.

Support for a possible positivity effect in decision processes comes from Lockenhoff and Carstensen (2007). In their study, older and younger adults selected information to examine about health choices by clicking on cues indicating information that was positive, negative, or neutral. As predicted, older adults selected and recalled a greater proportion of positive versus negative information compared to younger adults.

Hypotheses based on SST and relatively greater processing of positive than negative information imply that benefit information may be weighed relatively more than risk information in older compared to younger adults. If true, this would have potentially marked implications for consumers' processing of risk and benefit information about prescription drugs and risky financial choices that contain potential upsides but also marked risks. In one preliminary study, we showed younger and older adults information about a single prescription drug that had one benefit and two side effects (Peters, Borberg, et al., 2007). Each individual saw one level each of the benefit and side effects (half of the participants were shown high levels of the benefit; half were shown low levels; the same was done for both risks). By using a complete, between-subjects factorial design (2 benefit levels × 2 first-risk levels × 2 second-risk levels), we could then look at age differences in the use of numeric information about the benefit and the two side effects. No age differences existed in sensitivity to either side effect. However, individuals aged 50–88 were more sensitive to the high-versus-low levels of benefits compared to those aged 18–49. In the older age group, individuals shown a prescription with a higher benefit level were more likely to report intentions to use the drug than those shown a lower benefit level; the benefit levels did not influence intentions in the younger age group.

Alternatively, older adults may focus relatively more on affective information overall (both positive and negative information). Several effects on judgments and decisions might be observed if this is the case. First, losses may loom equally large or larger for older adults than for younger adults if both positive and negative information are accentuated. In addition, more affective sources of information such as anecdotal or hedonic (not utilitarian) information may receive greater weight (Dhar & Wertenbroch, 2000; Strange & Leung, 1999). Consistent with this, Blanchard-Fields found that older adults focus more than younger adults on emotional aspects of everyday problems (Blanchard-Fields, Chen, & Norris, 1997). Evidence suggested that less-numerate decision makers use explicit probabilities less and narrative information more than those who are more numerate (Dieckmann, Slovic, & Peters, 2009). Given that older adults are less numerate, it may well be the case that narratives, anecdotes, and other more verbal forms of information will have greater influence on their judgments and decisions.

Finally, incidental sources of affect (positive and negative moods; positive and negative primes) may influence older adults' judgments and decisions more than those of younger adults. An interesting study by Caruso and Shafir (2006) demonstrated that merely considering one's feelings has an impact on choices. Younger adult participants asked to consider their mood were more likely to choose a mood-relevant movie (a silly comedy) over a more highly rated dramatic movie compared to participants who had not thought about their feelings. SST suggests that older adults' feelings are more salient and accessible than are younger adults' feelings, leading to the prediction that older adults overall may rely more on emotional information when making choices. Thus, older adults should make relatively more choices that are mood relevant. This possibility remains to be tested.

Facilitating Better Decision Making

The science of what age differences in decision making exist and what processes underlie those differences will continue to be developed. Based on what we know today, however, what methods can be used to facilitate better decision making among our nation's older adults? One obvious possibility that comes directly from Tom Hess's (2000) work on older adults' selective use of their deliberative capacity is to increase motivation to use capacity by increasing the relevance and meaningfulness of the decision to the older adult (e.g., increasing personal accountability; Chen, 2004).

A second possibility, based on older adults' increased reliance on affective information, is to increase the affective meaning of information through how that information is presented. Peters et al. (2009) were interested in the processes by which decision makers bring meaning to dry, cold facts. We attempted to influence the interpretation and comprehension of information about health plan attributes by providing information in a form that can be used easily to evaluate the overall goodness or badness of a health plan. For example, in one of the studies older adult participants were presented with attribute information (quality of care and member satisfaction) about two health plans. The information was presented in bar chart format with the actual score displayed to the right of the bar chart (see Figure 4.1). The information for half of the subjects in each group was supplemented by the addition of evaluative categories (i.e., the category

Condition 1: Evaluative categories

Condition 2: No evaluative categories

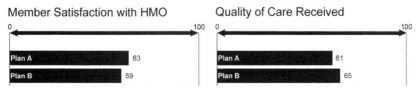

FIGURE 4.1
Example of evaluative categories in health plan choices of older adults.

lines plus labels that placed the health plans into categories of poor, fair, good, or excellent). The attribute information was designed such that Plan A was good on both attributes, while Plan B was good on quality of care but fair on member satisfaction. The specific scores for quality of care and member satisfaction were counterbalanced across subjects such that, for half of the subjects, the average quality-of-care scores were higher; for the other half, average member satisfaction scores were higher. We predicted and found that evaluative categories influenced the choices. Specifically, older adults preferred health Plan A more often when the categories were present (Plan A was always in the good evaluative category when the categories were present; see also Mikels et al., under review).

A third possibility based on the age-related declines in deliberative ability is to reduce the cognitive effort involved in processing information or doing some task. Studies have demonstrated, for example, that how information is presented may matter as much as what information is presented (Peters, Dieckmann, Dixon, Hibbard, & Mertz, 2007; Peters, Hibbard, et al., 2007). Showing only the most important information (or highlighting it), making key points easier to evaluate (order, summarize, interpret information), and generally requiring less cognitive effort and fewer inferences (e.g., do the math for them) can help elderly decision makers better understand and better use information.

Given that older adults demonstrate declines in deliberate efficiency and that comprehension and adherence in medical treatment is of great functional importance to them, efforts to aid their comprehension and decisions have focused in part, therefore, on how to support age-related declines in the efficiency of deliberative processes (Hibbard & Peters, 2003). Medication instructions that were well organized, explicit, and compatible with preexisting schemas about the task improved memory and were preferred over other formats, suggesting that they could improve medication adherence (Park, Willis, Morrow, Diehl, & Gaines, 1994). The use of external memory supports such as organizational charts and medication organizers have also been shown to be beneficial to older adults' adherence behaviors (Park, Morrell, Frieske, Blackburn, & Birchmore, 1991; Park, Morrell, Frieske, & Kincaid, 1992). Older adults demonstrated effective use of memory aids. They appeared to spontaneously use them to summarize or check information at the end of information search, as if to verify forgotten information, whereas younger adults appeared to use these same aids in the middle of a search, as if for planning rather than memory purposes (Johnson, 1997).

Finally, rather than reducing the cognitive effort involved, some methods may actually increase flexibility in processing information in decisions. Isen (2000) has shown that individuals induced into more positive moods (compared to neutral moods) process information more systematically if it helps them maintain their positive mood. Positive mood inductions also tend to lead to more creative and efficient decisions (Forgas, 1995; Isen, 2000; Mano, 1992). Such methods have not been tested with older adults, however. As a result, a study was conducted with older adult subjects (Carpenter, Peters, Isen, & Västfjäll, 2010). In the task, subjects were induced into a positive mood with a gift of candy; the rest received no gift. Subjects then completed a computer-based card task in which they won and lost money based on their choices. In the computer background, positive-mood subjects saw smiling suns; neutral-mood subjects saw control circles. Individuals in the positive-mood condition chose better from both gain and loss decks than neutral-mood subjects, suggesting that positive mood facilitated processing overall rather than highlighting positive information only in a mood-congruency effect. Concurrently, the positive-mood manipulation was associated with an increase in cognitive capacity (working memory; see also Yang & Isen, 2006). Understanding how affective processes influence cognitive flexibility and decision making may help researchers and policy makers improve how they present complex health, financial, and other important decisions to older adults.

Conclusion

In conclusion, older adults will process information in ways that are likely to be *different* from younger adults. Robust declines in deliberative capacity suggest that older adults will make worse decisions than younger adults in some situations. Deliberative decline is likely to be too simple a story, though, for three reasons. First, older adults appear to use their deliberative capacity selectively. Second, accumulated experience can compensate in part for age-related declines. And third, emotional focus appears to increase with age. As a result, older adults will make better decisions than younger adults in some situations.

Older adults, however, are faced with more decisions about vital health, financial, and other personal issues. At the same time, their proportion of the consumer population is growing, but our nation's resources are not necessarily growing with them. As a result, understanding ways to facilitate decisions of those who have attained more advanced ages may not only provide individual advantages for the older adult but also ultimately may prove beneficial to the population at large. At present, however, most research results (and advice) are based primarily on younger adults, and older adults, in all of their complexity, have been largely ignored.

Acknowledgments

This work was supported by grants from the National Science Foundation to the author (0517770 and 0339204). It is based in part on an earlier article (Peters, Hess, Västfjäll, & Auman, 2007). © 2007 John Wiley & Sons. Reprinted with permission.

References

Alhakami, A. S., & Slovic, P. (1994). A psychological study of the inverse relationship between perceived risk and perceived benefit. *Risk Analysis, 14,* 1085–1096.

Apter, A. J., Cheng, J., Small, D., Bennett, I. M., Albert, C., Fein, D. G., et al. (2006). Asthma numeracy skill and health literacy. *Journal of Asthma, 43,* 705–710.

Baker, D. W., Parker, R. M., Williams, M. V., Clark, W. S., & Nurss, J. (1997). The relationship of patient reading ability to self-reported health and use of health services. *American Journal of Public Health, 87,* 1027.

Baltes, P. B, & Baltes, M. M. (1990). Psychological perspectives on successful aging: The model of selective optimization with compensation. In P. B. Baltes & M. M. Baltes (Eds.), *Successful aging: Perspectives from the behavioral sciences* (pp. 1–34). Cambridge, UK: Cambridge University Press.

Bechara, A. (2005, November). Neural basis of decision-making and implications for older adults. In National Research Council (Ed.), *Papers from the workshop on decision making by older adults.* Washington, DC: National Academy of Sciences. Retrieved June 13, 2006, from http://www7.nationalacademies.org/csbd/bechara_paper.pdf

Bechara, A., Damasio, A., Damasio, H., & Anderson, S. (1994). Insensitivity to future consequences following damage to human prefrontal cortex. *Cognition, 50,* 7–15.

Bechara, A., Damasio, H., Tranel, D., & Damasio, A. R. (1997). Deciding advantageously before knowing the advantageous strategy. *Science, 275,* 1293–1294.

Bechara, A., Tranel, D., Damasio, H., & Damasio, A. R. (1996). Failure to respond autonomically to anticipated future outcomes following damage to prefrontal cortex. *Cerebral Cortex, 6,* 215–225.

Blanchard-Fields, F., Brannan, J. R., & Camp, C. J. (1987). Alternative conceptions of wisdom: An onion-peeling exercise. *Educational Gerontology, 13,* 497–503.

Blanchard-Fields, F., Chen, Y., & Norris, L. (1997). Everyday problem solving across the adult life span: Influence of domain specificity and cognitive appraisal. *Psychology and Aging, 12,* 684–693.

Bruine de Bruin, W., Parker, A. M., & Fischhoff, B. (2007). Individual differences in adult decision-making competence. *Journal of Personality and Social Psychology, 92,* 938–956.

Carpenter, S., Peters, E., Isen, A., & Västfjäll, D. (2010). *Positive mood facilitates working memory and complex decision making among older adults.* Manuscript in press.

Carstensen, L. L. (1993). Motivation for social contact across the life span: A theory of socioemotional selectivity. In J. E. Jacobs (Ed.), *Developmental perspectives on motivation: Nebraska symposium on motivation 1992* (Vol. 40, pp. 209–254). Lincoln: University of Nebraska Press.

Carstensen, L. L. (2001, January 2). On the brink of a brand-new old age. *New York Times.* Retrieved January 2, 2001, from http://www.nytimes.com/2001/01/02/opinion/02CARS.html

Carstensen, L. L. (2006). The influence of a sense of time on human development. *Science, 312,* 1913–1915.

Caruso, E. M., & Shafir, E. (2006). Now that I think about it, I'm in the mood for laughs: Decisions focused on mood. *Journal of Behavioral Decision Making, 19,* 155–169.

Charles, S., Mather, M., & Carstensen, L. L. (2003). Aging and emotional memory: The forgettable nature of negative images for older adults. *Journal of Experimental Psychology: General, 132,* 310–324.

Chasseigne, G., Grau, S., Mullet, E., & Cama, V. (1999). How well do elderly people cope with uncertainty in a learning task? *Acta Psychologica, 103,* 229–238.

Chasseigne, G., Lafon, P., & Mullet, E. (2002). Aging and rule learning: The case of the multiplicative law. *American Journal of Psychology, 115,* 315–330.

Chasseigne, G., Mullet, E., & Stewart, T. E. (1997). Aging and multiple case probability learning: The case of inverse relationships. *Acta Psychologica, 97,* 235–252.

Chen, Y. (2002). Unwanted beliefs: Age differences in beliefs of false information. *Aging, Neuropsychology, and Cognition, 9,* 217–228.

Chen, Y. (2004). Age differences in the correction of social judgments: Source monitoring and timing of accountability. *Aging, Neuropsychology, and Cognition, 11,* 58–67.

Chen, Y., & Blanchard-Fields, F. (2000). Unwanted thought: Age differences in the correction of social judgments. *Psychology and Aging, 15,* 475–482.

Chen, Y., & Sun, Y. (2003). Age differences in financial decision-making: Using simple heuristics. *Educational Gerontology, 29,* 627–635.

Chow, T. W., & Cummings, J. L. (2000). The amygdala and Alzheimer's disease. In J. P. Aggleton (Ed.), *The amygdala: A functional analysis* (pp. 656–680). Oxford, UK: Oxford University Press.

Damasio, A. R. (1994). *Descartes' error: Emotion, reason, and the human brain.* New York: Avon.

De Nardi, M., French, E., & Jones, J. B. (2006, October). *Differential mortality, uncertain medical expenses, and the saving of elderly singles* (NBER Working Paper No. W12554). Retrieved January 8, 2010 from http://ssrn.com/abstract=933599

Denburg, N. L., Buchanan, T. W., Tranel, D., & Adolphs, R. (2003). Evidence for preserved emotional memory in normal older persons. *Emotion, 3,* 239–253.

DeWalt, D. A., Berkman, N. D., Sheridan, S., Lohr, K. N., & Pignone, M. P. (2004). Literacy and health outcomes: A systematic review of the literature. *Journal of General Internal Medicine, 19,* 1228–1239.

Dhar, R., & Wertenbroch, K. (2000). Consumer choice between hedonic and utilitarian goods. *Journal of Marketing Research, 27,* 60–71.

Dieckmann, N. F., Slovic, P., & Peters, E. (2009). The use of narrative evidence and explicit probability by decision makers varying in numeracy. *Risk Analysis, 29,* 1473–1488.

Epstein, S. (1994). Integration of the cognitive and the psychodynamic unconscious. *American Psychologist, 49,* 709–724.

Estrada, C. A., Martin-Hryniewicz, M., Peek, B. T., Collins, C., & Byrd, J. C. (2004). Literacy and numeracy skills and anticoagulation control. *American Journal of the Medical Sciences, 328,* 88–93.

Fiedler, K. (2001). Affective influences on social information processing. In J. P. Forgas (Ed.), *Handbook of affect and social cognition* (pp. 163–185). Mahwah, NJ: Erlbaum.

Finucane, M. L., Alhakami, A., Slovic, P., & Johnson, S. M. (2000). The affect heuristic in judgments of risks and benefits. *Journal of Behavioral Decision Making, 13,* 1–17.

Forgas, J. P. (1995). Mood and judgment: The affect infusion model (AIM). *Psychological Bulletin, 117,* 39–66.

Frederick, S. (2005). Cognitive reflection and decision making. *Journal of Economic Perspectives, 19,* 24–42.

Fung, H. H., & Carstensen, L. L. (2003). Sending memorable messages to the old: Age differences in preferences and memory for emotionally meaningful advertisements. *Journal of Personality and Social Psychology, 85,* 163–178.

Goesling, B., & Baker, D. (2008). Three faces of international inequality. *Research in Social Stratification and Mobility, 26,* 183–198.

Goldman, D. P., & Smith, J. P. (2002). Can patient self-management help explain the SES health gradient? *Proceedings of the National Academy of Sciences of the United States of America, 99,* 10929–10934.

Good, C. G., Johnsrude, I. S., Ashburner, J., Henson, R. N. A., Friston, K. J., & Frackowiak, R. S. J. (2001). A voxel-based morphometric study of aging in 465 normal adult human brains. *NeuroImage, 14,* 21–36.

Hammond, K. R. (1996). *Human judgment and social policy: Irreducible uncertainty, inevitable error, unavoidable injustice.* New York: Oxford University Press.

Hershey, D. A., Walsh, D. A., Read, S. J., & Chulef, A. S. (1990). The effects of expertise on financial problem solving: Evidence for goal-directed, problem-solving scripts. *Organizational Behavior & Human Decision Processes, 46,* 77–101.

Hess, T. M. (2000). Aging-related constraints and adaptations in social information processing. In U. Von Hecker, S. Dutke, & G. Sedek (Eds.), *Generative mental processes and cognitive resources: Integrative research on adaptation and control* (pp. 129–155). Dordrecht, The Netherlands: Kluwer.

Hess, T. M., Germain, C. M., Rosenberg, D. C., Leclerc, C. M., & Hodges, E. A. (2005). Aging-related selectivity and susceptibility to irrelevant affective information in the construction of attitudes. *Aging, Neuropsychology, and Cognition, 12,* 149–174.

Hibbard, J. H., & Peters, E. (2003). Supporting informed consumer health care decisions: Data presentation approaches that facilitate the use of information in choice. *Annual Review of Public Health, 24,* 413–433.

Hibbard, J. H., Peters, E., Dixon, A., & Tusler, M. (2007). Consumer competencies and the use of comparative quality information: It isn't just about literacy. *Medical Care Research and Review, 64,* 379–394.

Hibbard, J. H., Peters, E., Slovic, P., Finucane, M. L., & Tusler, M. (2001). Making health care quality reports easier to use. *Journal of Quality Improvement, 27,* 591–604.

Hibbard, J. H., Slovic, P., Peters, E., Finucane, M., & Tusler, M. (2001). Is the informed-choice policy approach appropriate for Medicare beneficiaries? *Health Affairs, 20,* 199–203.

Isen, A. M. (2000). Positive affect and decision making. In M. Lewis & J. M. Havieland (Eds.), *Handbook of emotions* (2nd ed., pp. 417–435). London: Guilford.

Johnson, M. M. (1990). Age differences in decision making: A process methodology for examining strategic information processing. *Journal of Gerontology: Psychological Sciences, 45,* 75–78.

Johnson, M. M. S. (1993). Thinking about strategies: During, before and after making a decision. *Psychology and Aging, 8,* 231–241.

Johnson, M. M. S. (1997). Individual differences in the voluntary use of a memory aid during decision making. *Experimental Aging Research, 23,* 33–43.

Johnson, M. M. S., & Drungle, S. C. (2000). Purchasing over-the-counter medications: The impact of age differences in information processing. *Experimental Aging Research, 26,* 245–261.

Kahneman, D. (2003). A perspective on judgment and choice: Mapping bounded rationality. *American Psychologist, 58,* 697–720.

Kahneman, D., & Tversky, A. (1979). Prospect theory: An analysis of decision under risk. *Econometrica, 47,* 263–291.

Kensinger, E. A., Brierley, B., Medford, N., Growdon, J. H., & Corkin, S. (2002). Effects of normal aging and Alzheimer's disease on emotional memory. *Emotion, 2,* 118–134.

Kirsch, I. S., Jungeblut, A., Jenkins, L., & Kolstad, A. (2002). *Adult literacy in America: A first look at the findings of the National Adult Literacy Survey* (3rd ed., Vol. 201). Washington, DC: National Center for Education, U.S. Department of Education.

Kruglanski, A. W., Chun, W. Y., Erb, H.-P., Pierro, A., Mannetti, L., & Spiegel, D. (2003). A parametric unimodel of human judgment: Integrating dual-process frameworks in social cognition from a single-mode perspective. In J. P. Forgas, K. D. Williams, & W. von Hippel (Eds.), *Social judgments: Implicit and explicit processes* (pp. 137–161). Cambridge, UK: Cambridge University Press.

Labouvie-Vief, G. (2003). Dynamic integration: Affect, cognition, and the self in adulthood. *Current Directions in Psychological Science, 12,* 201–206.

Labouvie-Vief, G. (2005). Self-with-other representations and the organization of the self. *Journal of Research in Personality, 39,* 185–205.

Lipkus, I. M., Samsa, G., & Rimer, B. K. (2001). General performance on a numeracy scale among highly educated samples. *Medical Decision Making, 21,* 37–44.

Lockenhoff, C. E., & Carstensen, L. L. (2007). Aging, emotion, and health-related decision strategies: Motivational manipulations can reduce age differences. *Psychology and Aging, 22,* 134–146.

Loewenstein, G. F., Weber, E. U., Hsee, C. K., & Welch, E. S. (2001). Risk as feelings. *Psychological Bulletin, 127,* 267–286.

MacPherson, S. E., Phillips, L. H., & Della Sala, S. (2002). Age, executive function, and social decision making: A dorsolateral prefrontal theory of cognitive aging. *Psychology and Aging, 17,* 598–609.

Mano, H. (1992). Judgments under distress: Assessing the role of unpleasantness and arousal in judgment formation. *Organizational Behavior and Human Decision Processes, 52*, 216–245.

Mather, M. (2006). A review of decision-making processes: Weighing the risks and benefits of aging. In L. L. Carstensen & C. R. Hartel (Eds.), *When I'm 64* (pp. 145–173). Washington, DC: National Academies Press.

Mather, M., & Knight, M. (2005). Goal-directed memory: The role of cognitive control in older adults' emotional memory. *Psychology and Aging, 20*, 554–570.

McGrew, K. S., Wood, R. W., & Mather, N. (2001). *Woodcock-Johnson III*. Itasca, IL: Riverside.

Meyer, B. J. F., Russo, C., & Talbot, A. (1995). Discourse comprehension and problem solving: Decisions about the treatment of breast cancer by women across the life span. *Psychology and Aging, 10*, 84–103.

Mikels, J. A., Loeckenhoff, C., Maglio, S., Goldstein, M., Garber, A., & Carstensen, L. L. (2009). *Follow your heart or your head? The effects of affective versus deliberative decision strategies differ by age group.* Manuscript submitted for publication.

Murphy, S. T., & Zajonc, R. B. (1993). Affect, cognition, and awareness: Affective priming with optimal and suboptimal stimulus exposures. *Journal of Personality and Social Psychology, 64*, 723–739.

Mutter, S. A. (2000). Illusory correlation and group impression formation in young and older adults. *Journal of Gerontology: Psychological Sciences, 55B*, 224–237.

Mutter, S. A., & Pliske, R. M. (1994). Aging and illusory correlation in judgments of co-occurrence. *Psychology and Aging, 9*, 53–63.

Mutter, S. A., & Pliske, R. M. (1996). Judging event covariation: Effects of age and memory demands. *The Journals of Gerontology: Psychological Sciences, 51B*, 70–80.

Mutter, S. A., & Williams, T. W. (2004). Aging and the detection of contingency in causal learning. *Psychology and Aging, 19*, 13–26.

Osgood, C. E., Suci, G. J., & Tannenbaum, P. H. (1957). *The measurement of meaning.* Urbana: University of Illinois.

Park, D. C., Lautenschlager G., Hedden T., Davidson N. S., Smith A. D., &, Smith, P. K. (2002). Models of visuospatial and verbal memory across the adult life span. *Psychology and Aging, 17*, 299–320.

Park, D. C., Morrell, R. W., Frieske, D., Blackburn, B., & Birchmore, D. (1991). Cognitive factors and the use of over-the-counter medication organizers by arthritis patients. *Human Factors, 33*, 57–67.

Park, D. C., Morrell, R. W., Frieske, D., & Kincaid, D. (1992). Medication adherence behaviors in older adults: Effects of external cognitive supports. *Psychology and Aging, 7*, 252–256.

Park, D. C., Willis, S. L., Morrow, D., Diehl, M., & Gaines, C. L. (1994). Cognitive function and medication usage in older adults. *Journal of Applied Gerontology, 13*, 39–57.

Peters, E. (2006). The functions of affect in the construction of preferences. In S. Lichtenstein & P. Slovic (Eds.), *The construction of preference* (pp. 454–463). New York: Cambridge University Press.

Peters, E. (2008). Numeracy and the perception and communication of risk. In W. T. Tucker, S. Ferson, A. M. Finkel, & D. Slavin (Eds.), *Annals of the New York Academy of Sciences: Vol. 1128. Strategies for risk communication: Evolution, evidence, experience* (pp. 1–7). New York: New York Academy of Sciences.

Peters, E., Baker, D., Dieckmann, N., Leon, J., & Collins, J. (2010). *Explaining the education effect on health: A field of study in Ghana.* Manuscript submitted for publication.

Peters, E., Borberg, J., & Slovic, P. (2007, October). *Age and numeracy differences in the processing of risk and benefit information.* Paper presented at the 2007 annual conference of the Society for Medical Decision Making, Pittsburgh, PA.

Peters, E., Dieckmann, N., Dixon, A., Hibbard, J. H., & Mertz, C. K. (2007). Less is more in presenting quality information to consumers. *Medical Care Research and Review, 64,* 169–190.

Peters, E., Dieckmann, N. F., Västfjäll, D., Mertz, C. K., Slovic, P., & Hibbard, J. (2009). Bringing meaning to numbers: The impact of evaluative categories on decisions. *Journal of Experimental Psychology: Applied, 15,* 213–227.

Peters, E., Hess, T. M., Västfjäll, D., & Auman, C. (2007). Adult age differences in dual information processes: Implications for the role of affective and deliberative processes in older adults' decision making. *Perspectives on Psychological Science, 2,* 1–23.

Peters, E., Hibbard, J. H., Slovic, P., & Dieckmann, N. (2007). Numeracy skill and the communication, comprehension, and use of risk-benefit information. *Health Affairs, 26,* 741–748.

Peters, E., Lipkus, I. M., & Diefenbach, M. A. (2006). The functions of affect in health communications and in the construction of health preferences. *Journal of Communication, 56,* S140–S162.

Peters, E., & Slovic, P. (2000). The springs of action: Affective and analytical information processing in choice. *Personality & Social Psychology Bulletin, 26,* 1465–1475.

Peters, E., & Slovic, P. (2007). Affective asynchrony and the measurement of the affective attitude component. *Cognition and Emotion, 21,* 300–329.

Peters, E., Slovic, P., Västfjäll, D., & Mertz, C. K. (2008). Intuitive numbers guide decisions. *Judgment and Decision Making, 3,* 619–635.

Peters, E., Vastfjall, D., Slovic, P., Mertz, C. K., Mazzocco, K., & Dickert, S. (2006). Numeracy and decision making. *Psychological Science, 17,* 407–415.

Petty, R. E., & Wegener, D. T. (1999). The elaboration likelihood model: Current status and controversies. In S. Chaiken & Y. Trope (Eds.), *Dual-process theories in social psychology* (pp. 37–72). New York: Guilford.

Reyna, V. F. (2004). How people make decisions that involve risk: A dual-processes approach. *Current Directions in Psychological Science, 13,* 60–66.

Riggle, E. D. B., & Johnson, M. M. S. (1996). Age difference in political decision making: Strategies for evaluating political candidates. *Political Behavior, 18,* 99–118.

Rothman, R. L., Housam, R., Weiss, H., Davis, D., Gregory, R., Gebretsadik, T., et al., (2006). Patient understanding of food labels: The role of literacy and numeracy. *American Journal of Preventive Medicine, 31,* 391–398.

Salthouse, T. A. (1990). Cognitive competence and expertise in the aging. In J. E. Birren & K. W. Schaie (Eds.), *Handbook of the psychology of aging* (3rd ed., pp. 310–319). New York: Academic Press.

Salthouse, T. A. (2006). Mental exercise and mental aging: Evaluating the validity of the "use it or lose it" hypothesis. *Perspectives on Psychological Science, 1*, 68–87.

Schaie, K. W., & Zanjani, F. A. K. (2006). Intellectual development across adulthood. In C. Hoare (Ed.), *Handbook of adult development and learning* (pp. 99–122). New York: Oxford University Press.

Schwarz, N., & Clore, G. L. (1983). Mood, misattribution, and judgments of well-being: Informative and directive functions of affective states. *Journal of Personality and Social Psychology, 45*, 513–523.

Sentell, T. L., & Halpin, H. A. (2006). Importance of adult literacy in understanding health disparities. *Journal of General Internal Medicine, 21*, 862–866.

Shiv, B., & Fedorikhin, A. (1999). Heart and mind in conflict: The interplay of affect and cognition in consumer decision making. *Journal of Consumer Research, 26*, 278–292.

Simon, H. (1955). A behavioral model of rational choice. *The Quarterly Journal of Economics, 69*, 99–118.

Skurnik, I., Yoon, C., Park, D. C., & Schwarz, N. (2005). How warnings about false claims become recommendations. *Journal of Consumer Research, 31*, 713–724.

Sloman, S. A. (1996). The empirical case for two systems of reasoning. *Psychological Bulletin, 119*, 3–21.

Slovic, P., Finucane, M. L., Peters, E., & MacGregor, D. G. (2002). The affect heuristic. In T. Gilovich, D. Griffin, & D. Kahneman (Eds.), *Heuristics and biases: The psychology of intuitive judgment* (pp. 397–420). New York: Cambridge University Press.

Sorce, P. (1995). Cognitive competence of older consumers. *Psychology & Marketing, 12*, 467–480.

Staats, A. W., & Staats, C. K. (1958). Attitudes established by classical conditioning. *Journal of Abnormal & Social Psychology, 57*, 37–40.

Stanovich, K. E., & West, R. F. (2002). Individual differences in reasoning: Implications for the rationality debate? In T. Gilovich, D. W. Griffin, & D. Kahneman (Eds.), *Heuristics and biases: The psychology of intuitive judgment* (pp. 421–440). New York: Cambridge University Press.

Strange, J. J., & Leung, C. C. (1999). How anecdotal accounts in news and in fiction can influence judgments of a social problem's urgency, causes, and cures. *Personality and Social Psychology Bulletin, 25*, 436–449.

Streufert, S., Pogash, R., Piasecki, M., & Post, G. M. (1990). Age and management team performance. *Psychology and Aging, 5*, 551–559.

Strough, J., Mehta, C., McFall, J., & Schuller, K. (2008). Are older adults less subject to the sunk-cost fallacy than younger adults? *Psychological Science, 19*, 650–652.

U.S. Food and Drug Administration.(2009). *Facts about generic drugs.* Retrieved January 8, 2010 from http://www.fda.gov/Drugs/EmergencyPreparedness/BioterrorismandDrugPreparedness/

West, R. L. (1996). An application of prefrontal cortex function theory to cognitive aging. *Psychological Bulletin, 120*, 272–292.

Williams, M. V., Baker, D. W., Parker, R. M., & Nurss, J. R. (1998). Relationship of functional health literacy to patients' knowledge of their chronic disease. *Archives of Internal Medicine, 158*, 166–172.

Wilson, T. D., Dunn, D. S., Kraft, D., & Lisle, D. J. (1989). Introspection, attitude change, and attitude-behavior consistency: The disruptive effects of explaining why we feel the way we do. *Advances in Experimental Social Psychology, 22*, 287–343.

Wood, S., Busemeyer, J. R., Koling, A., Cox, C., & Davis, H. (2005). Older adults as adaptive decision-makers: Evidence from the Iowa gambling task. *Psychology and Aging, 20*, 220–225.

Yang, H., & Isen, A. M. (2006, November). *Differential effects of positive affect on working memory and short-term memory: Positive affect enhances working memory via improvement in controlled processing.* Paper presented at the annual meeting of the Psychonomic Society, Houston, TX.

Zajonc, R. B. (1980). Feeling and thinking: Preferences need no inferences. *American Psychologist, 35*, 151–175.

5

Do Workers Prepare Rationally for Retirement?

Gary Burtless

The Brookings Institution

Introduction

There are two views of workers' farsightedness in choosing a retirement age and implementing a lifetime saving plan. One view is that workers select their retirement age and saving strategy based on a rational and forward-looking plan. The plan is formed on the basis of good information about the worker's own preferences, the financial rewards from working, and the pros and cons of retiring at different ages. An opposing view is that many workers do not plan very far ahead in either choosing their retirement age or saving for retirement. Many use naïve rules of thumb when deciding when to leave work permanently, and a large minority do not have the ability to formulate a good saving plan or the self-command to stick to a sensible saving plan if one is proposed to them.

Economists who are optimistic about workers' planning abilities think the retirement age is usually the result of well-informed and farsighted deliberation. After workers have chosen the retirement age that seems most desirable, they accumulate savings so that they can afford to retire at the desired age. Furthermore, they invest their retirement savings in a way that is calculated to earn a good and tolerably safe return. According to this view, by the time workers get close to their desired retirement age they should have accumulated enough savings so that they can afford to stop working. If their retirement and saving plans have worked well, their annual consumption after retirement should be approximately the same as it was during years before they retired.

A number of empirical economists find this interpretation broadly consistent with available evidence about workers' behavior. Historical data on workers' retirement ages and savings patterns as well as survey findings on the level of workers' consumption before and after retirement seem consistent with farsighted planning on the part of most workers. Economists have found some evidence that the distribution of retirement ages within a given birth cohort is consistent with forward-looking behavior for at least some workers. Many workers retire when their health deteriorates or when there is an abrupt fall in the net return from working. This kind of decline occurs when workers are dismissed from long-held jobs. Usually, the workers who hold long-term jobs earn good wages as a result of job seniority and lengthy experience in a particular line of work. When they are dismissed from these jobs, many find it hard to locate a new job that pays as good a wage as the wage earned in the jobs they lost. Some workers also experience a drop in their net return from working when they reach the early or normal retirement age in a defined-benefit pension plan. A noticeable percentage of workers retires at this point. These retirement patterns conform to the basic economic model of retirement, which predicts that when there is a sharp decline in the economic payoff to employment older workers will exit the job market. Labor economists have also found evidence that long-term trends in the retirement age can be partially explained by changes in the retirement incentives built into employer and public pension plans. Thus, the aggregate-level evidence is consistent with the theory that many workers are choosing their retirement ages as a rational response to economic incentives.

The evidence on workers' saving behavior is more controversial. Many observers reject the idea that most workers have saved adequately for retirement. A number of analysts have published alarming studies showing that middle-aged and older U.S. workers face large saving shortfalls compared with the nest eggs they would need to maintain their consumption if they retired at the typical retirement age (Bernheim, 1992; Moore & Mitchell, 2000; Munnell, Webb, & Golub-Sass, 2007). This evidence has been challenged in a handful of studies of the wealth holdings of workers who are near the retirement age. Taking account of the year-to-year variability of workers' earnings, the uncertainty of life spans, and the pre- and postretirement spending obligations of individual workers, a few economists now argue that only a small percentage of workers near retirement have saved less than the optimal amount. Among those who have saved too little, the typical saving shortfall is found to be small (Engen, Gale, & Uccello, 1999; Hurd & Rohwedder, 2004; Scholz & Seshadri, 2008; Scholz, Seshadri, & Khitatrakun, 2006).

Although the evidence on retirement saving adequacy is open to dispute, behavioral economists have accumulated considerable survey and observational data to show that saving and investment are difficult for ordinary workers. When they are asked directly about their retirement plans and saving habits, a large percentage of workers report that they have given no thought to retirement, have saved too little for old age, and do not know whether they will be able to afford to retire. Few can accurately describe the risks or relative returns of the investments they hold in their retirement savings accounts. When asked to describe future benefits under their company-provided pension plans or Social Security, many workers show ignorance of the most basic provisions determining their future retirement income. If workers do not know how their pensions are calculated, it is a little hard to believe that they use information sensibly to choose an optimal retirement or saving strategy. Workers' saving patterns in company 401(k) plans are sensitive to small changes in the way their participation choices are presented to them. Many workers recognize that they ought to contribute to their retirement plan, but their actual decision to contribute can depend on minor details of an employer's 401(k) enrollment process. Workers' decisions about how to allocate their retirement savings across different kinds of investment products are frequently made with little knowledge of basic investment principles and are powerfully influenced by relatively minor changes in the way investment alternatives are described. In view of the fact that workers' saving and investment decisions are sensitive to minor administrative and presentational details, many observers are skeptical that workers' retirement saving behavior can be the result of deliberative and well-informed planning. Their saving may instead be the product of chance. Some workers have the good fortune to be employed by companies with a generous and sensibly designed pension plan. Less-fortunate workers hold jobs for which benefits are smaller, and the employer provides little guidance on how workers should save for old age.

Does it matter whether workers make retirement and savings decisions in a rational way? It does if workers' errors cause their well-being to fall well short of what it would be if they were good planners. Workers' welfare would be seriously harmed, for example, if those who had little savings decided to retire in late middle age and then faced severe deprivation after exhausting their retirement savings 15 years later. Workers' well-being would also be at risk if they saved too little for retirement or if they used up their retirement nest egg too quickly after they stopped working. Retirement systems that rely heavily on workers' ability to select a saving and investment strategy appear attractive if nearly all workers are skilled in these tasks. They seem less plausible if a large minority of workers perform one or both tasks badly.

This chapter considers what we have learned about the rationality and farsightedness of workers' retirement decisions. Do workers retire at a reasonable age? Do they save enough to afford the retirement ages they choose? Do they invest their retirement savings in a rational and prudent way? I first sketch briefly the standard economic model of lifetime labor supply and consumption and then consider how well the cross-sectional and historical evidence conforms to this model.

Planning the Retirement Age

Economists' standard theory of retirement rests on the life-cycle consumption model. The central idea in this model is that farsighted workers will rationally plan their consumption over a full lifetime. In devising their lifetime consumption plans, rational workers take account of the likely path of their labor earnings as they grow older and then prudently accumulate savings in anticipation of their retirement. The goal of a good consumption plan is to maximize one's lifetime well-being, subject to the constraint that lifetime consumption cannot exceed one's lifetime wealth. Lifetime wealth consists of a worker's initial assets and the present discounted value of anticipated labor earnings and other kinds of income that are not derived from initial assets or labor earnings. Rational workers will plan to avoid situations in which all of their lifetime wealth is consumed long before they expect to die.

A worker who successfully solves the consumption planning problem will plot out a desired path of consumption for each future year of life and will stick with the plan unless there is an unanticipated change in his or her financial outlook. The most advantageous plan will depend on the relationship between the worker's subjective rate of time preference and the interest rate that can be obtained on savings. The rate of time preference is a measure of the worker's impatience in consumption. If the worker's rate of time preference is equal to the market interest rate, the preferred consumption path will be basically level throughout the worker's life. If instead the rate of time preference is higher than the interest rate, the worker will attempt to shift consumption toward the early part of life, and consumption will fall as the worker grows older. Workers may wish to leave bequests to survivors, in which case they will consume all their lifetime wealth except the amount that they want to leave to heirs.

The life-cycle model emphasizes the single most important financial aspect of retirement, namely, the sharp drop or complete loss of earnings when employment ends in old age. A crucial implication of the life-cycle theory is that farsighted workers will simultaneously select both a retirement age and a pattern of lifetime consumption. Their choice will be decisively affected by the expected pattern of their wage income, the interest rate they pay on money they borrow, and the investment earnings they obtain on money they save. Another implication of the theory

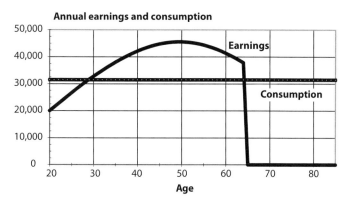

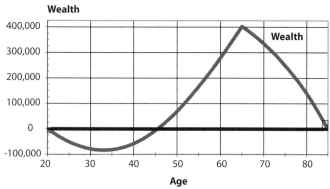

FIGURE 5.1
Life-cycle earnings, consumption, and wealth accumulation of a farsighted worker.

is that year-to-year changes in consumption should be much smaller than year-to-year changes in earnings, especially around the planned age of retirement. Workers with a farsighted plan will smooth consumption by saving and making withdrawals from their savings over the course of their careers.

Figure 5.1 shows one solution to the life-cycle consumption problem for a worker who expects to live to age 85, faces a 5% interest rate, chooses to retire at age 65, and has no bequest motive. The worker's potential wage is $20,000 a year when she enters the workforce at age 20, gradually rises to almost $46,000 a year when she reaches age 50, and then declines at later ages. The value of her expected lifetime earnings is a little more than $1.7 million, but her total lifetime consumption can be greater than this if she saves part of her earnings and invests her savings in an interest-bearing account that garners 5% a year. If she consumes her entire lifetime income (including anticipated interest earnings) steadily throughout her life, her annual consumption will be greater than her annual earnings until she is about 30. Her consumption will be less than her earnings in the middle of her career when her wages reach their peak. After she retires, her earnings will fall to zero, and she will live off accumulated wealth. The lower panel in Figure 5.1 shows the worker's wealth holdings at successive ages. Note that her nest egg is negative when she is young because she must borrow money to consume more than she earns. By age 30, the worker's wages exceed her annual consumption, and she can begin to repay some of her debts. At age 45, her debts are paid off and she begins to accumulate wealth. Her wealth holdings reach a lifetime peak at her retirement and then decline as her nest egg is drawn down to pay for old-age consumption.

Setting aside for a moment the effects of uncertainty, the life-cycle model can be used to analyze workers' choice of retirement age. To simplify, assume that workers stop working completely when they retire. If a worker's potential wages at each future age are known with reasonable certainty, the planning problem is to select the most satisfying combination of years at work and lifetime consumption that is available to the worker. Economists usually assume that, other things equal, workers would prefer to work fewer years (holding constant their lifetime consumption) and to consume more goods and services (holding constant their years at work). In other words, additional consumption of goods and services is a "good," while an additional year at work is a "bad." If workers postpone their retirement (accepting more of a bad), they can also consume more over their lifetime (a good). Of course, this characterization of the trade-off is not really accurate for people who enjoy their work and derive tremendous satisfaction from their accomplishments and social interactions on the job. Nonetheless, the theory is helpful in explaining retirement among the large number of people who dislike or eventually grow tired of working.

One reason workers retire is that their potential earnings decline in old age, so the payoff from accepting a longer work life eventually grows smaller with advances in age. When the payoff falls below the perceived value of the extra goods and services a worker can consume as a result of working longer, the worker will retire. Workers may also retire when they are involuntarily laid off and cannot find another job with wages, benefits, and working conditions as good as those in the job they lost. Poor health can spur retirement for two reasons. It may reduce the worker's potential wage, and it can make continued work less pleasant.

Company and government pension plans can affect the financial payoff from extra work, which is another reason employment can appear less attractive at older ages. Public and occupational pensions affect the lifetime trade-off between consumption and retirement in a complicated way. Their impacts on retirement depend on the contributions workers must make for the pensions they will receive and on the benefit formula and rules that link monthly pensions to a worker's past covered earnings.

In the United States, employers and workers currently pay a combined tax equal to 12.4% of wages into the Social Security system. The tax reduces workers' current wages by about 12% in comparison with the wages they would receive if the program did not exist. On the other hand, contributions allow a worker to earn credits toward a bigger public pension. The monthly pension goes up as the worker's covered lifetime wages increase. Whether the increase in the pension entitlement is large enough to compensate workers for their extra contributions is an empirical question. The answer varies from one worker to the next and at different stages in the same worker's career. Low-wage workers receive favorable treatment under the Social Security formula, so they usually receive a generous return on their contributions, especially in the early and middle years of a career. High-wage and long-service workers typically receive much lower returns. In fact, under many pension plans there may be a point in a worker's career when the pension becomes less valuable the longer the worker remains employed.

In some pension plans, this turning point can occur when the worker attains the earliest pension-claiming age. Assuming that workers cannot simultaneously work and collect a pension, workers who delay their retirement until after the earliest benefit-claiming age are at least temporarily passing up the opportunity to receive a pension. If a worker is entitled to $1,000 per month in pension, for example, the worker gives up $1,000 in retirement income every month he or she delays retirement past the benefit-claiming age. If the worker's regular monthly pay is $10,000, this represents a comparatively small sacrifice. But, if the wage is only $1,000 a month, the sacrifice is equal to 100% of her earnings. This worker's lifetime income is no higher if he or she works an additional year than if he or she retires unless there is an upward adjustment in future pensions to compensate for giving up a year's pension. If the pension formula provides an upward adjustment in pensions for workers who delay claiming benefits after the earliest benefit-claiming age, a crucial consideration is the size of the adjustment. If it is very small, say, an extra $10 per month, the worker is not fairly compensated for giving up 1 year of pension payments. In this case, the worker effectively faces a cut in wages if he or she works past the earliest benefit-claiming age. If the adjustment is large, the worker may not give up anything at all from working or may be financially better off.

This discussion assumes that workers cannot simultaneously work and collect a pension. Whether this is the case depends on the earnings test used in calculating the pension. A stringent earnings test forces workers to stop working or substantially reduce their hours to begin collecting a pension. Workers who earn more than a threshold level of earnings lose some or all of their monthly pensions. If pensioners are fairly compensated for this loss of benefits with an increase in future benefits, possibly after the pensioner leaves employment altogether, the temporary loss of pensions should in theory have little impact on pensioners' work effort. In the past, however, the short-run loss of Social Security benefits was not compensated by future pension increases, so the earnings test essentially represented a pure tax on Social Security recipients' earnings. A pension system that combines an earnings test with a pension-adjustment formula that does not fairly compensate workers when they delay claiming a pension offers a strong incentive for workers to cease working and start collecting pensions at the earliest benefit-claiming age.

Evidence

A large number of studies have tried to measure the impact of pension and other economic incentives on retirement. Excellent surveys of this literature have been written by Quinn, Burkhauser, and Myers (1990), Hurd (1990), Lumsdaine and Mitchell (1999), and Krueger and Meyer (2002). Many of the most widely cited retirement studies examined the impact of the Social Security system on U.S. retirement patterns. Economists have used two broad approaches to estimating the effects of pensions and other economic factors on the timing of retirement. One class of study relies on time series changes in pension incentives to identify the impact of incentives on some measure of labor supply in old age, usually labor force participation or the employment rate. A second relies on differences among workers at a particular point in time to disentangle the influence of detailed program incentives on individual workers. A few studies use the combination of both time series and cross-sectional variation to determine the effects of pension incentives based on longitudinal data for a representative sample of workers. The empirical studies cited in the literature reviews mentioned find considerable evidence that pension incentives and other economic factors have the predicted effects on the age of retirement. When workers become eligible for pensions that are high compared with their net earnings at work, they tend to retire. The higher the ratio of pensions to net earnings, the earlier retirement occurs. On the other hand, if increased wages and incentives in the pension formula make it financially attractive to delay retirement, workers tend to remain in the workforce. Poor health, a sudden deterioration in health, and involuntary layoff are associated with earlier retirement.

Time series data give some indication of the influence of the Social Security program on retirement. These data shed light on the relationship between the program's changing retirement incentives and the observed distribution of retirement ages (Burtless, 2006, pp. 136–48). The labor force participation rates of older American men fell substantially during the 20th century. The changing retirement incentives in Social Security help explain the trend as well as the clustering of retirements at ages that are critical to determining Social Security benefits. In 1940, Social Security had little if any influence on the distribution of retirement ages because benefits were not yet available for retired workers. Between 1941 and the late 1990s, workers eligible for Social Security who continued to work beyond age 65 gave up pensions for which they were not fairly compensated. The earnings penalty in the benefit formula encouraged workers to retire at age 65. Census Bureau estimates of labor force participation rates by exact year of age show a sharp increase between 1940 and 1960 in the percentage of men who withdrew from the labor force at age 65. Starting in 1961, age 62 became the earliest age at which American men could claim a reduced Social Security pension. Before 1961, men could not claim a pension until 65, and there was no evidence of clustering in retirements at age 62. By 1970, retirement was more common at 62 than at any other age except 65. By 1990, age 62 was the most popular age of retirement by a wide margin. In principle, the Social Security formula fairly compensates workers if they delay claiming a pension past age 62. However, a worker who heavily discounts the value of benefits in the distant future or who has short life expectancy would not regard the compensation as fair. Many of those workers would prefer to retire and claim a pension at age 62 rather than at a later age.

This kind of evidence is consistent with the view that some fraction of workers is sensitive to Social Security incentives when they retire. It is less obvious whether this shows most workers are choosing their retirement age on the basis of a farsighted and rational plan. Workers following a simple rule of thumb may retire as soon as a pension replaces a target percentage of their monthly pay. It does not require long-term planning to recognize this target is more likely to be achieved when the worker can first claim a Social Security pension. To be sure, the shifts in the peak of male retirement ages conform broadly with the shifting incentives provided by the U.S. Social Security program. The shift in behavior did not take place instantaneously after the change in Social Security incentives, however. For example, men were slow to respond to the availability of early pensions, which began in 1961. The percentage of men retiring at age 62 approximately doubled between 1970 and 1980, yet it is hard to see how the incentives for retirement at that particular age changed appreciably over the decade. The innovation in pension rules occurred in 1961 when early retirement benefits were first made available.

Axtell and Epstein (1999) argued that the slow evolution of retirement ages after the 1961 reform provides evidence that contradicts the view that workers are farsighted and well-informed in their choice of retirement age. They suggested instead that "imitative behavior and social interactions—factors absent from traditional economic models—may be fundamental in explaining the sluggish response to policy" (p. 162). They argued that only a small percentage of workers may have the capacity or willingness to understand program rules and interpret their meaning for the choice of an optimal retirement age. Axtell and Epstein suggested that most workers imitate the behavior of their "neighbors," that is, older relatives, colleagues at work, or actual neighbors whose retirement behavior can be directly observed. If an imitator's "neighborhood" happens to include one or more farsighted planners, it is more likely that the imitator will respond to new incentives in a farsighted way because the behavior imitated is more likely to be optimal. Axtell and Epstein showed how rational behavior can cascade through a social network, even though few members of the network may be farsighted or plan rationally for their retirements. Eventually, retirement patterns attain a new equilibrium in which the rational behavior predominates. It is not obvious, however, whether the optimal, farsighted behavior of a neighbor offers a good guide to one's own behavior. A neighbor who has accumulated greater wealth or who expects a shorter life span can comfortably retire at a younger age. Axtell and Epstein's model works best in explaining imitative behavior when agents face a common change in incentives. The change in availability of U.S. public pensions at age 62 is an example of such a change.

The pattern of retirement ages in a cross section of the population or in successive cross sections at different points in time suggests that at least some workers are sensitive to changes in the financial incentives to retire. It does not give us clear guidance on the percentage of workers who are farsighted and rational in their choice of a retirement age. The availability of longitudinal surveys of older workers allows researchers to ask people directly whether they have made retirement plans and selected an expected age of retirement. Information from later interviews can then be used to determine whether respondents follow through on their plans. Abraham and Hausman (2004) analyzed information from the 1992–2000 Health and Retirement Survey (HRS) to determine how frequently older workers reported a retirement plan and how often they stuck to those plans. Workers in the HRS were in their 50s and early 60s when the question on retirement plans was first posed. This seems like a point in life when long-term planners would have formulated some kind of retirement strategy. Abraham and Hausman reported that "the most common answer (38% of responses) was that the respondent had not given much thought to future work and retirement plans, or had no plans" (p. 9). Among workers who reported an expected retirement age or retirement strategy, a large percentage failed to follow through on their plans, even when the planned retirement was within 2 years of the date they were asked about their plans. Among respondents reporting that they would stop working altogether within 2 years of an interview, slightly more than one third were still at work in the next biannual interview. Among workers who claimed that they would never stop working, about one in seven had actually ceased working within 2 years. Of course, unexpected events may have intervened between the two surveys, disrupting the best-laid plans of rational workers.

Assuming that workers want to formulate a rational retirement strategy, a plausible starting point is to become familiar with the rules and benefit formulas governing the pension plans in which they are enrolled. The HRS provides a good source of information about older workers' knowledge of their pension plans. Workers were asked to describe some important features of their company plans, and their descriptions were compared to the descriptions of the same plan supplied by employers. Analysis of the workers' responses show startling discrepancies between workers' understanding and employers' descriptions of retirement plans (Gustman & Steinmeier, 2004). Only about one half of workers covered by a defined-contribution plan correctly identified the type of pension plan in which they were enrolled. Approximately the same percentage of workers enrolled in a defined-benefit plan correctly reported that their employer offered that form of pension. Even among workers who correctly stated that they were covered by a defined-benefit plan, only a minority accurately reported the youngest age at which they could claim pensions. For example, among workers in plans for which the early eligibility age was 55, only 40% of workers correctly reported this age. Slightly more than 20% believed that the early entitlement age was 62, and 7% thought it was 65 or higher.

Many workers are also uninformed about their future Social Security benefits. Rohwedder and van Soest (2006) examined HRS respondents' predictions of their Social Security benefits. Because respondents in the HRS are interviewed several times over more than a decade, most respondents' predictions can be compared with their actual benefits. Considering only the reports of respondents who claimed Social Security within 2 years of the interview, over one quarter of respondents reported that they did not know the probable amount of their benefit. Of the 73% who did volunteer an estimate, about one quarter overestimated their actual benefits by 10% or more, and a tenth overestimated their actual benefits by one third or more. Not surprisingly, respondents who made large overestimates of their Social Security benefits were also much more likely to experience sizable reductions in their consumption after they retired. Compared with respondents who had made more accurate benefit predictions, the retirees who had overestimated their benefits also reported greater worry about whether they would have enough income to get by in retirement. In this case, ignorance did not turn out to be bliss, at least after workers retired and learned that they had to survive on a smaller pension than expected.

How does misinformation affect retirement decisions? Chan and Stevens (2003) offered some revealing evidence. They focused their analysis on HRS respondents who worked in 1992 and were covered by a company pension plan according to the reports of their employers. Using the employer's description of the worker's pension entitlement, Chan and Stevens could reliably calculate the value of a pension if the worker retired immediately and compare that to the pension value if the worker retired at a future age. The average worker underestimated the value of the pension by about 55% of the amount reported by employers. Moreover, many workers offered wildly inaccurate estimates of the improvement in their pension if they delayed retirement to a later age. Using information from follow-up HRS interviews, Chan and Stevens found that workers' retirement choices were based on their (possibly inaccurate) interpretation of pension rules. For people with accurate information, retirement choices were closely aligned with the financial incentives in their plan. If a worker's understanding of the plan rules was in error, the retirement decision was often based on serious misunderstanding.

Thus, the evidence on workers' pension knowledge casts doubt on the theory that the great majority of workers has gathered reliable information about pension incentives and devised a rational, farsighted plan about when to retire.

Saving for Retirement

The life-cycle model provides some clear predictions about how wealth is accumulated over a career and how workers should respond to unexpected events. The theory implies that workers should build up savings in anticipation of retirement and then draw down their wealth after they retire. It makes a clear distinction between (unanticipated) changes in flows of income that can be expected to last and changes that are only temporary. An unexpected income improvement that is permanent, such as an earnings gain that accompanies a promotion, will have a much bigger impact on a worker's consumption than an improvement that is only temporary, such as a one-time bonus for outstanding job performance. A fully anticipated drop in income, such as the one that accompanies a planned retirement, should have no effect on consumption.

Some evidence supports this theory (Lusardi & Browning, 1996). Most empirical research suggests that the life-cycle model is correct in emphasizing that households discount short-run fluctuations in their income when determining current consumption, and that retirement is one important motive for saving. There is competing evidence, however, that consumption is more volatile and closely related to current income changes than would be the case if there were complete smoothing of consumption over full lifetime resources. As the life-cycle theory predicts, we observe a tendency among many workers to steadily, but gradually, build up their wealth, increasing their rates of saving in peak earning years and as they approach retirement. The life-cycle theory's implication that consumers have a target wealth-income ratio that increases with age up to retirement also seems to be valid for many households.

Nonetheless, some economists are skeptical of the theory because simple versions of it are not very successful in accounting for important aspects of personal saving. For example, many workers enter retirement without any assets. A certain fraction of workers who do have assets continue to add to them after they retire. Neither fact is easy to reconcile with simple versions of the life-cycle model. Thaler (1994) offered a number of arguments against accepting the life-cycle model as a full explanation for retirement timing and lifetime saving. One of these is that solving the problem of optimizing both the retirement age and the path of lifetime consumption is hard. Workers do not get an opportunity to improve on their performance of this difficult task through constant repetition. Most workers will retire only once in their lives. The difficulty of the problem and the absence of opportunities to improve on previous performance mean that many people will fail to fully optimize. Thaler also pointed out that a good saving strategy involves self-control. Workers are required to postpone something that is pleasant—current consumption—to obtain a benefit that is far in the future. There is abundant psychological evidence that most people have serious problems exercising consistent self-control. In this case, a failure of self-control is likely to lead to undersaving.

Empirical research has focused on two questions about saving and retirement. Do workers typically accumulate enough savings so that they can live comfortably during retirement? Is there evidence to support the prediction that consumption changes little after retirement occurs?

Saving Before Retirement

The first question has remained unresolved because of disagreement over what constitutes adequate saving for retirement. One well-documented fact is that many Americans reach old age with little savings (Diamond & Hausman, 1984). This finding has been confirmed in many studies over the years. Lusardi (2001) tabulated the wealth holdings of HRS respondents who were not retired at the time of their first interview in 1992. Since these workers were between 50 and 61 years old, it is reasonable to assume that most of them were within a decade of retirement. Active workers in the bottom tenth of the HRS wealth distribution had no wealth at all except the promise of a Social Security pension. Even workers at the 25th percentile had essentially no financial market wealth. These workers' nonfinancial wealth holdings, including equity in a home or business, defined-contribution pension plans, and vehicles amounted to about $41,000 (in 2007 U.S. dollars). Lusardi calculated that if all of this wealth could be sold and converted into a lifetime annuity, it would provide workers with an income of less than $300 a month. One quarter of workers 50–61 years old in the HRS had even less wealth than this. One reason for low savings is that many workers have given little or no thought to retirement. Lusardi reported that the median wealth holdings of workers who have thought "hardly at all" about their retirement is less than one half the median wealth of workers who have thought "some" or "a lot" about retirement. In later analysis of the wealth holdings of a younger group of workers, Lusardi and Beeler (2007) confirmed the importance of planning in wealth accumulation. In 2004, nonplanners had accumulated substantially less wealth than workers who reported doing some planning. The wealth differences were large even when the researchers took account of the effects of many other determinants of workers' wealth, including income and demographic characteristics.

Although the fraction of older workers with little or no wealth may seem surprisingly high, is it high enough to cause us to reject the hypothesis that the great majority of workers save rationally for retirement? For some workers, the optimal rate of preretirement saving is zero or close to zero. Most workers who earn low or erratic wages throughout their careers will qualify for a Social Security pension or social assistance benefits. Their expected monthly benefits may equal or exceed the average net pay they received during their career. Since some of these workers are not eligible for social assistance unless their savings are low, it does not make sense to accumulate much wealth before retirement. The availability of Social Security, social assistance, and company-provided defined-benefit pensions means that the optimal amount of savings depends crucially on workers' expectations regarding retirement income aside from earnings on their own savings. Workers who expect pensions or assistance payments to replace a large percentage of their net earnings have much less need for savings than workers who do not anticipate such benefits.

Bernheim (1992, 1995) published two widely cited studies showing that many Americans nearing retirement, including high-wage workers, face large shortfalls in retirement saving. He calculated workers' optimal saving levels, taking into account the number of their current and anticipated dependents, earnings, expected Social Security and occupational pension benefits, and other factors. Other researchers have reached similar conclusions, often based on much better survey data. Moore and Mitchell (2000) examined the 1992 wealth holdings of HRS respondents and calculated the additional saving they would need to retire without any loss of consumption at retirement. This calculation took into account the Social Security and pension benefits that workers could obtain if they continued working. The calculations were repeated for two potential retirement ages, 62 and 65, the two ages that are most common. Moore and Mitchell showed that the median HRS household would have to increase its saving rate by 16% of earnings to maintain constant consumption after retirement at age 62. If retirement were delayed for three additional years to 65, the required extra savings for the median worker would represent 7% of earnings. When Moore and Mitchell compared required savings rates to actual saving rates among households approaching retirement, they found that actual saving rates typically fell far short of the required rate. Warshawsky and Ameriks (2001) reached a similar conclusion about the adequacy of household saving.

In an analysis of wealth adequacy, Munnell, Webb, and Delorme (2006) calculated the percentage of Americans who will have enough retirement income to substantially replace their preretirement income if they retire at age 65. As the authors noted, their assumption regarding the retirement age may be optimistic since about half of American workers retire before age 63. Using comprehensive pension and wealth data from the Survey of Consumer Finances and an optimistic forecast of future saving, the analysts projected that 35% of Americans born between 1946 and 1954 and 44% of those born in 1955–1964 will experience sizable declines in spendable income after retirement. Interestingly, the predicted percentage of workers facing a shortfall is considerably lower among workers enrolled in defined-benefit pension plans than it is among workers in defined-contribution plans. In a defined-benefit plan, employers are responsible for setting aside and investing retirement savings on behalf of their employees. In a defined-contribution plan, workers usually choose the total percentage of wages to set aside in a pension plan. Workers also determine the portfolio allocation of the investment funds. Those enrolled in defined-contribution plans often have the right to borrow against their fund balances while they are employed with the sponsoring employer and to liquidate their retirement savings (with a tax penalty) when they change employers. The finding that workers in defined-benefit plans face less risk of inadequate retirement incomes than workers in defined-contribution plans may imply that strong precommitment devices are needed to force workers to save for long-term goals like retirement. If workers apply time-inconsistent discount rates when dividing current income between immediate consumption and retirement saving, the constraints in a defined-benefit plan may be more effective than those in a defined-contribution plan in enforcing a disciplined saving strategy (Laibson, Repetto, & Tobacman, 1998).

Other analyses of wealth surveys have produced a more reassuring picture of wealth adequacy. A number show that comparatively few workers have clearly undersaved, and the typical amount of undersaving is small. One reason for the conclusion is that these studies explicitly took account of the income uncertainty workers face in their preretirement years and the life-span uncertainty they face after retirement. Earnings uncertainty is important for an obvious reason. If workers cannot borrow, they must save a large percentage of their earnings in high-income years to ensure that their families do not have to reduce their consumption in low-earning years. In the simplest version of the life-cycle model, economists assume that annual earnings will rise and fall over a worker's career in a completely predictable way (see Figure 5.1). In the real world, earnings are not predictable. Rational planners will save less than the full amount needed to completely smooth consumption under every contingency, and this will mean that large, unexpected income reductions will sometimes cause workers to use much of their planned savings before they retire. Workers and retirees also face uncertainty about when they will die. If workers die at an unexpectedly early age, their retirement savings will go unused and will not contribute much to their lifetime happiness. If they live to a very advanced age, they may deplete all their savings and face many years of low consumption. Rational workers will make saving choices that balance these risks, but for many farsighted workers, the combination of a rational choice and unexpected events will sometimes mean their wealth is lower than they hoped or expected.

Engen et al. (1999) considered whether the observed distribution of wealth holdings seems consistent with the distribution that would be observed if each household responded to unexpected earnings changes and life-span uncertainty in an optimal way. The researchers did not actually observe the past sequence of earnings for any member of their sample, but they used information from other sources to derive reasonable estimates of typical year-to-year variability in earnings. Combining this information with data about the worker's current earnings and survival probabilities in future years, they simulated the range of wealth holdings that would be observed if workers responded optimally to a simulated sequence of earnings fluctuations and the known probabilities of future death. Their simulations suggested that many prudent and rational savers will have little or no savings if they experienced a big, unpleasant earnings surprise. Engen et al. concluded that there is probably some systematic undersaving in a few population groups, but the shortfall in saving is modest compared with earlier estimates. This conclusion was corroborated in studies by Scholz et al. (2006) and Scholz and Seshadri (2008). These studies used HRS data to calculate optimal saving accumulations based on workers' actual lifetime earnings histories, derived from Social Security records. The optimal accumulations were then compared with wealth holdings reported by the same workers. Scholz et al. concluded that less than one fifth of HRS households have lower saving than their optimal targets, and the saving shortfall of those households is typically quite small. The results of Scholz and Seshadri, which covered a younger cohort of workers, are similar.

Postretirement Income and Consumption

These findings do not prove that the saving behavior of American workers is farsighted and rational. They demonstrate instead that it is difficult to rule out the hypothesis that saving choices are farsighted and rational for an overwhelming majority of workers. Many people would find this conclusion more credible if analysts could point to clear evidence that retirees enjoy adequate income or consumption in old age. A commonly used benchmark for income adequacy is the official poverty line. The Census Bureau has tracked poverty rates among the aged and nonaged since 1959. In that year, many aged households did not receive Social Security pensions; others collected very small pensions. Under the official poverty definition, 35.2% of America's population 65 and older was poor in 1959 compared with just 17.0% of adults between 18 and 64. As the Social Security system matured and public retirement benefits grew, the poverty rate of the aged population fell much faster than it did among the nonaged. Between 1993 and 2002, the old-age poverty rate was essentially indistinguishable from the poverty rate of those 18 to 64 years old. Since 2004, it has been more than one percentage point below the rate of nonelderly adults. (Historical statistics on U.S. poverty rates by age are reported on the U.S. Census Bureau Web site, http://www.census.gov/hhes/www/poverty/histpov/hstpov3.html.) The old-age poverty rate is even lower if we measure well-being using consumption rather than income (Meyer & Sullivan, 2007, Table 1). Under one interpretation, the long-term trend toward low poverty rates among America's elderly is reassuring. Recent generations of the aged have accumulated enough pensions and savings so that they are now no more likely to be poor than adults who are less than 65. Another view, however, is that the relative good fortune of the elderly is mainly due to generous (and compulsory) public pensions and social assistance. Without public pensions, a large percentage of the population over 65 would be judged poor (Smeeding & Williamson, 2001). Compulsory saving and government redistribution, not farsighted planning, might explain the low poverty rate of the elderly.

Does worker consumption decline after retirement? Most evidence suggests it does, at least for a sizable minority of retirees. The implications of this decline are disputed, however. Hausman and Paquette (1987) were among the first economists to find strong evidence of a drop in consumption following retirement. Looking solely at food consumption among families represented in the Longitudinal Retirement History Survey (LHRS), Hausman and Paquette found that retirement led to a decline in expenditures on food of about 14% of preretirement consumption. For the workers who were forced to leave their jobs because of a layoff or deterioration in health, the drop in consumption was even bigger—an additional 9% of preretirement food consumption. For workers who had accumulated below-average wealth, the drop in food expenditures was larger still. Using survey data on British household consumption, Banks, Blundell, and Tanner (1998) also found persuasive evidence for a fall in consumption in the period immediately after retirement.

An important question is whether the fall in consumption is anticipated by workers and is the result of a farsighted and rational consumption plan. Some decline in consumption might be explained by lower spending requirements for people who no longer need to work and who now have the time to produce at home what they once purchased in the market. Some of the drop in consumption after retirement is at least partly anticipated. Hurd and Rohwedder (2004) used interview responses in the HRS to compare respondents' preretirement expectations of consumption after retirement with the actual experiences of workers who had already retired. These researchers confirmed that consumption falls at retirement, with an average decline of about 15–20% of preretirement consumption. They also showed, however, that this fall in consumption is largely anticipated by workers. In fact, the reported decline in consumption among workers who had already retired is a bit smaller than the average decline predicted by workers who had not yet retired.

Direct Evidence on the Rationality of Saving Decisions

As we have seen, it is hard to rule out rationality and farsightedness based solely on observing workers' saving accumulation just before retirement and their income and consumption patterns before and after retirement. Many workers accumulate wealth that is low in relation to their earnings, and a large minority appears to experience a drop in consumption immediately after they retire. Nonetheless, the observed wealth distribution and pattern of consumption before and after retirement could be the result of an internally consistent, farsighted, and rational plan. The discussion so far shows that it is difficult using standard survey evidence to rule out rationality in saving behavior. Even the most anomalous combination of earnings, wealth, and consumption can usually be explained as the result of an internally consistent set of preferences and a worker's rational response to unanticipated past events, expected future events, and uncertainty about future earnings and life spans.

However, behavioral economists have developed evidence that sheds light on workers' reasoning at the time they make decisions about retirement saving. In some of these studies, economists have documented short-sightedness or irrationality in workers' saving behavior. Many case studies focused on workers' decisions to participate in a company retirement plan. In some defined-contribution pension plans, workers only receive an employer contribution to their accounts if they make a voluntary contribution to the plan from their own wages. For example, workers might be required to contribute at least 3% of their salaries before their employers will make a 3% contribution to their accounts. Workers who are liquidity constrained may refrain from contributing to the plan because the value of receiving income today outweighs the value of collecting a larger future pension. Although this choice may not seem sensible to people who place a premium on securing a good retirement income, it is nonetheless rational for workers who place a high value on current versus future consumption.

The decision to pass up an employer's contribution is *not* farsighted or rational, however, if the worker does not have to make any sacrifice in current consumption to obtain the contribution. Choi, Laibson, and Madrian (2005) collected information on workers who faced precisely this kind of choice. They analyzed 401(k) plans in which some workers were allowed to make immediate, penalty-free withdrawals from their pension accounts after employers made matching contributions to the accounts. In this case, workers could elect to make 3% salary contributions that were matched by 3% contributions from their employers, and workers were immediately allowed to withdraw their employers' contributions. Thus, workers could make voluntary contributions without sacrificing any immediate consumption. In spite of the obvious advantage of making voluntary contributions up to the employer's contribution limit, the researchers found that about half of eligible workers failed to do so. They calculated that undersaving workers sacrificed an average of 1.3% of their annual salaries by failing to take maximum advantage of the employer's contribution.

Employers' experiments with enrollment procedures in 401(k) plans also shed light on the rationality of workers' saving behavior. When 401(k) plans were first introduced in the 1980s, it was common for employers to require workers to make a positive election before they were enrolled in the plan. Enrollment rates were often low under this procedure. An alternative procedure is to automatically enroll new workers in the 401(k) plan unless they make a positive election to remain outside the plan. Madrian and Shea (2001) examined the effects of switching the enrollment process from "opt in" to "opt out." In principle, the default option should have little impact on either participation or workers' saving rates. In practice, the effect on enrollment was large. At one company, only 20% of new employees initially enrolled in the firm's 401(k) before the change in the enrollment procedure. When the default option was changed so that new employees were automatically enrolled, the initial enrollment rate jumped to 90%. Among employees who remained on company payrolls for 3 years, 401(k) enrollment under the new procedure was 98% versus only 65% under the old procedure. For a sizable minority of workers, a small change in the 401(k) enrollment procedure produced a big impact on participation rates and retirement saving. In follow-up research at other companies making the switch from opt in to opt out of a 401(k) plan, analysts found little evidence that workers were dissatisfied with their savings under the new enrollment process. Even though the new procedure resulted in a much higher 401(k) enrollment rate, the percentage of enrolled workers who later dropped out of the plan was approximately the same before and after the switch in procedures (Choi, Laibson, Madrian, & Metrick, 2006).

Other evidence of undersaving comes from workers' own assessments of their saving behavior. Laibson et al. (1998) cited polling evidence showing that 76% of U.S. respondents believe that they should be saving more for retirement. In another survey, sponsored by Merrill Lynch, a polling firm found self-reported shortfalls in retirement saving among workers between 29 and 47 years old. Compared with their target saving rate, more than three quarters of respondents reported saving too little of their income. The median reported gap between respondents' target saving rate and their actual saving amounted to 10% of household income (Laibson et al., 1998, p. 94). Unfortunately, workers' assessments of their retirement saving needs are not precise. Only about 4 in 10 U.S. workers have performed any calculation of the wealth accumulation needed to sustain their living standards after they retire (Helman, Copeland, & VanDerhei, 2006, p. 1).

Allocation of Retirement Saving

Workers who elect to set aside part of their wages in retirement savings accounts usually must decide how to invest their savings. How good a job do they do? To answer this question, analysts must first establish what a good retirement portfolio would look like. Many economists believe modern finance theory offers a simple solution to the worker's asset allocation problem. Canner, Mankiw, and Weil (1997) argued that the mutual fund separation theorem has a straightforward implication for savers: "More risk-averse investors should hold more of their portfolios in the riskless asset. The composition of risky assets, however, should be the same for all investors" (p. 181). According to the theorem, investors should hold a portfolio that consists of a riskless or safe short-term security (Treasury bills) and a mutual fund that holds all risky assets in proportion to their weight in the market. The investor's only important investment decision is the allocation of the overall portfolio between the safe asset and the composite risky asset. This allocation depends on the investor's risk aversion, but it does not depend on the investor's age or retirement status. As Canner and colleagues recognized, however, few professional investment advisors recommend a saving strategy based on this insight (see also Jagannathan & Kocherlakota, 1996; and Ameriks & Zeldes, 2004). Instead, almost all advisors suggest savers should invest more heavily in equities if they are less risk averse and young and gradually shift their asset allocation toward bonds if they are more risk averse or closer to retirement.

The disagreement between finance economists and professional investment advisors makes it impossible to assess workers' investment choices against ideal portfolios appropriate for savers at different ages. It is easier to evaluate some other aspects of their investment behavior. All analyses of investor behavior in employer-sponsored defined-contribution pension plans show that American workers trade little, almost certainly too little. Few 401(k) participants exchange one kind of asset for another, and it is uncommon for workers to reallocate their new contributions among the investment alternatives available to them (Agnew, Balduzzi, & Sundén, 2003; Ameriks & Zeldes, 2004). In a 10-year panel of observations in a large defined-contribution pension fund, Ameriks and Zeldes found that only 53% of workers made any change in their allocation of new contributions, and only 27% made a change to the allocation of assets already held in their accounts. This means that most workers' portfolio allocations change over time in response to realized returns on the different assets held in their portfolios. For example, workers who consistently allocate 50% of their new contributions to a diversified equity fund and 50% to a bond fund will see the stock-bond allocation of their portfolio vary widely over time if the relative returns on stocks and bonds differ. In the 1990s, stock returns were much higher than bond returns, so savers who failed to rebalance their portfolios ended the decade with a much higher proportion of their savings in stocks (the risky asset) and a much smaller proportion in bonds (the less-risky asset). Most investment advisors recommend that savers rebalance their portfolios about once a year to maintain the risk profile of their holdings, but few retirement savers follow this advice.

A serious problem, at least for a large minority of worker investors, is lack of financial knowledge. A 1995 survey of U.S. mutual fund purchasers found that more than one quarter were unaware that it is possible to lose money on investments in a bond mutual fund. Only a minority of investors reported knowing the cost of owning the mutual funds in their portfolio. An even smaller percentage realized that higher fund expenses were likely to reduce investors' net returns. About one investor in five thought higher fund expenses would actually boost net returns (Alexander, Jones, & Nigro, 1998). Economists have found considerable evidence that workers who are not financially literate are much less likely to invest in stocks (van Rooij, Lusardi, & Alessie, 2007). Unlike the well-informed and fully rational saver imagined by classical economists, many actual savers do not take the trouble to become informed about the pros and cons of different kinds of investments, although the payoff from doing so would be substantial. Poorly informed savers invest little or none of their retirement savings in equities and other risky assets, even though nearly all economists and financial planners think such investments should receive at least some weight in a sensible retirement portfolio.

Analysts have uncovered several aspects of worker investment behavior that raise questions about their capacity to align their portfolios with their long-term goals. Many workers allocate too much of their retirement savings to a single stock, and to a particularly risky one. An investment option open to many U.S. retirement savers is stock in the company where they work. According to Schlomo Benartzi (2001), about a quarter of American workers' discretionary retirement savings is invested in the stock of their employers. Many individual workers invest all or nearly all of their pension savings in their employer's stock. From the point of view of risk management, this is a dubious savings strategy. First, the risk of owning a single stock is much greater than that of holding a diversified portfolio, such as that offered by an equity mutual fund. Second, the future performance of an employer's stock and the worker's wage earnings are likely to be positively correlated. If a worker is laid off because his or her employer falls on hard times, the employer's share price will probably decline at the same time. It is hard to understand why financially savvy workers would want to compound the misfortune of job loss by losing most of their retirement savings at the same time.

Many workers show little evidence that they have carefully weighed their investment options or made a knowledgeable decision about their saving allocation. A sizable percentage of workers leave contributions in the default investment option under their employer retirement plan (Choi, Laibson, & Madrian, 2004). It is hard to believe the funds are left untouched because the default allocation corresponds to the worker's optimal choice. Workers remain in the default option investment plan, regardless of whether it is a low-risk money market fund or a moderate-risk stock-bond hybrid fund. The risk/expected return characteristics of the two investment options are different, so workers' persistence in remaining in the default option is explained by inertia or lack of knowledge rather than by the happy coincidence of worker preferences and the risk characteristics of the default option.

Finally, many investors are excessively swayed by the packaging of the investment choices offered to them. In principle, well-informed investors should select a portfolio of assets because its risk and expected return characteristics correspond closely to those they desire. In practice, some investors will prefer to invest in Option B if it is presented as an intermediate alternative between Options A and C but will instead choose Option C when it is presented as the intermediate alternative between Options B and D. If Options B and C are both available on different menus of investment alternatives, investors should always prefer B over C or C over B, regardless of the risk and return characteristics of the other investment options on the menu. Careful experiments by Benartzi and Thaler (2002) showed, however, that some workers' preferences are decisively affected by extreme and intermediate alternatives that are offered on the menu. Workers who know little about investment are apparently guided in their portfolio allocation by factors that should be irrelevant to their decision.

Implications for Policy

Many proposals to reform the U.S. retirement system rest on the theory that workers will make informed and sensible choices if offered complete freedom to choose their retirement age, saving rate, and investment strategy. Under this assumption, popular with professors of economics and finance, workers select their retirement age and lifetime saving plan based on farsighted evaluation of the potential risks and rewards of different retirement and saving options. This assumption is probably valid for some workers but is unlikely to be true for most of them. Many observers, including a few economists, are skeptical that workers think about retirement and savings in the farsighted and logical way just described. One reason that the government requires workers to participate in Social Security, that companies provide pensions, and that unions agitate for more generous pensions is lack of confidence that workers will make sensible provision for old age on their own. The basic rationale for employer and government pensions is that it is better to organize retirement saving collectively rather than to rely on the unaided efforts of individual workers.

A traditional defined-benefit pension helps solve three problems that most workers face as they prepare for retirement. First, the plan automatically sets aside a portion of current compensation as savings in a retirement account. Money in that account only becomes available when the worker is old or retired. Workers do not have to rely on their own judgment to select a retirement saving rate, and they do not have to rely on self-discipline to stick with the saving plan they adopt. Second, the money set aside in the retirement plan is managed by specialists who are knowledgeable about investing. Workers are not asked to rely on their own investment expertise, which may be limited. Third, when workers reach the end of their careers, their retirement nest eggs are converted into monthly annuity payments that last for the remainder of their lives. Workers do not need to worry about living too long or spending their nest egg so fast that they exhaust their retirement savings before they die.

A mandatory defined-contribution pension solves one the three problems just mentioned by requiring workers or employers to contribute a fraction of wages to a pension fund. It may not solve the other two problems. A voluntary defined-contribution pension, such as the ones offered in most 401(k) plans, may not solve any of the three problems. In most 401(k) plans, it is left to workers to decide how much if anything to contribute to the plan. Under voluntary plans, workers can and do elect to save too little. Workers are asked to decide for themselves how to invest their retirement savings, usually from a menu of investment options selected by their employer. Many workers are not competent to make investment decisions, and the poor performance of their investments reflects this fact. When workers' employment under a defined-contribution plan ends, they may not be offered the option to buy a life annuity. If their retirement nest egg is kept in an ordinary investment account rather than converted into an annuity, retirees face the risk that they may outlive their savings.

Societies that rely on workers to make their own decisions about retirement saving and investment have made a reasonable choice if workers make these decisions competently. The same choice looks riskier when a large fraction of workers bases saving and investment decisions on incomplete or incorrect information, short time horizons, and bad reasoning. Voluntary defined-contribution pensions require workers to assume more responsibility to save for retirement, to allocate their pension savings across different investment options, and to plan the timing of asset withdrawal during retirement. If we adopt a worker-directed defined-contribution plan, we should be confident that most workers will make prudent decisions. Serious planning errors, when the worker is employed or retired, can lead to serious hardship if the worker's error is a big one. By the time a retired worker discovers he or she has saved too little or has invested unwisely, the worker may have little opportunity to undo the mistake by increasing his or her saving rate or going back to work.

One reason most retired workers currently receive adequate incomes, regardless of their preretirement preparations, is the safety net provided by public assistance and Social Security. If this safety net is scaled back and the nation's employers continue to shift from old-fashioned defined-benefit plans into 401(k) defined-contribution plans, the nation should consider a new set of rules for these plans that reflect what we know about worker decision making. Many workers will accumulate more retirement savings when retirement contributions are automatically deducted from their wages. Workers' retirement savings will obtain better risk-adjusted returns when they are automatically invested in a prudent and diversified portfolio and when the portfolio is automatically rebalanced to ensure that its risk characteristics remain appropriate for retirement savers. Because many workers are myopic and invest little effort in learning about financial products or their long-term income needs, strong signals should be provided in the retirement plan to indicate a reasonable saving rate, a prudent investment allocation, a sensible age for claiming benefits, and a prudent rule for withdrawing funds after retirement.

Beshars, Choi, Laibson, and Madrian (2005) suggested that company pension plans should have sensible default rules, that is, rules that automatically determine outcomes unless overridden by a worker's instructions. If a prudent retirement saving plan requires a combined employee-employer contribution equal to 8% of wages, the default contribution rate in a plan should be 8%. Workers who wish to contribute more or less than 8% of their salaries should be required to submit instructions to override this default. Research shows that automatic enrollment in a voluntary pension plan can significantly increase participation rates, and high default contribution rates can significantly boost retirement saving. The same approach can be used to steer less-informed workers into appropriate investment portfolios and into annuities after they retire.

The recommendations of Beshars et al. (2005) are reasonable if defined-contribution pensions will supplement a basic Social Security pension that is large enough to remove full-career workers from poverty after they retire. If Social Security benefits are too low to achieve that goal, something stronger than good default rules will probably be needed.

Acknowledgments

The chapter is based on a presentation for "The Ageing Consumer Conference 2008: Perspectives from Psychology and Economics," Ross School of Business, University of Michigan, Ann Arbor, May 3–4, 2008. The views are the author's alone and do not reflect those of The Brookings Institution.

References

Abraham, K. G., & Hausman, S. N. (2004) *Work and Retirement Plans among Older Americans* (Pension Research Council Working Paper). Philadelphia: Pension Research Council, Wharton School.

Agnew, J., Balduzzi, P., & Sundén, A.E. (2003) Portfolio Choice, Trading, and Returns in a Large 401(k) Plan. *American Economic Review, 93*, 193–215.

Alexander, G. J., Jones, J. D., & Nigro, P. J. (1998) Mutual Fund Shareholders: Characteristics, Investor Knowledge, and Sources of Information. *Financial Services Review, 7*, 301–316.

Ameriks, J., & Zeldes, S. P. (2004) *How Do Household Portfolio Shares Vary with Age?* (Working paper). New York: Columbia University Graduate School of Business.

Axtell, R. L., & Epstein, J. M. (1999) Coordination in Transient Social Networks: An Agent-Based Computational Model of the Timing of Retirement. In H. J. Aaron (Ed.), *Behavioral Dimensions of Retirement Economics*. Washington, DC: Brookings Institution, 161–183.

Banks, J., Blundell, R., & Tanner, S. (1998) Is There a Retirement Savings Puzzle? *American Economic Review, 88,* 769–788.

Benartzi, S. (2001) Excessive Extrapolation and the Allocation of 401(k) Accounts to Company Stock. *Journal of Finance, 56,* 1747–1764.

Benartzi, S., & Thaler, R. H. (2002) How Much Is Investor Autonomy Worth? *Journal of Finance, 57,* 1593–1616.

Bernheim, B. D. (1992) *Is the Baby Boom Generation Preparing Adequately for Retirement?* New York: Merrill Lynch.

Bernheim, B. D. (1995) *The Merrill Lynch Baby Boom Retirement Index: Update '95, Technical Report.* New York: Merrill Lynch.

Beshars, J., Choi, J. J., Laibson, D., & Madrian, B. C. (2005) *The Importance of Default Options for Retirement Saving Outcomes: Evidence from the United States* (Working Paper 43/05). Moncalieri, Italy: Center for Research on Pensions and Welfare Policies.

Burtless, G. (2006) Social Norms, Rules of Thumb, and Retirement: Evidence for Rationality in Retirement Planning. In K. W. Schaie and L. L. Carstensen (Eds.), *Social Structures, Aging, and Self-Regulation in the Elderly* (pp. 123–160). New York: Springer.

Canner, N., Mankiw, N. G., & Weil, D. N. (1997) An Asset Allocation Puzzle. *The American Economic Review, 87,* 181–191.

Chan, S., & Stevens, A. H. (2003) *What You Don't Know Can't Help You: Pension Knowledge and Retirement Decision Making* (NBER Working Paper 10185). Cambridge, MA: National Bureau of Economic Research.

Choi, J. J., Laibson, D., & Madrian, B. C. (2004) Plan Design and 401(k) Savings Outcomes. *National Tax Journal, 57,* 275–298.

Choi, J. J., Laibson, D., & Madrian, B. C. (2005) *$100 Bills on the Sidewalk: Suboptimal Saving in 401(k) Plans* (NBER Working Paper No. 11554). Cambridge, MA: National Bureau of Economic Research.

Choi, J., Laibson, D., Madrian, B. C., & Metrick, A. (2006) Saving for Retirement on the Path of Least Resistance. In E. McCaffrey and J. Slemrod (Eds.), *Behavioral Public Finance: Toward a New Agenda* (pp. 304–352). New York: Russell Sage.

Diamond, P. A., & Hausman, J. A. (1984) Individual Retirement and Savings Behavior. *Journal of Public Economics, 23,* 81–114.

Engen, E. M., Gale, W. G., & Uccello, C. E. (1999) The Adequacy of Household Saving. *Brookings Papers on Economic Activity, 2,* 65–165.

Gustman, A. L., & Steinmeier, T. L. (2004) What People Don't Know About Their Pensions and Social Security: An Analysis Using Linked Data From the Health and Retirement Study. In W. G. Gale, J. B. Shoven, and M. J. Warshawsky (Eds.), *Private Pensions and Public Policies* (pp. 57–119). Washington, DC: Brookings Institution.

Hausman, J. A., & Paquette, L. (1987) Involuntary Early Retirement and Consumption. In G. Burtless (Ed.), *Work, Health and Income Among the Elderly* (pp. 151–175). Washington, DC: Brookings Institution.

Helman, R., Copeland, C., & VanDerhei, J. (2006) *Will More of Us Be Working Forever? The 2006 Retirement Confidence Survey* (EBRI Issue Brief No. 292). Washington, DC: Employee Benefit Research Institute.

Hurd, M. D. (1990) Research on the Elderly: Economic Status, Retirement, and Consumption and Saving. *Journal of Economic Literature, 28,* 565–637.

Hurd, M. D., & Rohwedder, S. (2004) *The Retirement-Consumption Puzzle: Anticipated and Actual Declines in Spending at Retirement* (Working Paper 2004-069). Ann Arbor: Michigan Retirement Research Center.

Jagannathan, R., & Kocherlakota, N. R. (1996) Why Should Older People Invest Less in Stocks Than Younger People? *Federal Reserve Bank of Minneapolis Quarterly Review, 20,* 11–23.

Krueger, A. B., & Meyer, B. D. (2002) Labor Supply Effects of Social Insurance. In A. J. Auerbach and M. Feldstein (Eds.), *Handbook of Public Economics* (Vol. 4, Chapter 33). Amsterdam: Elsevier.

Laibson, D. I., Repetto, A., & Tobacman, J. (1998) Self-Control and Saving for Retirement. *Brookings Papers on Economic Activity, 1,* 98–172.

Lumsdaine, R., & Mitchell, O. S. (1999) New Developments in the Economics of Retirement. In O. Ashenfelter and D. Card (Eds.), *Handbook of Labor Economics* (Vol. 3, Part 3, 3261–3307). Amsterdam: North Holland.

Lusardi, A. (2001) *Explaining Why So Many People Do Not Save* (Center for Retirement Research Working Paper 2001-05). Chestnut Hill, MA: Center for Retirement Research at Boston College.

Lusardi, A., & Beeler, J. (2007) Explaining Saving Behavior Between Cohorts: The Role of Planning. In B. Madrian, O. Mitchell, and B. Soldo (Eds.), *Redefining Retirement: How Will Boomers Fare?* (pp. 271–295). Oxford, UK: Oxford University Press.

Lusardi, A., & Browning, M. (1996) Household Saving: Micro Theories and Micro Facts. *Journal of Economic Literature, 34,* 1797–1855.

Madrian, B. C., & Shea, D. F. (2001) The Power of Suggestion: Inertia in 401(k) Participation and Savings Behavior. *Quarterly Journal of Economics, 116,* 1149–1525.

Meyer, B. D., & Sullivan, J. X. (2007) *Consumption and Income Poverty for Those 65 and Over* (Working Paper 07-21). Chicago: Harris School of Public Policy, University of Chicago.

Moore, J., & Mitchell, O. S. (2000) Projected Retirement Wealth and Saving Adequacy. In O. S. Mitchell, B. Hammond, and A. Rappaport (Eds.), *Forecasting Retirement Needs and Retirement Wealth* (pp. 68–94). Philadelphia: University of Pennsylvania Press.

Munnell, A. H., Webb, A., & Delorme, L. (2006) *A New National Retirement Risk Index.* Chestnut Hill, MA: Center for Retirement Research, Boston College.

Munnell, A. H., Webb, A., & Golub-Sass, F. (2007) *Is There Really a Retirement Savings Crisis? An NRRI Analysis.* Chestnut Hill, MA: Center for Retirement Research, Boston College.

Quinn, J. F., Burkhauser, R. V., & Myers, D. A. (1990) *Passing the Torch: The Influence of Economic Incentives on Work and Retirement*. Kalamazoo, MI: Upjohn Institute for Employment Research.

Rohwedder, S., & van Soest, A. (2006) *The Impact of Misperceptions About Social Security on Saving and Well-Being* (Research Paper No. WP 2006-118). Ann Arbor: Michigan Retirement Research Center.

Scholz, J. K., & Seshadri, A. (2008, August) *Are All Americans Saving "Optimally" for Retirement?* Paper presented at the 10th Conference of the Retirement Research Consortium, Washington, DC.

Scholz, J. K., Seshadri, A., & Khitatrakun, S. (2006) Are Americans Saving "Optimally" for Retirement? *Journal of Political Economy, 114*, 607–643.

Smeeding, T. M., & Williamson, J. (2001) *Income Maintenance in Old Age: What Can Be Learned From Cross-national Comparisons?* (**LIS** Working Paper No. 263). Luxembourg: Luxembourg Income Study.

Thaler, R. H. (1994) Psychology and Savings Policies. *The American Economic Review, 84*, 186–192.

van Rooij, M., Lusardi, A., & Alessie, R. (2007) *Financial Literacy and Stock Market Participation* (NBER Working Paper 13565). Cambridge, MA: National Bureau of Economic Research.

Warshawsky, M., & Ameriks, J. (2001, May–June) What Does Financial Planning Software Say About Americans' Preparedness for Retirement? *Journal of Retirement Planning*, 27–37.

6

New Choices, New Information: Do Choice Abundance and Information Complexity Hurt Aging Consumers' Medical Decision Making?

Stacy L. Wood
University of South Carolina

Judith A. Shinogle
University of Maryland, Baltimore County

and

Melayne M. McInnes
University of South Carolina

Introduction

In recent years, researchers, public policy makers, and consumers alike have been captivated by the paradox of "too much choice." This paradox argues that, while choice is typically good, an overabundance of choice can be surprisingly bad, overwhelming us with an informational overload (Huffman & Kahn 1998; Scammon 1977), making us anxious about our decisions (Garbarino & Edell 1997), slow (or unable) to decide (Dhar 1997; Greenleaf & Lehmann 1995; Iyengar & Lepper 2000), and dissatisfied with our outcomes (Botti & McGill 2006; Schwartz 2004). In one choice paradox study, researchers examined consumers buying jam in a grocery store. Iyengar and Lepper (2000) demonstrated that consumers were attracted to larger (24 jams) versus smaller (6 jams) displays but were less likely to choose from the larger set of jams. The "paradox" in the choice paradox emerges because the downside of having many options runs counter to economic axioms that more choice is always better than less. Economic theory argues that, with more choice, individuals should be more likely to find options that suit heterogeneous preferences and confer greater utility (Lancaster 1990).

However, with increasing demonstrations of the "more-is-less" phenomenon (e.g., Iyengar, Huberman, & Jiang 2004; Iyengar & Lepper 2004; List 2002, 2003, 2004; Peters Dieckmann, Dixon, Hibbard, & Mertz 2007), public policy makers and consumers have taken note. For policy makers, employee participation in firm 401K savings plans provide a compelling example. Concern over low savings rates in 401K plans have prompted policy makers and firms (which cannot offer this tax-deferred savings option unless a fixed percentage of their employees voluntarily enroll) to look for ways to increase employee participation. The intuitive impulse, and one in keeping with economic tenets, is to expand the choices available to workers in hopes that additional choices would attract greater interest and enrollment. Given the paradox of too much choice, this would be exactly the wrong policy—firms should instead decrease the number of investment options. Iyengar, Huberman, and Jiang (2004) tested this counterintuitive premise using data on 401K participation from a nationwide financial firm and found that the number of choices offered was negatively correlated with the likelihood of participation. Similarly, participation rates in 401K plans increased 10 to 20 percentage points when workers were offered a collapsed set consisting of the status quo versus one choice with a preselected asset allocation and savings rate (Beshears et al. 2006).

How are aging consumers impacted by the paradox of too much choice? Are the elderly especially susceptible to the negative outcomes that arise from cognitive overload or decisional inertia when choices and their attendant information are overwhelming? One area in which this question is especially pertinent is medical decision making. How aging consumers make decisions about health care options is consequential both for them and for society. And, medical decisions often involve complex and abundant choice information. In this domain, we examine the weaknesses and (more importantly) the strengths of seniors in information-rich health care decisions.

Aging Consumers' Response to Complexity and Abundance in Health Care Decisions

Consumers, especially older adults, often find themselves facing complex and consequential health decisions. These decisions range from choice of insurance coverage to healthy lifestyle choices to decisions about treatment options for specific conditions. The importance of such decisions is reflected in the number of different academic areas in which they are investigated; these include medicine, pharmacy, economics, exercise science, consumer behavior, and social psychology. For example, research on shared decision making (SDM) explores medical treatment decision making as an interaction between physician and patient and is a broad field of inquiry with a variety of perspectives (Moumjid 2007) that is growing into its own research and financing area as a potential means for controlling health care cost growth (Wennberg, O'Connor, Collins, & Weinstein 2007). This diversity of intradisciplinary research provides for a rich body of work, but one downside is that generalizable findings about health decisions can be difficult to integrate and compare.

In general, health decisions are characterized by five key elements: (a) multiple choices, (b) abundant choice information, (c) information and options that change over time, (d) uncertainty, and (e) important consequences. For example, a consumer deciding what to do after a diagnosis of gastroesophageal reflux disorder (GERD) may consider lifestyle (diet and exercise) changes, over-the-counter (OTC) antacids, several prescription drug treatments (including proton pump inhibitors, alginic acid, H_2 receptor blockers, prokinetics, and sucralfate), endoscopic devices, or surgery as treatment options that differ in cost of time and money, expected efficacy, and potential side effects.

When we look broadly at research about how the elderly in particular make health-related decisions, two somewhat divergent pictures emerge. First, and more commonly, research identifies many ways in which the elderly are vulnerable consumers and decision makers. A large literature exists on how to determine minimal thresholds of decisional capacity in the aged as such assessments have both legal and ethical implications when older individuals make critical health and financial decisions (Moye & Marson 2007). Aging consumers can be hampered in decision making by diminishing cognitive capacity (Yoon 1997). Diminution of working memory capacity (Light 1991; Salthouse 1991) may be especially problematic when decision makers compare alternatives (Cole & Houston 1987; Roedder John & Cole 1986). Cole and Balasubramanian (1993) found that elderly consumers did not search nutritional information as intensively as younger consumers when shopping for cereal in a grocery store setting and subsequently chose less-appropriate cereals. However, when the same choice task was given in a laboratory setting where participants could write down information acquired during the search process, age-related differences disappeared. In some choice environments, lack of detailed information processing may be due to older consumers' greater reliance on schematic processing (Yoon 1997). This is important in health care contexts as ability to process detailed numerical information is a key predictor of comprehension of health plan choices (Hibbard, Peters, Dixon, & Tusler 2007).

Aging individuals often show worse memory for the context in which information is conveyed (e.g., the physical setting, emotional context, or speaker; McIntyre & Craik 1987) and have difficulty in locating relevant information in information-rich contexts (Cole & Gaeth 1990). Source errors can be dangerous; Skurnik, Yoon, Park, and Schwarz (2005) found that older consumers were especially prone to recalling repeated false claims as true. Older adults also focused more on emotionally meaningful information and goals (Fung & Carstensen 2003) and subsequently responded more positively to affective advertising appeals than younger cohorts (Drolet, Williams, & Lau-Gesk 2007; Williams & Drolet 2005), and emotional intensity may explain deviations from optimal choice behavior (Araña, León, & Hanemann 2008). This may make them more vulnerable to "predatory" persuasion environments characterized by strong social pressure (Hill & Kozup 2007) and may have important ramifications for seniors' financial decisions. Older consumers are found to pay higher interest rates for borrowing and more fees compared to their middle-aged counterparts in a broad array of financial markets (Agarwal, Driscoll, Gabaix, & Laibson 2007). In light of aging consumers' perceived vulnerability, health care practitioners are cognizant of and proactive in attempts to remedy older individuals' diminished physical (e.g., visual and auditory) and cognitive capacities when communicating important health information and decision inputs (Spotts & Schewe 1989).

In addition to ability-based health decision impediments, aging consumers are often viewed as a vulnerable constituency because of financial concerns. A small number of patients account for the lion's share of medical spending in the United States; the top 10% of spenders tended to be elderly and female. Of the U.S population, 5% account for nearly 50% of health care expenditures, with many seniors having persistent high costs. And, while the elderly only account for 13% of the U.S. population, they account for 36% of all health care expenditures (Agency for Healthcare Research and Quality 2006). Elderly patients have a higher probability of increasing health problems and fewer future opportunities for generating income to pay for medical care (White-Means 1989). Not surprisingly, research has shown that older health care consumers are more willing than younger consumers to trade off health care quality for lower prices (Jackson & Jensen 1984). Elder self-neglect is a relatively small, but disturbing, phenomenon that may have financial influences (Gruman, Stern, & Caro 1997). Financial limitations and other individual characteristics (such as technological literacy) may also limit seniors' easy access to online information resources.

However, extant research on health and medical decision making also identifies a more proactive and agentic view of aging consumers. Aging patients report wanting to be active participants in medical decision making and desire more information in making those decisions (Chang, Lee, Kim, & Lee 2008). Medicare-eligible consumers actively compared alternatives for their physician services, and their level of "doctor shopping" is independent of income (White-Means 1989). The increased need for information in such situations should be reflected in increased information search. While seniors appear to search less diligently for choice information in some contexts (Cole & Balasubramanian 1993; Yoon 1997), they have also been observed to engage in higher levels of information search. Lumpkin and Festervand (1988) found that elderly consumers use more independent and marketer-supplied information than nonelderly consumers, and Boscarino and Stelber (1982) observed that elderly decision makers rely more on informal information sources than did the nonelderly.

Greater information search and desire for decision agency may reflect elderly patients' greater preference for control in medical contexts than younger patients (Tangsrud & Smith 2000). Age-related differences in desired control may be a function of decision-making processes. Health decisions often create conflict through the necessity of making emotional trade-offs (Luce 1998). Shared medical decision making can serve to reduce felt decisional conflict by patients (Kremer 2007); if aging patients are more impacted by emotional decision inputs (Williams & Drolet 2005), the reduction of felt conflict may be especially important to them and drive increased decision engagement.

How can we reconcile these two views of the aging health care consumer? Some research illustrates seniors' vulnerability in medical domains in which cognitive, social, and financial concerns inhibit decision makers' ability to navigate complex choices and abundant information. Other research painted a picture of an active and engaged decision maker who confidently tackles information-rich and emotionally charged decisions. We suggest here that seniors demonstrate both strengths and weaknesses in medical decision making that are a function of individual and environmental characteristics. In the next section, we outline these characteristics to provide an expanded perspective on aging health care consumers.

Good Strengths, Bad Weaknesses, and Ugly Decisions

As noted, many health-related decision contexts are downright "ugly" in their multitudinous, uncertain, emotionally charged, and information-laden options. All consumers face a challenging task in such an environment. However, also as noted, many are concerned about aging consumers' special vulnerability in such situations.

TABLE 6.1

Characteristics of Older Consumers That Facilitate or Inhibit Decision Making in Health-Related Choices

Strengths	Weaknesses

• Expertise effects
  Confidence and self-efficacy
  Increased information search and elaboration
  Impression management
  High intrinsic and situational involvement
• Positive search ratio (benefits to costs)
	• Potential for reduced cognitive capacity
	• Potential for reduced visual/auditory capacity
	• Use of entrenched heuristics and schemas
	• Limited use of technology
	• Potential for apathy or self-neglect

In Table 6.1, we outline the "bad" (weaknesses) and the "good" (strengths) of older health care consumers. The weaknesses have been described and are the pervading view of aging decision makers across several literatures. However, we propose an expanded view of the senior decision maker by positing several (perhaps overlooked) strengths that may facilitate seniors' decision making in information-rich environments. Many of these strengths reflect insights from the expertise literature (Alba & Hutchinson 1987, 2000). Expertise is a function of both familiarity (number of experiences) and objective knowledge or skill (Alba & Hutchinson 1987). After a long life's experience (and subsequently increasing knowledge) of health care, aging consumers may reasonably be viewed as "expert patients." More than younger consumers, they may be more likely to have greater real and perceived expertise in health care domains.

In environments that have the potential for the effects of too much choice, the critical factor for good decision making is the ability and motivation to process large information loads for a number of choices. If we view aging health care consumers as expert patients, this conceptualization creates a framework in which the strengths and weaknesses of expert information search and subsequent decision making may be used to predict times when aging consumers demonstrate better and worse choices. The expertise literature chronicles both the benefits of expertise for decision making (Alba & Hutchinson 1987; Brucks 1985) and, conversely, "curses of expertise" (Camerer & Johnson 1991; Shanteau 1992; Wood & Lynch 2002). As we argue, aging consumers' proactive desire for shared decision making may be a result of increased benefits and decreased costs of search.

Repeated experience with a decision domain and increasing knowledge of the product options and vocabulary lead to increased consumer expertise (Alba & Hutchinson 1987). This expertise may be "real," such as when it leads to improved knowledge, choices, or skills (Wood & Lynch 2002), or may be "perceived," such as when individuals self-report strong levels of subjective knowledge (Moreau, Lehmann, & Markman 2001).

Expertise has many benefits for decision making. First, experts are often confident about their ability to make choices and find information. An individuals' confidence increases with mere exposure to information (Oskamp 1965) and with increased familiarity with domain-specific concepts (e.g., "feeling-of-knowing" phenomenon; Reder & Ritter 1992). This confidence may facilitate individuals' feelings of self-efficacy and prompt actions or decisions (Bandura 1977).

Increased expertise also facilitates decision making as it makes consumers more efficient in information search and learning (Brucks 1985; Johnson & Russo 1984); for example, to gather new information effectively, an individual must "know what they don't know" (Miyake & Norman 1979). Knowledge of the vocabulary of a consumption domain (e.g., knowing what a "trans fat" or a "co-pay" is) helps consumers better understand their own preferences (West, Brown, & Hoch 1996). In this way, older patients may feel more confident in asking questions in health information forums in which one must ask questions of knowledgeable others. Experts should also be able to elaborate more from the information that they find (Alba & Hutchinson 1987). Because of existing knowledge structures, experts can better draw inferences about the underlying association between two presented facts (Haviland & Clark 1974), and this accurate inference making should enrich the value of gathered choice information (Broniarczyk & Alba 1994).

If older consumers perceive themselves as expert patients with a wealth of experience and knowledge, this perceived identity may motivate them to engage in behaviors that present this self-image to others (Jones & Pittman 1982). *Impression management* refers to a general motivation to manage one's interactions with others to best communicate a desired identity (Schlenker & Weigold 1990). Expertise forms one potential basis of identity (Schlenker & Weigold 1992). For example, a wine enthusiast may be motivated to use vintner terminology, buy expensive boutique wines, and learn about new vineyards and regions to present and maintain a cohesive image of him- or herself as a wine expert. Individuals who enjoy expertise in a particular domain as part of their identity are often referred to as *market mavens* and actively participate in word-of-mouth communication and information sharing (Feick & Price 1987). Some older patients may see themselves as experts in certain conditions, such as diabetes or rheumatoid arthritis, or may perceive a more broad expertise in "knowing doctors" or "knowing how the system works" akin to a specialized type of marketplace metacognition (Wright 2002). In such cases, impression management motivations may encourage older consumers to seek out health information, especially regarding new products or programs (such as Medicare Part D), since they will enjoy their status as experts and sharing this knowledge with others.

For experts to learn the information that they find and generate, they must expend effort (Wood & Lynch 2002), and one factor that motivates this effort is involvement in the product category (Alba & Hutchinson 1987). *Product involvement* is defined as the personal relevance or importance of the product class to the consumer (Beatty & Smith 1987). With high involvement, consumers rely on more analytical information processing in making choices, and with low involvement, consumers are persuaded more by quick heuristics and catchy slogans (Petty & Cacioppo 1986). Involvement can be either intrinsic (e.g., interest in cars may be due to a long-standing hobby) or situational (e.g., interest in cars may be due to the need to buy a new car; Celsi & Olson 1988). Increased situational and intrinsic involvement in health and health care is an almost axiomatic consequence of old age. With greater involvement, we should observe that aging consumers are more motivated than their younger counterparts to learn about health-related choices.

Several of the described benefits that accrue to experts in a choice context are driven by information search behaviors. These phenomena are consonant with the economic model of consumer search behavior (Moorthy, Ratchford, & Talukdar 1997; Ratchford 1982). In this model, consumers search for choice information as long as the costs of search do not exceed the perceived benefits of new information. Here, expertise again plays a role. Experts often have lower search costs (search is easier or more efficient) and more potential benefit from information because they can make better use of it (Moorthy et al. 1997). For seniors, lower search costs may arise both from their expertise and from other situational characteristics, such as lower cost of time (especially for those who are retired) and more frequent and longer access to health care professionals. Similarly, for seniors, the benefits of information search may arise not only from "expert enrichment" such as better consumption vocabularies, more elaboration, and more involvement but also from increased price sensitivity and other factors that make health decisions more consequential for older consumers. In this way, aging consumers may search for more information because of a positive benefit-to-cost ratio of search compared to younger consumers.

An Application to the Medicare Prescription Drug Plan

The introduction of the Medicare Prescription Drug Discount Card Program is a compelling example of a new health care decision faced by aging consumers that is characterized by an abundance of complex choice information. This program, the precursor drug benefit for Medicare Part D, began in June 2004 and offers seniors the chance to purchase prescription drugs at discounted prices. Policy makers were pleased by the enthusiastic response from providers—over 70 different discount card programs were available when the program was launched. Unfortunately, response from consumers did not match the enthusiasm of providers. While 3.9 million enrollments were reported initially, nearly 75% of these were automatic enrollments for seniors who had managed care plans or state pharmacy assistance programs (CMS, *Medicare News*, July 30, 2004).

The Medicare Prescription Drug Program (Part D) was introduced in 2006. An AP-Ipsos poll suggested that many seniors found the new program confusing—as one illustration of this, the government increased the number of workers at their help line from 150 to 4,000 soon after enrollment began (Lester 2006). In this program, seniors in traditional Medicare (nonmanaged care) can choose a private drug insurance plan, and with many providers on board, the program provides consumers with a variety of choices while facilitating competition among providers. Indeed, in both programs, introducing choice and competition is the hallmark of the policy reform. A wide array of choices should better meet the needs of beneficiaries with heterogeneous preferences and promote competition among providers to find innovative ways to reduce cost. A finding that more choices undermine participation would be a serious challenge to the design of these programs. It is not surprising, then, that choice demotivation effects were specifically cited as one reason for low initial enrollment rates in the prescription drug program. In a 2005 *New York Times* editorial, Barry Schwartz wrote that the low enrollment rates in the prescription drug program should serve as a cautionary tale for other government programs that promoted individual choice:

> There is now accumulating evidence that choice isn't always good. Whether people are choosing jam in a grocery store, essay topics in a college class, or even potential partners in an evening of "speed dating," the more options they have, the less likely they are to make a choice. In other words, increasing options induces people to opt out of choosing altogether, and this comes into play when people decide how to invest their money for retirement. … The appropriately abysmal early public response to the administration's Medicare prescription drug choice plan provides ample reason to suspect that many people will not regard being able to choose their Social Security investment instruments as a blessing.

Was the paradox of too much choice at the heart of the lackluster response to the Medicare Prescription Drug program? Were aging consumers befuddled and frozen in the face of multiple information-rich choices? The strengths and weaknesses described suggest that many factors may have influenced seniors' decision making in this context. Individual diminution in cognitive abilities or ability to access necessary information may have made the complex decision impossible for some seniors. However, many of the strengths of senior decision making—focusing primarily on the motivation and ability to engage in information search—should be observed in this particular choice context.

Some survey data were supportive. In a survey of seniors, of those who said they did not plan to sign up for cards, only 14% cited as a reason that it was too difficult to choose among the variety of the cards offered (Kaiser Family Foundation/Harvard School of Public Health 2004). Most seniors reported being able to find answers to their questions and liked having alternative insurers to choose among despite facing too many alternatives (Heiss, McFadden, & Winter 2006). Heiss, McFadden, and Winter (2006) found that, while there was some evidence that seniors relied too heavily on short-term costs, seniors were "surprisingly" well calibrated in terms of enrollment and the amount they were willing to pay.

In an experimental economic study, we also found results suggesting that choice (and choice information) abundance was not to blame for poor enrollment in the Medicare Prescription Drug Discount Card Program, and that senior decision makers may be better able to make complex decisions than they are often given credit (McInnes, Shinogle, & Wood 2008). Specifically, our study was designed to test whether reducing the number of choices offered in the Medicare Prescription Discount Card Program would result in increased participation. We conducted our test in a laboratory environment that allowed for the control of potential confounds (such as the endogeneity at issue in past 401K studies) in which participants (average age 76) were asked to make a hypothetical choice framed in the rich contextual narrative of the discount card purchase choice. While drug purchases in the study were hypothetical, any savings generated through the purchase of the discount card were paid to participants in cash at the end of the study; these amounts were commensurate with real savings (~$45 for the optimal choice) and thus nontrivial. The relevant choice information given to participants (e.g., discount card choices, drug prices, and pharmacy availability) was based on actual information obtained from the Medicare Web site for four common drugs purchased by seniors. Congruent with past research protocols used to study this effect, participants were given a choice of either 6 discount card options or 24 discount card options.

Our study (McInnes et al. 2008) found no evidence that restricting the number of choices would improve participation in Medicare discount card programs. Participation rates did not differ between small and large card choice set conditions. This suggests that simply reducing the number of card options available in this Medicare program may not increase participation among seniors. Further, and importantly, our results lend caution to applying findings on choice demotivation found in a context in which consequences are small to those in which choices are consequential.

Importantly, we also found a surprising effect of choice set size on choice confidence and satisfaction (McInnes et al. 2008). First, consumers who chose in a small set (6 cards) were no more likely to feel satisfied or confident in their choices than those who chose among a greater set of options (24 cards). The paradigm of too much choice would suggest that consumers with more choice would report greater uncertainty and expended effort and potentially less satisfaction. However, participants reported a high degree of confidence with no difference by treatment. Participants reported that they did not find the choice extremely confusing or "hard" and tended to disagree with the statement that "there was too much information." These findings are congruent with the proposition in this chapter of expertise-based confidence in senior decision makers.

At the end of the protocol, our participants were asked about whether they would consider switching plans as new cards became available (McInnes et al. 2008). Surprisingly, we found that the participants who had more choices in the first round were more likely to seek new information and were more likely to consider switching. While this finding runs counter to the notion of too much choice, it is consistent with the previously described economic view of experts' information search. While the large set (24 cards) was accompanied by a very large amount of information, this information may have been desired by decision makers with much to gain from processing it and relatively low costs of processing. Having benefited from the process once, those in the large set condition may have felt more interested in looking into future options. From a policy-making perspective, this result suggests that when consumers expend a larger amount of decision-making effort in making an initial choice, this does not necessarily mean that those consumers are going to be the most "loyal" to or entrenched in the decision. Rather than an overwhelmed "never again!" attitude, consumers who faced the large 24-card choice set seemed to feel more confident about their future ability or interest in making a taxing consumer decision.

This willingness-to-switch result speaks to the important issue of status quo bias in health plan choice. The price effects on demand of health insurance plans tends to be lower for incumbent employees compared to new hires in examining health plan choice (Strombom, Buchmueller, & Feldstein 2002), and there is evidence of lower health plan switching for people with longer attachments to health plans than those new to market (Frank & Lamiraud 2008). The willingness to consider new options has significant economic consequences. Frank and Lamiraud (2008) found that those who switched health plans paid on average 15% to 16% less in health insurance premiums.

Conclusion

There are many challenges that face the aging decision maker, especially in the realm of health care and medical decision making. In medical domains, factors that promote consumers to search for health care options and information benefit all consumers by increasing competition and reducing prices (Pauley & Satterthwaite 1981). However, contrary to many perspectives that frame the aging as vulnerable consumers, seniors may have many decision-making strengths that are unique to the health domain. Because of their potential to be expert patients, seniors may be more confident, involved, and able to benefit from heavy-duty information search in complex choice environments and may also have greater reason to search because of more consequential financial outcomes and lower cost of time. The introduction of Medicare programs for prescription drugs provided a compelling case in which to examine these issues. While the choice paradox explanation may dominate in the public press, results from surveys and our laboratory study suggested that choice overload was not the primary reason for seniors' lackluster response to these programs. As such, our results would caution any policy interventions that reduced the number of choices as a way to encourage increased enrollment (McInnes et al. 2008).

We offer an expanded view of the aging health care consumer; while previously studied weaknesses and vulnerability do exist, we suggest that several strengths do as well. Many of these strengths are based on seniors' long experience and subsequent expertise in health decisions. However, while this focus on expertise illustrates several reasons for seniors to thrive in medical decision making compared to younger consumers, expertise has its dark side as well. In the judgment and decision-making literature, several "curses of expertise" have been identified in which experts demonstrated poor learning (Bettman & Park 1980; Wood & Lynch 2002), poor performance (Camerer & Johnson 1991), and poor prediction (Shanteau 1992). However, many of these demonstrations were task specific (e.g., Johnson & Russo 1984; Shanteau 1992) and occurred when experts relied too heavily on old theories or schemas (Shanteau 1992; Wood & Lynch 2002). Not surprisingly, aging consumers use schemas more extensively (Yoon 1997), and in some cases, this may be a function of their expertise. Interestingly, another effect noted may be influenced by expertise. As noted, aging individuals often make source errors about the context in which information was conveyed (e.g., the physical setting, emotional context, or speaker; McIntyre & Craik 1987). Yet, Alba and Hutchinson (1987) stated that experts may often make source errors because increased elaboration can lead to inferential assumptions about multiple pieces of information, while memory for specific sources fades. These issues suggest that more research is needed to fully understand unique expertise effects in seniors' medical decision making. Future research that explores expertise effects in aging consumers' decision making may highlight new points of vulnerability that come, ironically, from consumers' superior knowledge.

Acknowledgments

We thank Aimee Drolet, Carolyn Yoon, Norbert Schwarz, and participants of the 2008 Perspectives on Consumer Aging conference for valuable comments and insights. Our research that is cited in this chapter was partially funded through National Science Foundation grant SES-0214290, the PhRMA Foundation Research Starter Grant, and the Moore School of Business, University of South Carolina. Since this writing, the first author accepted an endowed chair at the College of Management, North Carolina State University.

References

Agency for Healthcare Research and Quality (2006, June), High Concentration of U.S. Health Care Expenditures, *Research in Action*, 19.

Agrawal, Sumit, John C. Driscoll, Xavier Gabaix, & David Laibson (2007), *The Age of Reason: Financial Decisions Over the Lifecycle* (NBER Working Paper No. 13191). Cambridge, MA: National Bureau of Economic Research.

Alba, Joseph W., & J. Wesley Hutchinson (1987), Dimensions of Consumer Expertise, *Journal of Consumer Research, 13*, 411–454.

Alba, Joseph W., & J. Wesley Hutchinson (2000), Knowledge Calibration: What Consumers Know and What They Think They Know, *Journal of Consumer Research, 27*, 123–156.

Araña, Jorge E., Carmelo J. León, & Michael W. Hanemann (2008), Emotions and Decision Rules in Discrete Choice Experiments for Valuing Health Care Programmes for the Elderly, *Journal of Health Economics, 27*, 753–769.

Bandura, Albert (1977), Self-efficacy: Toward a Unifying Theory of Behavioral Change, *Psychological Review, 84*, 191–215.

Beatty, Sharon, E., & Scott M. Smith (1987), External Search Effort: An Investigation Across Several Product Categories, *Journal of Consumer Research, 14*, 83–95.

Beshears, John, James J. Choi, David Laibson, & Brigitte C. Madrian (2006), *Simplification and Saving* (NBER Working Paper No. 12659). Cambridge, MA: National Bureau of Economic Research.

Bettman, James R., & C. Whan Park (1980), Effects of Prior Knowledge and Experience and Phase of the Choice Process on Consumer Decision Processes: A Protocol Analysis, *Journal of Consumer Research, 7*, 234–248.

Boscarino, Joseph, & Steven R. Stelber (1982), Hospital Shopping and Consumer Choice, *Journal of Health Care Marketing, 2,* 15–23.

Botti, Simona, & Ann L. McGill (2006), When Choosing Is Not Deciding: The Effect of Perceived Responsibility on Satisfaction, *Journal of Consumer Research, 33,* 211–219.

Broniarczyk, Susan M., & Joseph W. Alba (1994), The Role of Consumers' Intuitions in Inference Making, *Journal of Consumer Research, 21,* 393–407.

Brucks, Merrie (1985), The Effects of Product Class Knowledge on Information Search Behavior, *Journal of Consumer Research, 12,* 1–16.

Camerer, Colin F., & Eric J. Johnson (1991), The Process-Performance Paradox in Expert Judgment: How Can Experts Know So Much and Predict So Badly? In *Toward a General Theory of Expertise: Prospects and Limits,* ed. Karl A. Ericsson, New York: Cambridge University Press, 195–217.

Celsi, Richard L., & Jerry C. Olson (1988), The Role of Involvement in Attention and Comprehension Processes, *Journal of Consumer Research, 15,* 210–224.

Centers for Medicare and Medicaid Services (2004), Medicare Prescription Drug Card Enrollment Surpasses 4 Million Mark, *Medicare News,* July 30 press release.

Chang, Soo Jung, Kyung Ja Lee, In Sook Kim, & Won Hee Lee (2008), Older Korean People's Desire to Participate in Health Care Decision Making, *Nursing Ethics, 15,* 73–86.

Cole, Catherine A., & Siva K. Balasubramanian (1993), Age Differences in Consumers' Search for Information: Public Policy Implications, *Journal of Consumer Research, 20,* 157–169.

Cole, Catherine A., & Gary J. Gaeth (1990), Cognitive and Age Related Differences in the Ability to Use Nutritional Information in a Complex Environment, *Journal of Marketing Research, 27,* 175–184.

Cole, Catherine A., & Michael J. Houston (1987), Encoding and Media Effects on Consumer Learning Deficiencies in the Elderly, *Journal of Marketing Research, 24,* 55–63.

Dhar, Ravi (1997), Consumer Preference for a No-Choice Option, *Journal of Consumer Research, 24,* 215–231.

Drolet, Aimee, Patti Williams, & Loraine Lau-Gesk (2007), Age-Related Differences in Responses to Affective Versus Rational Ads for Hedonic Versus Utilitarian Products, *Marketing Letters, 18,* 211–221.

Feick, Lawrence F., & Linda L. Price (1987), The Market Maven: A Diffuser of Marketplace Information, *Journal of Marketing, 51,* 83–97.

Frank, Richard G., & Karine Lamiraud (2008), *Choice, Price Competition and Complexity in Markets for Health Insurance* (NBER Working Paper No. 13817). Cambridge, MA: National Bureau of Economic Research.

Fung, Helene H., & Laura L. Carstensen (2003), Sending Memorable Messages to the Old: Age Differences in Preferences and Memory for Advertisements, *Journal of Personality and Social Psychology, 85,* 163–178.

Garbarino, Ellen C., & Julie A. Edell (1997), Cognitive Effort, Affect, and Choice, *Journal of Consumer Research, 24,* 147–158.

Greenleaf, Eric A., & Donald R. Lehmann (1995), Reasons for Substantial Delay in Consumer Decision Making, *Journal of Consumer Research, 22,* 186–199.

Gruman, Cynthia, Alan Stern, & Francis G. Caro (1997), Self-Neglect Among the Elderly: A Distinct Phenomenon, *Journal of Mental Health and Aging*, 3, 309–322.

Haviland, Susan E., & Herbert H. Clark, (1974), What's New? Acquiring New Information as a Process of Comprehension, *Journal of Verbal Learning and Verbal Behavior*, 13, 512–521.

Heiss, Florian, Daniel McFadden, & Joachim Winter (2006), Who Failed to Enroll in Medicare Part D, and Why? Early Results, *Health Affairs*, 25, 344–354.

Hibbard, J., E. Peters, A. Dixon, & M. Tusler (2007), Consumer Competencies and the Use of Comparative Quality Information: It Isn't Just About Literacy, *Medical Care Research and Review*, 64, 379–394.

Hill, Ronald Paul, & John C. Kozup (2007), Consumer Experiences With Predatory Lending Practices, *Journal of Consumer Affairs*, 41, 29–46.

Huffman, Cynthia, & Barbara E. Kahn (1998), Variety for Sale: Mass Customization or Mass Confusion? *Journal of Retailing*, 74, 491–513.

Iyengar, Sheena S., & Mark R. Lepper (2000), When Choice Is Demotivating: Can One Desire Too Much of a Good Thing? *Journal of Personality and Social Psychology*, 79, 995–1006.

Iyengar, Sheena, S., Gur Huberman, & Wei Jiang (2004), How Much Choice Is Too Much: Determinants of Individual Contributions in 401K Retirement Plans, In *Pension Design and Struction: New Lessons from Behavioral Finance*, ed. Olivia S. Mitchell & Stephen Utkus, Oxford: Oxford University Press, 83–95.

Jackson, Bill, & Joyce Jensen (1984), Majority of Consumers Support Advertising of Hospital Services, *Modern Healthcare*, 14, 93–97.

Johnson, Eric J., & J. Edward Russo (1984), Product Familiarity and Learning New Information, *Journal of Consumer Research*, 11, 542–550.

Jones, Edward E., & Thane S. Pittman (1982), Toward a General Theory of Strategic Self-Presentation, in *Psychological Perspectives on the Self*, ed. Jerry Suls, Hillsdale, NJ: Erlbaum, 231–262.

Kaiser Family Foundation/Harvard School of Public Health (2004), Views of New Medicare Drug Law: A Survey of People on Medicare, http://www.kff.org/medicare/upload/Views-of-the-New-Medicare-Drug-Law-Toplines.pdf

Kremer, Heidemarie (2007), It's My Body: Does Patient Involvement in Decision Making Reduce Decisional Conflict? *Medical Decision Making*, 27, 522–532.

Lancaster, Kelvin (1990), The Economics of Product Variety: A Survey, *Marketing Science*, 9, 189.

Lester, Will (2006), Poll: Medicare drug program difficult to understand, Associated Press, accessed at: http://www2.ljworld.com/news/2006/jan/23/poll_medicare_drug_program_difficult_understand/, January 23, 2006.

Light, Leah L. (1991), Memory and Aging: Four Hypotheses in Search of Data, *Annual Review of Psychology*, 42, 333.

List, John A. (2002), Preference Reversals of a Different Kind: The More Is Less Phenomenon, *American Economic Review*, 92, 1636–1643.

List, John A. (2003), Does Market Experience Eliminate Market Anomalies? *Quarterly Journal of Economics*, 118, 41–71.

List, John A. (2004), Neoclassical Theory versus Prospect Theory: Evidence from the Marketplace, *Econometrica*, 72, 615–625.

Luce, Mary Frances (1998), Choosing to Avoid: Coping With Negatively Emotion-Laden Consumer Decisions, *Journal of Consumer Research*, 24, 409–433.

Lumpkin, James R., & Troy A. Festervand (1988), Purchase Information Sources of the Elderly, *Journal of Advertising Research, 27*, 31–44.

McInnes, Melayne M., Judith A. Shinogle, & Stacy L. Wood (2008), *Too Much Choice: Does It Explain Low Participation Rates in the Medicare Prescription Drug Discount Program?* (Working Paper, University of South Carolina, Columbia, SC).

McIntyre, John S., & Fergus I. Craik (1987), Age Differences in Memory for Item and Source Information, *Canadian Journal of Psychology/Revue Canadienne de Psychologie*, Special Issue: Aging and Cognition, *41*, 175–192.

Miyake, Naomi, & Donald Norman (1979), To Ask a Question, One Must Know Enough to Know What Is Not Known, *Journal of Verbal Learning and Verbal Behavior, 18*, 357–364.

Moorthy, Sridhar, Brian T. Ratchford, & Debabrata Talukdar (1997), Consumer Information Search Revisited: Theory and Empirical Analysis, *Journal of Consumer Research, 23*, 263–277.

Moreau, C. Page, Donald R. Lehmann, & Arthur B. Markman (2001), Entrenched Knowledge Structures and Consumer Response to New Products, *Journal of Marketing Research, 38*, 14–29.

Moumjid, Nora (2007), Shared Decision Making in the Medical Encounter: Are We All Talking About the Same Thing? *Medical Decision Making, 27*, 539–546.

Moye, Jennifer, & Daniel C. Marson (2007), Assessment of Decision-Making Capacity in Older Adults: An Emerging Area of Practice and Research, *Journals of Gerontology Series B: Psychological Sciences & Social Sciences, 62B*, 3–11.

Oskamp, Stuart (1965), Overconfidence in Case-Study Judgments, *Journal of Consulting Psychology, 29*, 261–265.

Pauly, Mark V., & Mark A. Satterthwaite (1981), The Pricing of Primary Care Physicians' Services: A Test of the Role of Consumer Information, *Bell Journal of Economics, 12*, 488–506.

Peters, Ellen, Nathan Dieckmann, Anna Dixon, Judith H. Hibbard, & C. K. Mertz (2007), Less Is More in Presenting Quality Information to Consumers, *Medical Care Research & Review, 64*, 169–190.

Petty, Richard E., & John T. Cacioppo (1986), The Elaboration Likelihood Model of Persuasion, *Advances in Experimental Social Psychology, 19*, 123–205.

Rahhal, Tamara A., Cynthia P. May, & Lynn Hasher (2002), Truth and Character: Sources That Older Adults Can Remember, *Psychological Science, 13*, 101.

Ratchford, Brian T. (1982), Cost-Benefit Models for Explaining Consumer Choice and Information Seeking Behavior, *Management Science, 28*, 197–212.

Reder, Lynne M., & Frank E. Ritter (1992), What Determines Initial Feelings of Knowing? Familiarity With Question Terms, Not With the Answer, *Journal of Experimental Psychology: Learning, Memory, and Cognition, 18*, 435–451.

Roedder John, Deborah, & Catherine A. Cole (1986), Age Differences in Information Processing: Understanding Deficits in Young and Elderly Consumers, *Journal of Consumer Research, 13*, 297–315.

Salthouse, Timothy A. (1991), Mediation of Adult Age Differences in Cognition by Reductions in Working Memory and Speed of Processing, *Psychological Science, 2*, 179–183.

Scammon, Debra L. (1977), Information Load and Consumers, *Journal of Consumer Research, 4*, 148–155.

Schlenker, Barry R., & Michael F. Weigold (1990), Self-Consciousness and Self-Presentation: Being Autonomous Versus Appearing Autonomous, *Journal of Personality and Social Psychology, 59*, 820–828.

Schlenker, Barry R., & Michael F. Weigold (1992), Interpersonal Processes Involving Impression Regulation and Management, *Annual Review of Psychology, 43*, 133.

Schwartz, Barry (2004), *The Paradox of Choice*. NY: Harper Collins Publishers, Inc.

Schwartz, Barry (2005), Choose and Lose, *New York Times*, January 5.

Shanteau, James (1992), Competence in Experts: The Role of Task Characteristics, *Organizational Behavior & Human Decision Processes, 53*, 252–266.

Skurnik, Ian, Carolyn Yoon, Denise C. Park, & Nobert Schwarz (2005), How Warnings About False Claims Become Recommendations, *Journal of Consumer Research, 31*, 713–724.

Small Number of Patients Account for Most Healthcare Spending (2006), *Healthcare Strategic Management, 24*, 7.

Spotts, Harlan E., Jr., & Charles D. Schewe (1989), Communicating With the Elderly Consumer: The Growing Health Care Challenge, *Journal of Health Care Marketing, 9*, 36–44.

Strombom, B. A., T. C. Buchmueller, & P. J. Feldstein (2002), Switching Costs, Price Sensitivity and Health Plan Choice, *Journal of Health Economics, 21*, 89–116.

Tangsrud, Robert, Jr., & Malcolm C. Smith (2000), Control-Related Motivations, Capabilities, and Preferences Among Patients, *Journal of Business Research, 48*, 259–266.

Wennberg, J. E., A. M. O'Connor, E. D. Collins, & J. N. Weinstein (2007), Extending the P4P Agenda, Part 1: How Medicare Can Improve Patient Decision Making and Reduce Unnecessary Care, *Health Affairs. 26*, 1564–1574.

West, Patricia M., Christina L. Brown, & Stephen J. Hoch (1996), Consumption Vocabulary and Preference Formation, *Journal of Consumer Research, 23*, 120–135.

White-Means, Shelley I. (1989), Consumer Information, Insurance, and Doctor Shopping: The Elderly Consumer's Perspective, *Journal of Consumer Affairs, 23*, 45–64.

Williams, Patti, & Aimee Drolet (2005), Age-Related Differences in Responses to Emotional Advertisements, *Journal of Consumer Research, 32*, 343–354.

Wood, Stacy L. & John G. Lynch Jr. (2002), Prior Knowledge and Complacency in New Product Learning, *Journal of Consumer Research, 29*, 416–426.

Wright, Peter (2002), Marketplace Metacognition and Social Intelligence, *Journal of Consumer Research, 28*, 677–682.

Yoon, Carolyn (1997), Age Differences in Consumers' Processing Strategies: An Investigation of Moderating Influences, *Journal of Consumer Research, 24*, 329–342.

7

The Aging Consumer and Intergenerational Transmission of Cherished Possessions

Carolyn Folkman Curasi
Georgia State University

Linda L. Price
University of Arizona

and

Eric J. Arnould
University of Wyoming

Introduction

As the population of developed countries ages, we witness some processes and phenomena that shed new light on the aging consumer, consumer identity work, and intergenerational transmission of cherished possessions. During the last half of the 20th century, individuals in more developed countries, in historical terms, enjoyed unprecedented wealth. With new-found affluence, the inevitable question of what to do with all of these possessions when one reaches life's twilight becomes newly prominent.

We stumbled on the ubiquity of the disposition dilemma among older populations when informants spontaneously raised the issue of their struggle with deciding what to do with their cherished possessions. Since the publication of our earlier research (Curasi, Price, & Arnould 2004; Price, Arnould, & Curasi 2000), interest in this phenomenon in the popular press as well as in academic venues has grown. In this chapter, we explore the precipitating life events, emotions, and strategies associated with older consumers' transmission of their special possessions. Our research helps distinguish possessions singled out by consumers as being "cherished" or "priceless." Perhaps more than other possessions, it is the meanings for family identity (Epp & Price 2008) that these items hold that have made them special to their caretakers and not their potential exchange value. Thus, our interpretation focuses on the meanings of these special possessions. Earlier literature examined involuntary disposition of cherished possessions, precipitated by passively experienced events, such as a debilitating illness or a move to a nursing home, but little consumer research has tapped the theoretical insights to be gained from a focus on the voluntary disposition of cherished possessions.

Intergenerational Transmission in Families

The meanings of family and kinship in late modern consumer culture are dynamic, fashioned, and refashioned to suit changing circumstances (Löfgren 1984; Smart & Neale 1999; Stacey 1990; Yanagisako 1984). An accelerated tendency for people to construct their families out of diverse households and sets of relationships developing at different times and in disparate contexts is shown by the sharp rise in the number of blended family households in the United States (Bumpass, Raley, & Sweet 1995; Morgan 1996; Smart & Neale 1999).

Kin relationships remain important, negotiated between members over time and changing circumstances and embedded in the personal biographies of the people concerned (Finch & Mason 1993, 2000). Contemporary consumers still express adherence to a familial kin group and want to feel that they contribute actively to it (Gutierrez, Price, & Arnould 2008; Miller 1998; Smart & Neale 1999). In consumer societies in which individuals construct their lives without many fixed points, close relationships remain central to identity and well-being (Arnould & Price 2000; Finch & Mason 2000; Gergen 2000). Relational family practices—rites of passage, reunions, dinners, family dramas, and calendrical rituals for instance—are enduring, affectively charged sources of self-identity recorded in our newspapers and expressed in personal narrative (Cheal 1988; Epp & Price 2008; McGlone, Park, & Smith 1998; Morgan 1996; Neville 1984; Otnes, Lowrey, & Shrum 1997; Wallendorf & Arnould 1991; Yu, Burns, & Veeck 2006).

The elective quality of identity and family and the continuing importance of family practices lead us to speculate about links between family practices and inherited possessions. Family has long been recognized as crucial to the reproduction of social systems. Transmission of domestic property in particular expresses and symbolizes the boundaries of kinship groups and power within those boundaries (Douglass 1984; Finch & Mason 2000; Goody 1976; Judge & Hrdy 1992; Laslett & Wall 1972; Marcus & Hall 1992; Rosenfeld 1979).

Finch and Mason's (2000, p. 161) interviewees seemed more engaged emotionally with inherited individual keepsakes (often objects of no value) than with material assets. Individuals in families they studied displayed a clear stake in the symbolic significance of these items. And, British and American inheritors of cherished possessions and heirlooms claimed they are charged with qualities of previous owners (see also Grayson & Shulman 2000; McCracken 1988; Sussman, Cates, & Smith 1970; Tobin 1996; Unruh 1983). Such objects also symbolize descendants' relationships with their deceased kinsfolk. Finally, research indicates inherited objects provide vehicles for animating memories—creating, shaping, and sustaining them (Finch & Mason 2000; Grafton-Small 1993; Katriel & Farrell 1991).

In sum, research on cherished possessions and heirlooms in late modern families raises the following research questions: Positive contamination of the object through prolonged contact with a respected elder kinsperson helps preserve cherished objects for one generation, but what of subsequent generations? Are inherited emblems of family relationships an important source of family identity, difference, and distinction? Do middle-class Americans seek to collect and pass forward their ancestors' history and achievements? Do individuals act as guardians of special objects for future generations? Do guardians use inherited objects to convey values and meanings of significance to their kin, and if so, how? Do consumers use heirloom objects as signs of imagined values? May heirloom objects become inalienable (Godelier 1999; Weiner 1992)?

Research Activity

Kinship and social class provided the sampling frame boundaries for this investigation. Kinship is the predominant pattern of wealth transference in the United States (Judge & Hrdy 1992; Schneider 1980; Sussman et al. 1970), and the middle class comprises the largest economic segment of consumers in North America (Kacapyr 1996). Interviews with multiple generations examined whether and how cherished possessions are kept within families across different generations.

In composite, and consistent with the idea that contemporary families have an elective quality, our informant families exhibited numerous divorces, remarriages, deaths, and elements of discord. More than half our informants talked about at least one divorce. Some families lived in close geographic proximity, but others lived far apart, and most had moved one or more times. Although the majority of our informants resided in the southeastern United States at the time of the interviews, informants living in Ohio, Illinois, New York, and California were also interviewed. Most of our informants lived in urban areas, but a small number lived in smaller rural communities. We represented a wide spectrum of white ethnic backgrounds and included families that had lived in the United States for several generations and families that immigrated within the preceding two generations. A few of our informants were middle-class African American, and a few had Spanish as a first language. We did not explicitly investigate changing prosperity of families across generations, but overall our informant families had experienced upward or stable economic circumstances. That is, to our knowledge we did not interview informants whose families were worse off than a generation ago.

Research reported here is based on multiple data sets. It began with semistructured interviews with 80 older consumers, focusing on their cherished possessions and inherited objects. Depth interviews with 38 informants within 15 family groups, representing 26 intergenerational dyads, comprise a second data set. A third set of 70 semistructured interviews representing 35 intergenerational dyads spread between males and females of three generations supplemented our primary interviews.

Analysis focused on understanding common and contrasting structures in the informants' emic representations of practices and meanings associated with cherished possessions and of strategies used to keep objects within the family (Wallendorf & Arnould 1991). Three types of analyses were employed: analyses focused on an informant, between informants within a family, and between informants across our sample of middle-class North Americans (Thompson 1997). Details of data collection, analysis, and discussions of procedures to guarantee credibility and trustworthiness are available (Curasi et al. 2004; Price et al. 2000).

Findings

Disposition of Special Possessions

Figure 7.1 provides a framework of the disposition process organized around five fundamental areas that became pivotal in the disposition process as we examined our data. We wanted to understand (a) the events or informant characteristics that triggered the disposition of cherished possessions; (b) the emotions associated with disposition and the relationship of those emotions to disposition decisions; (c) the meanings associated

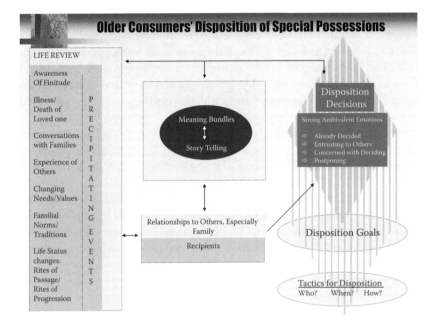

FIGURE 7.1
The heuristics that guide the decisions of who, when, and how to transfer cherished possessions.

with the special possessions that older consumers decided to transfer; (e) the disposition goals of these informants; and (f) the tactics consumers employed to accomplish their goals. That is, we were interested in understanding the heuristics that guide the decisions of who, when, and how to transfer cherished possessions.

Events or Informant Characteristics That Trigger Disposition

We found that the question of whether older consumers considered what to do with their cherished possessions rests on a complex, idiosyncratic interplay of informants' sense of their own mortality, of the meanings they associated with their cherished possessions, and of their relationship to others, especially family members. Only a handful of our informants claimed not to have given much thought to transferring some of their cherished possessions to a loved one. But, even these individuals, after prompting, revealed that they had, in fact, given some thought to the future of their possessions, but that they were not yet ready to part with them. The vast majority of our informants, however, displayed active, agentic thinking about disposition closely linked to creative acts of reminiscence and what gerontologists refer to as "life review" (Butler 1963, 1974).

In late adulthood, life review, including reminiscence, often becomes frequent. It is during this life review process that people construct life narratives to help them to answer questions related to the meaning of their life and to assist them in constructing an enduring legacy. Mnemonically rich special possessions are often pivotal in this narrative process focused on explaining the meaning of one's life and on the possibility of crafting a legacy.

Our informants typically described a confluence of circumstances that collectively precipitated their feelings of the inevitability of their own mortality, motivating them to make these disposition decisions. Mary, who was 77 years old, married, and in good health, is illustrative. Her concern was prompted by her husband's quadruple heart bypass surgery, her mother's death, the death of friends, and reading the obituaries. Regardless of their own age or health status, informants repeatedly discussed a spouse's illness or death as a crucial precipitating event leading to thoughts about the disposition of their cherished possessions.

Life status changes can also be a precipitating event, leaving older consumers with things they no longer need or use. Especially if these items are meaningful, consumers' first recourse is to try to give these things to their children. As this woman explained:

> I keep telling my children, "If you want something, take it." They say, "Hold it." I say, "No." We are reaching a point that we don't need all this that we have. We need to get rid of it. And we are. Slowly. ... And this one son that lives here in Jacksonville Beach didn't have dishes, and I told him, I think he ought to take those. And they are very nice. It's more of a complete set than the ones we have here. ... It serves 12 people. And I think to myself, I'd rather have less. We do not entertain that much anymore. So, I am doing that. Every time the children want something or say they like something. (Iris, married, 78)

In other cases, special events such as rites of passage and progressions (marriage, graduation, and 21st birthdays) can stimulate gift giving via transferring a cherished possession. Transferring objects during a life status change can weave the new caretakers' life story into the meaning and story of a cherished possession, and in this way the meaning of the object may become implicated in multiple identity narratives (Epp & Price 2008).

In sum, we found that there are a number of precipitating events that seem to help initiate or trigger thoughts of disposition of cherished possessions. Prominent in our data were precipitating events that helped initiate an awareness of finitude, or a sense of one's own mortality, coupled with the life review process, which both play a key role in prompting disposition decisions.

Meanings

Informants' discussions of their cherished possessions illustrated the link also between cherished possessions and meaningful elements of life stories. Consider Julie, for example. She was 76 years old and had been widowed for about a decade. In addition to the loss of her husband, she had lost several other family members as well. Nevertheless, she was extremely active and not preparing to die anytime soon. When asked if she had thought about disposing of her special possessions, she replied:

> The jewelry was bought in Japan when my husband was in the Air Force. He was stationed there for a couple of years in the 1950s. ... The jewelry has the strongest feelings for me because my husband is not with me anymore. ... The jewelry that I gave to my granddaughter was something that my husband had given to me before he died. It was very close to me, but I really wanted my granddaughter to have it. ... Of course, it will be sad since I know it will not be done until I am close to death. I want the people who are going to receive them to enjoy them but not really at my expense. I will just leave them to my kids in my will, or they will just know to have them. I think they already know.

The vast majority of our informants discussed at least one possession that served as a narrative mnemonic life token, a totem of identity, or an emblem of kinship structure and family continuity (see Grandpa Louie's tale in this chapter). Among the many meanings of special possessions, the theme comprising narrative mnemonic life tokens was the most salient for our informants. Life stories provide special possessions with meaning, and special possessions revitalize older consumers' life stories. Understanding older consumers' disposition decisions requires an understanding of these stories (Katriel & Farrell 1991; Korosec-Serfaty 1984). Our informants spontaneously linked cherished possessions with life review and used them as a narrative scaffolding to create a personal and resilient sense of identity. With these stories, older consumers answered the questions of the meaning of their life and explained their personal legacy. In so doing, they also often crafted a type of symbolic immortality for themselves, weaving stories of themselves to their cherished possessions. In turn, they hoped that their loved ones would remember their stories and retell them long into the future.

Sheila was forthright in expressing her desire for symbolic immortality and in her hope to accomplish it through objects that substituted for her (Godelier 1999; Tobin 1996; Unruh 1983). Although her son was not yet married, Sheila had thought about things he should give his future wife and had thought about his children:

And I want your children and wife to remember me, and their children, etc. I want to be part of their lives. Someday someone would say, this bracelet came from my Great, Great, Great, Grandmother Sheila [laughing]. I guess I'm silly, but I am sentimental. I wish I had things from my grandparents, particularly things I could wear like jewelry pieces or rings. That would mean a lot to me.

Cherished possessions of older consumers often mark indexicality (Grayson & Shulman 2000), an indelible contextual association with a specific time, place, and people as with Julie's Japan-bought jewelry. Janice, widowed and age 78, also illustrated object indexicality. When asked what possessions she valued most, she replied:

My jewelry. All of it was given to me from my deceased husband, Richard. I love all of them, but I'm particularly fond of three pieces: the small silver cross, the silver ring, and the Escara bracelet. Each one of them were given to me from Richard throughout the years. I wear the silver cross around my neck, and I got that at age 18 when we were still dating. The silver ring with a small white diamond I received on our engagement at age 20, and that I still wear. The same year that Richard died, he gave me the Escara golden bracelet on no particular occasion. I was 66 at the time. These items are strictly of sentimental value.

As Janice demonstrated, many of our informants discussed their cherished possessions as a record of their life history and indicated indexical value with the term *sentimental*, as distinct from monetary or exchange value. For many informants, mnemonic and narrative qualities of cherished possessions extended their individual and collective sense of self and of the lineage forward through time.

Goals

With a long story accompanying its meaning, Virginia, who was in her 80s, talked about disposing of an urn. She voiced her hopes that "sentimental" meanings will preserve it and frustration that all the urn's meanings cannot be transferred to her daughter, but the overall goal was transfer of an object bundled with meanings particular to the family:

It's because of the family feelings. I have a white urn with pastel flowers on it. I remember it because I went with my grandmother to her friend's house. She would take care of her house when she was gone. Mrs. Norman. She gave it to my grandmother for looking after her house. I remember the walk to the house with my grandmother. She loved flowers and pretty things. She had beautiful things in her house.

> I remember the walk home with the urn and my grandmother. ... I can picture it in my grandmother's house and then in my mother's house, and now it sits in my house. I hope someday it will be in my daughter's house. It is sad that she did not know my grandmother, though. She barely knew my mother. I had children when I was older, and we didn't live close to my family anymore. I hope she has sentimental attachment to some of these family things. ... I hope my kids will feel as strongly about my possessions as I have, but I don't think that is possible since they haven't lived my life. (Virginia, divorced, 84)

Many of our informants hoped that these cherished items would stay within their family lines for perpetuity.

Tactics

Kinship distance, gender, closeness, appreciation of mnemonic associations, valuing of the use value of objects, and control (see Maddie's quote below) are all tactical considerations in intergenerational transmission expressed by our informants.

Maddie wanted to transfer the object not only to a particular gender but also to someone with whom she was close. She considered kinship distance in her deliberations. Implied here is the idea that a close relationship also entails a history of conveying feelings and experiences, including previous communications about the cherished item. However, aesthetic appreciation and mnemonic associations also figured into her calculations about the individual to whom she should transfer the pin.

> I have thought about it. I have two boys though. I guess if one of their wives wanted it I could give it to them. I am just not too close to them. Maybe I could give it to my granddaughter. She lives so far away. Next time I see her maybe I'll bring it up and see what she thinks. It is beautiful and maybe she would appreciate it. I wonder if she will think it is too old fashioned and out of date. I just love it! ... She will not have the memories I do when she looks at it. (Maddie, married, 60s)

Often, disposition decisions are made during the older consumer's lifetime so that the original owner can live to see the new owner enjoy their cherished possessions as Diane, age 70, and later Iris, age 78, both explained:

> I love to give things to my children, if they like something. My Mother-in-law used to be that way toward me. If I went into her home and admired something, she'd want to give it to me. And I found myself doing the same thing. I think to see someone enjoy something that you've enjoyed would be nice, rather than waiting until you're dead to pass them out. (Diane, widowed, 70)

> It is, if they like something, you know, I would rather they take it
> now. You know how it happens, when you are dying, everyone comes
> in. There is always a fight involved. I don't care what, there's always a
> fight over it. We would rather they get it before and enjoy it while we
> are still around. And not fuss about it later. (Iris, married, 78)

Many informants, in fact, such as Charlie, viewed themselves as caretakers for cherished family possessions. Charles was 67 years old and
living in his own home. To ensure that a cherished possession would be
transferred forward through the family lineage, Charlie repeated a transfer ritual. He used a family tradition to pass forward to his son a favorite
set of golf clubs that his father had given to him. Charles talked about
missing them, but remarked, "I knew this was what my father did for me,
so I did it for my son."

Emotions

Our informants illustrated ambivalent and complex emotions when talking about disposition of their cherished possessions, with both strong
positive and strong negative feelings characterized.

Iris explanation vividly illustrates emotional triggers:

> Tell you what, I go to estate sales all the time. And when I go, every
> time I go I realize that I have to do something. I must get rid of what
> I have. It is so *sad* [her emphasis], and there are these beautiful items
> that are being sold. They are practically giving them away. And people
> look at them, and these are people that cherished things, like we did
> in the past. And then you look, and think, look what is happening to
> them. Obviously, their children didn't want them. And people think
> nothing of it, and they try to bring the price down. And I think of
> these people, and of how they must have felt. They had all of this, and
> it meant so much to them. So, every time I go, I think: That's not going
> to happen to me. (Iris, married, 78)

Associated with these emotions is the older consumer's desire to exert
some control over the future life of the cherished objects. By deciding to
whom a cherished possession will be given, older consumers can help to
ensure the future they desire for their cherished possessions long after
they are gone.

Grandpa Louie broke down after describing some of his cherished
possessions, tools that had belonged to his father and a coin collection.
Alluding to the personal competencies symbolically represented in these
objects, he said, "[I'm] happy in one sense and sad in another. I am happy
that someone is going to get the coins and treasure them, and I am even
okay that no one would want my old junky tools, but I am sad because

I am old." Thinking about the objects evidently saddened some informants by evoking thoughts of past times and selves, works (collections), and departed loved ones (Belk 1991a, 1991b; Grayson & Shulman 2000; Richins 1994).

Our informants often faced disposition with some dread. Their fear was linked to mingled concerns about loss of self-identity, erasure of family traditions, absence of receptive recipients, or changes in family structure that threatened the worth of the objects as they are transferred from one complexly storied life to another. Ambivalence was also linked to anxieties about the future, as if the real value of cherished possessions lies in their ability to extend the past into the future. Such strong feelings help us account for the complexity of the tactics referred to here and represented in Figure 7.1.

Preserving Family Heirlooms

What becomes of cherished objects passed on to succeeding generations? First, if not already a legacy of a previous generation, is a change in the state of the cherished object. Progressing from one generation to the next makes a cherished object into an heirloom. Next, if previous caretakers' tactics have been successful, new caretakers seem to engage in curatorial consumption (McCracken 1988), designed to preserve family heirlooms. Our informants often discussed a single object that they described as a family heirloom. They felt that these rare family items should be preserved; it was their claim to an ancestral past and family accomplishments (Weiss 1997). This desire for tokens of family continuity was widespread in our data, as was the competition that ensued to be the caretaker of the family heirloom and to pass it forward to future generations. How do they do this?

Sacred objects like heirlooms encompass both a visible, material component and immaterial elements (stories of origin, secret chants, spells, and names; Godelier 1999; Weiner 1992). Informants who strategized to create heirlooms from their cherished objects thus recognized the crucial role of storytelling in transferring heirlooms successfully. An excellent illustration surrounded a ring that Teresa, age 72, wanted to become inalienable. The ring was a gift from Teresa's late husband, Jeff, and she told a detailed, emotional, and romantic story of how she came to have the ring. She planned to pass this to her only daughter, Patricia, age 45, with whom she had a close affective relationship, noting, "She has always seen it on me. The ring will always remind her of me after I am gone. To me that is important." Here, she recognized the legitimating potential of her own contamination of the ring and the amalgamated stories and meanings that her daughter Patty will bundle with the ring. Telling the story of the object helped Teresa relive an important moment in her own history that coincided with a historical moment in time (the end of World War II) and brought into the present a departed loved one (Price et al. 2000). Moreover, she told the story for tactical reasons as well.

Consider also Robert, a caretaker of a ring that had been in his family for generations. He told us about the ring:

> I have a solid gold ring, which I inherited from my father, which was his grandfather's ring that he brought back from California during the California Gold Rush. The ring weighs approximately 2 ounces, is solid gold, and very, very, soft. ... The ring simply means a link to the past. My father's grandfather walked to California from Indiana behind an ox team and spent 5 years in California working basically as a hired hand. There is kind of a family history about him being in California during the Gold Rush years and experiencing that along with the Wild West and Indians. Along the way there was some talk about meeting some famous characters, like Peg Leg Smith, and to witness an Indian massacre of a wagon train. So, every time I look at the ring I appreciate it more because I know what he had to go through walking all the way to California to pursue a dream.

Storytelling was one of the most common means used by consumers to ensure that family members all understood the significance of their family heirlooms. By repeatedly telling the history of cherished possessions, family members come to understand the prominence of these items within their lineage. These stories are often told repeatedly, that is, ritualistically, at family celebrations. They emerge as a tactic for establishing and maintaining the special significance of the object to the family or group (Weiner 1994). Often, the older, current caretaker invests extra effort in ensuring that the future caretaker is well versed in the cherished possession's origin story. And, the timing of the transfer of the object often rests on the current guardian's evaluation of the effectiveness of the retelling of the possession's story. Also evaluated is the potential guardian's commitment and dedication to preserving the object for future generations (Weiner 1994).

When the stories associated with the cherished possessions are shared with family members, those stories become part of the item's meaning bundle. Significantly, such items can become iconic representations of family identity, such as being the kind of family that overcomes adversity represented in Robert's story (Epp & Price 2008). Cherished possessions tend to have layers of meanings and often are layered with stories from the different generations that have held the object, as diagrammed in Figure 7.2. A caretaker's personal association with a family heirloom can

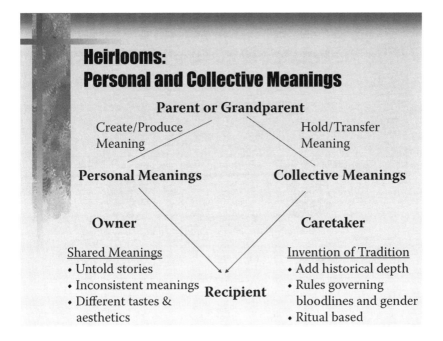

FIGURE 7.2
Cherished possessions tend to have layers of meanings and often are layered with stories from different generations that have held the object.

also become part of the history of the item with another layer of meanings discussed during any ritualized use, maintenance, or storytelling.

As Weiner (1992) insisted, along with the stories, objects must be preserved, and rituals of use, display, and maintenance that give these possessions moral force must be passed forward as well if heirlooms are to become potentially inalienable possessions, revered items withheld from the market against all enticements, as depicted in Figure 7.3.

Our informants provided numerous illustrations of how, as objects changed in status, their display and usage altered. Josie, 83, described a sword that belonged to her grandfather, a Civil War veteran. He carried it with him at the battle of Vicksburg. She inherited it when she was only 3 because she was "his namesake and his favorite grandchild" and planned to pass it on to her grandson (her son John's son and namesake). Although Josie had stories about the sword, she had no memories of her grandfather with the sword and only vague recollections of him (lack of contamination). Nevertheless, she preserved the sword, hid it when she left town, and saw it as a proud, distinct family possession to be kept by future generations.

A story about a collection of china, recently transformed from cherished object to heirloom and perhaps inalienable object, illustrates altered use and display to denote its status. Julie, age 21, described her mother's care

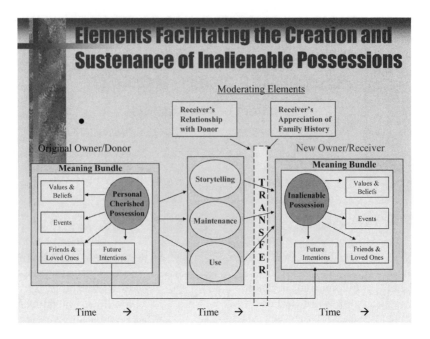

FIGURE 7.3
Along with the stories, objects must preserved, and rituals of use, display, and maintenance that give these possessions moral force must be passed forward as well if heirlooms are to become potentially inalienable possessions.

in packing her great-grandmother's china as a signal of its singularity of meaning:

> And um, I just know they are very special to her, because every time we move and I help pack she makes sure. She wants me to be careful and not to break them. If they were to break you know, I ... they probably would be irreplaceable and she'd be upset about it. I mean you may be able to find something like that but it's just not the same once it's given to you.

The china that Carol (Julie's mother) can remember her grandmother using "on holidays when all the family got together" was now prominently displayed in the china cabinet in "one of the first rooms you see when you enter my house" but was not for use, "just to admire and cherish." Carol, age 55, explicitly framed the amalgam of meanings associated with the china, indicating with respect to her grandmother and mother, "So, you know, I've got something, a little bit of something from both of them." She continued, noting, "then they will also be an extension of myself, too, because they will have truly been passed from generation to generation. ... I would like to pass them along to one of my children one day." Indeed,

Julie would like to inherit this china. To her, the china manifested and legitimated a meaningful collective identity—family unity. She readily endorsed and hoped to reproduce this value with her own children, "Um, they kind of just uh, to me it means family, it means unity. How we all still get along after all these years." Julie observed that she would follow her mother's pattern of use: "Well, I, I wouldn't use it, I'd have it simply for show. Just to show it. I'd have it in my china cabinet, and I would tell everybody the story how it went from generation to generation."

As objects move from alienable object to heirloom and on to inalienability, caretakers are likely to encase them in protected environments, subject them to ritualized use, and limit who handles them. Maria, age 49, explicitly noted in an interview with her daughter, Claire, that as she came to understand the significance of an object to the family, her own use of that object changed:

> Your grandmother gave me the bracelet her mother gave her when she was born. I remember it from when I was little. I always loved it, and Mama would let me wear it around the house if I asked. She gave it to me at my 46th birthday party. I cried because it meant a lot to me. I always wanted it. … She also told me to cherish it and give it to you when the time was right. … It's a dress-up bracelet, so I only wear it on special occasions. It's funny because when I was younger, when I would wear it when I was little, I would have worn it everyday all day. Now I see the importance in the bracelet, and like your grandmother said, I will cherish it.

Similarly, Claire's grandmother, Frances, age 78, treasured crystal she inherited from her Aunt M (who was like a mother to her). She also indicated the narrowing of storage, use, and access that accompanied its conversion from alienable to inalienable.

> Not everyone can touch the crystal but they don't want to because they are nervous they will break it. So they admire it in the china cabinet. … You might even one day have one of the crystal pieces in your house. If you do take care, I mean if you don't want it give it to someone in the family. … When I moved I made sure those things were not broken when I moved, that they were packed by packers. Thank God they were not broken.

Guardianship

Weiner (1992) remarked:

Someone must attest to the authentication of a possession and to the history that surrounds it. And even when there are few inalienable possessions, someone must decide about their transmission within or, when necessary, outside the group. Those whose knowledge is honored by others enhance or diminish what an inalienable possession represents. (p. 104)

In contrast to work that has emphasized role withdrawal and simple disposition with age (Csikszentmihalyi & Rochberg-Halton 1981), many of our informants assumed an active management role with regard to heirlooms. Some informants embraced the idea of guardianship, as in the following comment from Joanna, who was in her late 60s, as she described her pleasure with being chosen as the caretaker of a bracelet that had belonged to a favorite grandmother:

My grandmother died when I was a freshman in high school. She and I were really close. I think that added to my interest in a lot of her items. She passed on to me a bracelet that my grandfather had made for her when he was in the Navy. It means the world to me. Its something I could never replace. I was glad that out of the six grandkids, she recognized that I was the one that would treasure it the most. ... I guess it's a minor detail, but when you think about it, it's really the backbone of one's heritage and family identity.

Previous research on guardianship of heirlooms, including McCracken's (1988) descriptive study of a contemporary caretaker, emphasized kinship. Thus, one might expect our data to display patterns of guardianship distributed by kinship role. Previous research argued that gender also should exert a powerful role in assigning guardianship. However, we might also expect guardianship of heirlooms to exhibit an elective quality in our late modern society (Giddens 1992; Smart & Neale 1999).

As in the example in this section, our results showed that the preferred guardian for an heirloom object is generally a same-gender descendent (rather than an opposite-gender descendent) or a same-gender affine (kin through marriage). Amanda, age 22, speculated that if she inherits it, she will pass her grandmother's ring to her daughter, if she has one, and to a daughter-in-law or granddaughter if she does not. For her part, Sheila, age 50, lamented that she had no daughters to whom to give her jewelry, and she hoped for granddaughters and wanted to be sure that a daughter-in-law earned her trust before passing any jewelry her way. These cases are typical.

As is true in traditional societies, informants take guardianship of inalienable possessions seriously. Edith, age 65, instilled in all her children the belief that family heirlooms are precious and must be preserved along with their fragile texts. Her son, Stanley, age 28, was acting to preserve and pass on the watch he inherited from his grandfather. He remarked:

> Starting now, even before the children, I would like to think about the objects that I would consider leaving to my children and the reasons why. I feel that they deserve an explanation as to why I would leave them the objects. This can be more special than the objects themselves.

Edith, emphasizing the family identity connotations of heirlooms, even counseled the interviewer:

> Treasure any heirlooms that your family may give to you as they hold great memories and associations with your family and its members. … The events that transpire throughout your life and objects that you acquire are what make up your life.

Edith clearly opined that guardianship of inalienable wealth provides identity and links current generations to a stream of ancestors that constitute their social distinction (Epp & Price 2008). She and her children felt responsible for preserving family objects and communicating their power and meaning to future generations.

Other informants consistently acknowledged obligations and responsibilities to keep objects out of the market, teach others their stories, and socialize future caretakers. Clara was a 29-year-old single mother of a young daughter. Like her grandmother, now in her 70s, whom we also interviewed, she judged that certain objects should be kept in the family. Clara described her daughter as like her—"she values things." After supporting that claim with several stories, she concluded:

> And that's the other thing, I think it's *my duty* to raise her to value not only the things of the present but the things of the past. And if I, if I teach her right, I won't have to worry about where those items go. (emphasis added)

With heirlooms come responsibilities for the ritualized use of heirloom objects mentioned. Several instances in our data depicted ritual obligations to the greater family unit accompanying guardianship of heirlooms. Commonly, these ritual obligations have to do with "keeping the family history," "keeping the family together," or a combination of these two themes.

Melinda, age 43, was the caretaker of a marble-topped table inherited from her grandmother, who tellingly was "always the one that pulled us together as a family." When Melinda inherited the table, she discovered her siblings expected her to take on their grandmother's kin-keeping role:

> It was interesting that one of my cousins ... shortly after Grandmother passed away and we were all together and he said, "Now Melinda, you're the matriarch of the family." And, I thought that was really interesting, and it scared me a little bit that he thought of me that way because Grandmother always was the one that pulled us all together as a family. ... It was because of Grandmother that we all congregated together to really be with her, you know, because she was just so special. So, I think that was kind of interesting that he had looked to me that I was going to, you know, be able. And, that's a lot of responsibility. (Melinda, married, 43)

Melinda observed that this was a difficult job because her grandmother's three sons did not get along well. Still, her cousin looked to her as the matriarch of the family. Symbolically, the guardian of this table was charged with using the power imbued in it to keep the family together. Melinda, like the tribal caretakers of inalienable wealth (Godelier 1999; Weiner 1992) should use the table to benefit the whole kin group, in this case her extended family.

Transmission and Inalienable Wealth

We found interesting parallels between heirloom objects and sacred possessions in tribal societies anthropologists called *inalienable wealth*. One characteristic of inalienable wealth is its capacity to speak to and for an individual's or a group's social identity and affirm felt differences between one person or group and another (Weiner 1992, p. 43; Weiner 1994). Thus, in our data, we found comments like the following, which referred to a 102-year-old watch that still "runs perfectly to the second":

> That was really a masterpiece kind of thing, and I know when I see my mother wear it that she is connecting with her own family ... and so I think it was not just a family heirloom as much as it was a symbol of the kind of people they were. They were precise ... they valued things; they hung onto things and after going through the depression, they placed a lot of value on something like a fine watch. (Linnea, 45 years old)

A second characteristic of inalienable wealth is legitimating power derived from origins thought to lie "in some sacred, changeless order"

(Godelier 1999, p. 124). Thus, in our data, we found references to heirloom Christian texts and, in the following excerpt, specific reference to the heirloom as a source of legal legitimacy:

> The Bible, I always remember it being in the family. My grandparents, and then my mother was the oldest daughter, so she got it, and then I got it and I will pass it to my oldest daughter. So it's at least four generations right now. ... Because that Bible is so old, and it has all of the births and deaths and marriages. So it is used as a legal register. (Della, 93 years old)

Third, caretakers fear loss of inalienable possessions because loss places at risk the special knowledge and attributes that define the group (Kirsch 2001, p. 177).

> Yes, I have leather suitcases. I forgot about them until we started talking about them. They were my grandparents. They were leather bound everywhere; um, they are in mint condition with silk lining. They are heavy even when nothing is in them. I'm afraid to even use them because I'm afraid that they will get stolen. ... They will be passed down through my generation, kids hopefully. (Phyllis, 32 years old)

Fourth, caretakers possess inalienable objects but do not have ownership of them; instead they are owned by the lineage, that is, by the family (Godelier 1999; Radin 1993; Weiner 1992). Our data provided evidence that these items have porous ownership boundaries:

> My mother left me household items like dishes, which are very valuable today. ... The dishes remind me of my mother. They've been passed down through the family tree. ... I plan on passing my mother's dishes to my daughters to continue the tradition. ... Certain things like my mother's dishes, I will never get rid of. But I will pass them on to my daughters. (Ginny, widowed, 72)

As with Melinda's table mentioned in this chapter, inalienable objects may be used, but the positive effects that emanate from the powers contained in these objects must be shared with the group (Godelier 1999, p. 122). Thus, in our data we found that heirlooms may be used to stimulate collective memories and moral tales:

> Interviewer: Are there any special occasions that you think you would bring out the blankets to share with people?

Informant: When we have family gatherings at my house, I would love to bring out the quilt to show the family and all sit around and talk about our memories. I feel that would be a very special time to share the quilt. (Jan, 31 years old)

Finally, there are aspects of inalienable possessions that demarcate group membership both via inclusion and through exclusion. On the one hand, for objects to remain inalienable, the normative social order and reality legitimated by these objects must be accepted and shared by the members of the group. Our informants' emic understanding of this principle was typically encoded in remarks about the "importance" of family and family "history":

There are a lot of memories associated with each of these teacups, and my daughter would love to hold onto those memories and share them with her children and grandchildren. I realize that the significance of the teacup set from my father will not be the same for someone else, but my daughter places a lot of importance on family and the history of our family.

On the other hand, while people outside the group may decode some of the public meanings of inalienable wealth, the sacred meanings shared by members of the group resist expression and representation and thus are relatively inaccessible to outsiders (Godelier 1999). Themes of family unity, overcoming adversity, craftsmanship, and so on have been evoked here. Dorothy, 75, discussed the fragile sacred meanings of inalienable wealth. She received a christening dress from her mother-in-law, who in turn received it from hers. Dorothy christened her two sons in it and prevailed on her daughter-in-law to christen her first son in it. She was unsure whether her second grandson was christened in it. According to tradition, someone outside the family (affine) must keep the heirloom in the family. Therefore, the heirloom's status as an inalienable possession is precarious. Dorothy, separated by kinship and geographical distance from her daughter-in-law, expressed considerable anxiety about the future of the object, asking "How can we [the older generation] pass this caring about cherished things on?"

Discussion

The purpose of this research was to extend knowledge about connections between cherished objects, heirlooms, and inalienable wealth broached anecdotally in previous research and of necessity how older consumers managed their cherished possessions. We specifically aimed to identify practices differentiating these items. In this way, we sought to explore behaviors not previously theorized in consumer culture and to inspire investigation of the domain of inalienability. Our data showed that heirlooms passed from one generation to another differed from individuals' cherished objects. Heirlooms reflected contamination with a previous owner and affective intergenerational ties between owners. Inalienable wealth differed from heirlooms by virtue of being actively invested with the properties summarized (see also Curasi et al. 2004). Our point was not to reify the terms cherished possessions, heirlooms, or inalienable wealth but to insist on useful analytical differences between these constructs.

Of course, first our research showed unequivocally that some, if not all, middle-class Americans seek to collect and pass forward the history, achievements, and identities of ancestors. Data presented also affirmed that positive contamination of the object through prolonged contact with a respected elder kinsperson helped preserve cherished objects for one generation. However, successful transfers between generations foreground object meanings through storytelling and employed tactics to mobilize kinship distance, closeness, and caretaking tendencies in target recipients. But, many informants were very concerned about the preservation of heirlooms in subsequent generations. Our research showed that storytelling and distinctive practices of use and display are necessary, if not sufficient, conditions for preserving heirlooms. We also found that heirlooms were an important source of personal identity and family distinction, a fact evident across tales of Civil War swords, Gold Rush rings, 200-year-old watches, and many more prosaic items. Finally, it may not be stretching the analogy to claim that some heirloom objects became inalienable wealth, objects whose sacred status requires that they be held back from market logic and market exchange at all costs.

Perhaps from the standpoint of theorizing old age, our research led to a different perspective on older consumers from the image of cognitive deterioration and increased vulnerability, typical of consumer behavior research (Moschis 1994). In our research, we discovered that older consumers acted as conscientious and proactive guardians of special objects for future generations, even when they were surprised when called on to do so. They employed stories, ritualized use, storage and display, and meaning matching with potential heirs to protect these objects. And, they tried to use cherished inherited objects to convey values and meanings of significance to their kin.

Acknowledgments

This research was funded in part by a research grant from the Research Council, University of South Florida, and from the Institute on Aging, University of South Florida. We would also like to thank Kent Grayson; graduate students at the University of Nebraska; participants in the Sheth Research Camp, University of Pittsburgh; and seminar participants at University of Connecticut, University of California Irvine, and at the Australian Graduate School of Management for comments on earlier versions of the manuscript.

References

Arnould, Eric J., & Linda L. Price (2000), Authenticating Acts and Authoritative Performances: Questing for Self and Community, in *The Why of Consumption: Contemporary Perspectives on Consumer Motives, Goals and Desires*, eds. S. Ratneshwar, David Glen Mick, & Cynthia Huffman, London: Routledge Press, 140–163.

Belk, Russell W. (1991a), The Ineluctable Mysteries of Possessions, *Journal of Social Behavior and Personality, 6*, 17–55.

Belk, Russell W. (1991b), Possessions and the Sense of Past, in *Highways and Buyways: Naturalistic Research from the Consumer Behavior Odyssey*, ed. Russell W. Belk, Provo, UT: Association for Consumer Research, 114–130.

Bumpass, Larry L., Kelly R. Raley, & James A. Sweet (1995), The Changing Character of Stepfamilies: Implications of Cohabitation and Nonmarital Childbearing, *Demography, 32*, 425–437.

Butler, Robert N. (1963), The Life Review: An Interpretation of Reminiscence in the Aged, *Psychiatry, 26*, 65–75.

Butler, Robert N. (1974), Successful Aging and the Role of the Life Review, *Journal of the American Geriatrics Society, 22*, 529–535.

Cheal, David (1988), *The Gift Economy*, London: Routledge.

Csikszentmihalyi, Mihaly, & Eugene Rochberg-Halton (1981), *The Meaning of Things: Domestic Symbols and the Self*, Cambridge, UK: Cambridge University Press.

Curasi, Carolyn, Linda Price, & Eric Arnould (2004), How Individuals' Cherished Possessions Become Families' Inalienable Wealth, *Journal of Consumer Research, 31*, 609–622.

Douglass, William (1984), Sheep Ranchers and Sugar Growers: Property Transmission in the Basque Immigrant Family of the American West and Australia, in *Households*, eds. Robert McC. Netting, Richard R. Wilk, & Eric J. Arnould, Berkeley: University of California Press, 109–129.

Epp, Amber M., & Linda L. Price (2008), Family Identity: A Framework of Identity Interplay in Consumption Practices, *Journal of Consumer Research, 35*, 50–70.

Finch, Janet, & Jennifer Mason (1993), *Negotiating Family Responsibilities*, London: Routledge.

Finch, Janet, & Jennifer Mason (2000), *Passing On: Kinship and Inheritance in England*, London: Routledge.

Gergen, Kenneth J. (2000), *The Saturated Self*, New York: Basic Books.

Giddens, Anthony (1992), *The Transformation of Intimacy*, Cambridge, UK: Polity Press.

Godelier, Maurice (1999), *The Enigma of the Gift*, Chicago: University of Chicago Press.

Goody, J. (1976), Introduction, in *Family and Inheritance: Rural Society in Western Europe 1200–1800*, eds. J. Goody, J. Thirsk, & E. P. Thompson, Cambridge, UK: Cambridge University Press.

Grafton-Small, Robert (1993), Consumption and Significance: Everyday Life in a Brand-New Second Hand Bow Tie, *European Journal of Marketing*, 27, 38–45.

Grayson, Kent, & Donald Shulman (2000), Indexicality and the Verification Function of Irreplaceable Possessions: A Semiotic Analysis, *Journal of Consumer Research*, 27, 17–30.

Gutierrez, Kelli, Linda Price, & Eric Arnould (2008), Consuming Family Dinner Time, in *Advances in Consumer Research*, Volume 35, eds. Angela Y. Lee & Dilip Soman, Duluth, MN: Association for Consumer Research, 189–190.

Judge, Debra S., & Sarah Blaffer Hrdy (1992), Allocation of Accumulated Resources Among Close Kin: Inheritance in Sacramento, CA, 1890–1984, *Ethology and Sociobiology*, 13, 495–522.

Kacapyr, Elia (1996, October), Are You Middle Class? *American Demographics*, 31–35.

Katriel, Tammar, & Thomas Farrell (1991), Scrapbooks as Cultural Texts: An American Art of Memory, *Text and Performance Quarterly*, 11, 1–17.

Kirsch, Stuart (2001), Lost Worlds: Environmental Disaster, 'Culture Loss,' and the Law, *Current Anthropology*, 42 (April), 167–199.

Korosec-Serfaty, Perla (1984). The home from attic to cellar. *Journal of Environmental Psychology*, 4, 303–321.

Laslett, Peter, & Richard Wall (1972), *Household and Family in Past Time*, Cambridge, MA: Cambridge University Press.

Löfgren, Orvar (1984), Family and Household: Images and Realities: Cultural Change in Swedish Society, in *Households*, eds. Robert McC. Netting, Richard R. Wilk, & Eric J. Arnould, Berkeley: University of California Press, 446–470.

Marcus, George E., with Peter Dobkin Hall (1992), *Lives in Trust: The Fortunes of Dynastic Families in Late Twentieth-Century America*, Boulder, CO: Westview.

McCracken, Grant (1988), Lois Roget: Curatorial Consumer in a Modern World, in *Culture and Consumption*, Bloomington: Indiana University Press, 44–56.

McGlone, F., Allison Park, & Kate Smith (1998), *Families and Kinship*, London: Family Policy Studies Centre.

Miller, David (1998), *A Theory of Shopping*, Ithaca, NY: Cornell University Press.

Morgan, David H. J. (1996), *Family Connections: An Introduction to Family Studies*, Cambridge, MA: Blackwell.

Moschis, George P. (1994), *Marketing Strategies for the Mature Market*, Westport, CT: Greenwood.

Neville, Gwen Kennedy (1984), Learning Culture Through Ritual: The Family Reunion, *Anthropology and Education Quarterly*, 15, 151–166.

Otnes, Cele, Tina Lowrey, & L. J. Shrum (1997), Toward an Understanding of Consumer Ambivalence, *Journal of Consumer Research, 24,* 80–93.

Price, Linda L., Eric J. Arnould, & Carolyn F. Curasi (2000), Older Consumers' Disposition of Special Possessions, *Journal of Consumer Research, 27,* 179–201.

Radin, Margaret (1993), *Reinterpreting Property,* Chicago: University of Chicago Press.

Richins, Marsha (1994), Special Possessions and the Expression of Material Values, *Journal of Consumer Research, 21,* 522–533.

Rosenfeld, Jeffrey (1979), Old Age, New Beneficiaries: Kinship, Friendship, and (Dis)Inheritance, *Sociology and Social Research, 64,* 86–98.

Schneider, David M. (1980), *American Kinship: A Cultural Account,* Chicago: University of Chicago Press.

Smart, Carol, & Bren Neale (1999), *Family Fragments,* Cambridge, UK: Polity Press.

Stacey, Judith (1990), *Brave New Families: Stories of Domestic Upheaval in Late Twentieth Century America,* New York: Basic Books.

Sussman, Marvin B., Judith N. Cates, & David T. Smith (1970), *The Family and Inheritance,* New York: Sage.

Thompson, Craig J. (1997), Interpreting Consumers: A Hermeneutical Framework for Deriving Marketing Insights from the Texts of Consumers' Consumption Stories, *Journal of Marketing Research, 34* (November), 438–455.

Tobin, Sheldon S. (1996), Cherished Possessions: The Meaning of Things, *Generations: Journal of the American Society on Aging, 20,* 46–48.

Unruh, David R. (1983), Death and Personal History: Strategies of Identity Preservation, *Social Problems, 30,* 340–351.

Wallendorf, Melanie, & Eric J. Arnould (1991), 'We Gather Together': Consumption Rituals of Thanksgiving Day, *Journal of Consumer Research, 18,* 13–31.

Weiner, Annette B. (1992), *Inalienable Possessions: The Paradox of Keeping-While-Giving,* Berkeley, CA: University of California Press.

Weiner, Annette B. (1985), Inalienable Wealth, *American Ethnologist, 12,* 210–227.

Weiner, Annette B. (1994), Cultural Difference and the Density of Objects, *American Ethnologist, 21,* 391–403.

Weiss, Brad (1997), Forgetting Your Dead: Alienable and Inalienable Objects in Northwest Tanzania, *Anthropological Quarterly, 70,* 164–173.

Yanagisako, Syliva Junko (1984), Explicating Residence: A Cultural Analysis of Changing Households Among Japanese-Americans, in *Households,* eds. Robert McC. Netting, Richard R. Wilk, & Eric J. Arnould, Berkeley: University of California Press, 330–352.

Yu, Hongyan, Alvin C. Burns, & Ann Veeck (2006), The Meanings of Family Dinners for Young, Affluent Families in Urban China, in *Advances in Consumer Research,* Volume 33, eds. Connie Pechmann & Linda Price, Duluth, MN: Association for Consumer Research, 606.

Section 3

Older Consumers in the Marketplace

8

Comprehension of Marketing Communications Among Older Consumers

Carolyn M. Bonifield
University of Vermont

and

Catherine A. Cole
University of Iowa

Introduction

According to the U.S. Census Bureau (http://www.census.gov), as of 2009 approximately 39 million Americans were aged 64 and older. Both new products and advertising directed toward this age group have increased over the past few years as companies such as Whirlpool, GE, Sony, L'Oreal, and Microsoft have shifted their product development and advertising strategies to target older consumers more aggressively (Glader 2008; Schechner & Kumar 2009). Both researchers and practitioners are interested in better understanding this rapidly growing older market.

In this chapter, we identify the individual, task, and contextual characteristics that influence older consumers' comprehension of marketing communications (see Bonifield & Cole 2007; Yoon, Cole, & Lee 2009 for more general reviews). We present these as research propositions in Table 8.1. We draw primarily on applications for advertising but also discuss applications for product warnings, for which a warning is "designed to alert people about potential dangers related to a particular object or environment" (Rousseau, Lamson, & Rogers 1998, p. 644).

Comprehension is an important topic for several reasons. First, prior research estimated that miscomprehension is fairly high in the general population. According to Jacoby and Hoyer (1989), consumers miscomprehend approximately one third of all mass media messages. Rogers, Lamson, and Rousseau (2000) reviewed literature on warnings and concluded that even a good warning may not be understood and complied with by many perceivers. Second, comprehension is important because it affects persuasion (Bradley & Meeds 2004). In fact, the multiplicative comprehension elaboration model, discussed by Wyer (2002), suggests that the probability that someone will be persuaded by a message is a multiplicative function of the probability of comprehending and the probability of generating positive elaborations (Wyer 2002). In this model, as comprehension decreases, persuasion decreases.

Background

To better inform decisions about how to design messages that are easily comprehended, we review the growing body of literature in marketing and psychology that examines how individual, task, and contextual characteristics affect older consumers' comprehension from an information-processing perspective (Cole & Gaeth 1990; Cole & Houston 1987; Gaeth & Heath 1987; Law, Hawkins, & Craik 1998; Rousseau et al. 1998; Skurnik, Yoon, Park, & Schwarz 2005; Yoon 1997; Yoon, Lee, & Danziger 2007). Underlying this review are models of comprehension and aging, which are discussed next.

Models of Comprehension and Aging

Current models of text processing recognize that text must be processed within a limited capacity cognitive system or working memory. To comprehend text, the perceiver must perceptually encode input, identify lexical elements such as nouns and verbs, determine syntactic and semantic relationships between these elements, and develop an understanding. The perceiver uses linguistic context and world knowledge to frame and interpret the input (Stine & Wingfield 1987; Was & Woltz 2007). Stine-Morrow, Miller, & Hertzog (2006) presented a model of self-regulated language processing (SRLP) that argues that the receiver plays an active role in the comprehension process by explicitly or implicitly allocating resources to construct meaning from language, depending on the receiver's own processing capacity, knowledge, and goals as well as the characteristics of the task and the context.

When processing text, the receiver constructs three basic levels of comprehension: the surface form, the propositional text base, and the situation model. All three levels have been studied in advertising research. The surface form corresponds to comprehension of the actual words and syntax that were employed in the text. Bradley and Meeds (2004), for example, investigated the effects of using defined or undefined technical language in an advertisement on comprehension and persuasion. The propositional text base is an abstract representation of the information explicitly conveyed in the text. Advertising and product warning research on claim comprehension has been conducted at the text base level (e.g., Cowley 2006). The situation model is a global understanding of what the text is about (Radvansky, Zwaan, Curiel, & Copeland 2001). Research on how advertising characteristics affect comprehension of a story that spans several ads in a campaign is research done at the situation model level (e.g., Luna 2005).

Regarding the effects of aging, several studies show that aging does not affect one's ability to update the situation model during comprehension. However, aging can affect propositional text base processing. In other words, younger adults are often better at remembering what the text said, but older adults are often better than younger adults at remembering what the text is about (Radvansky et al. 2001; Stine-Morrow, Loveless, & Soederberg 1996). In the Radvansky et al. (2001) study, after reading a text passage (length of 58–85 sentences), younger participants (ages 18–26), when compared to older participants (ages 61–96), were significantly more accurate on recognition tasks requiring use of surface form or propositional text base information but significantly less accurate on a task requiring use of the situation model.

Age differences that emerge in text base processing are at least in part attributable to age-related declines in cognitive mechanics; however, there is considerable heterogeneity in the rate of change in these mechanics (Stine-Morrow et al. 2006). The implicated cognitive mechanics include changes in processes such as working memory capacity or processing speed, reductions in attentional resources (Craik & Byrd 1982), failure to inhibit irrelevant information (Hasher, Zacks, & May 1999), and reduced ability to spontaneously generate associations between pieces of information (Naveh-Benjamin 2000). For example, age differences in comprehension of spoken material may arise because older adults have trouble remembering earlier presented material to keep communication in context (Light & Capps 1986).

In contrast, the age-invariant situation model processing may occur because older adults have a different resource allocation policy than younger adults. For example, older adults may devote a larger proportion of their processing to the situation models than younger adults, whereas younger adults may devote a larger proportion of their processing resources to the propositional text base than do older adults (Adams, Smith, Nyquist, & Perlmutter 1997). Adams et al. suggested that age

TABLE 8.1

Summary of Propositions

P1	Age differences in comprehension of marketing communications material will be smallest for situation model forms of comprehension and largest for the propositional text base or surface form of comprehension.
P2	Age differences in comprehension of marketing communications material will be larger for television and radio than for print media.
P3	Age differences in claim comprehension will be smaller for simple explicit claims and larger for implicit complex claims or for claims with pragmatic implications.
P4	Age differences in comprehension of marketing communications material will be larger for factual than for emotional information.
P5	There will be age differences in judgments about text/visual information consistency and in comprehension of symbols in warnings, especially when the visual information is unfamiliar.
P6	Age differences in comprehension will be smaller when the information is clearly presented in a consistent location or without competing visual/auditory information, but age differences in comprehension will increase when the information is inconspicuous or surrounded with distracting information.
P7	The effects of repetition may depend on the level of comprehension assessed: Increased repetition of visual elements and story elements across an ad series will reduce age differences in comprehension of the situation model, but increased repetition of specific claims will make older adults more vulnerable to the truth effect than younger adults and will increase age differences in comprehension at the text base level.
P8	Age differences in comprehension will be smaller for familiar domains in which consumers possess knowledge and when consumers can easily access this knowledge, but larger for unfamiliar domains and when knowledge is harder to access (e.g., telephone solicitations).
P9	Age differences in comprehension will be smaller when all adults are able and motivated to use systematic processing.

differences in resource allocation policies may emerge because there are age differences in developmental tasks. Younger adults may be motivated to acquire facts, while older adults are motivated to integrate facts into the big picture.

The research on comprehension models and aging provided evidence for our first proposition (P1) in Table 8.1: Age differences in comprehension of marketing communications materials will be relatively small for comprehension at the level of the situation model and larger for the propositional text base or surface form of comprehension.

Task Characteristics Affecting Comprehension

Mode of Message Transmission

The mode of message transmission (e.g., radio, television, or print) is important because speech taxes processing resources more than print does. An auditory message requires that the listener keep pace with the rate of speech input. In addition, unlike written messages, speech messages are physically present only transiently. In contrast, when the information is in print form, the reader can control both the rate of input and reread sections as needed. For example, Abernathy and Adams-Price (2006) found no age differences in younger and older adults' comprehension of complex drug information when it was presented within print advertisements. Regarding television, Cole and Houston (1987) compared 18- to 45-year-olds with 60- to 91-year-olds and found that older adults performed significantly worse on recall and recognition tests after exposure to 30 minutes of news and commercials than younger adults. They speculated that the pattern of results occurred because younger adults are better able than older adults to distinctively encode television communications, which are rich in auditory and visual dimensions. Our second proposition (P2) states that age differences in comprehension of marketing communications material will be larger for television and radio than for print media.

Claim Format

Marketers use a variety of claims to inform consumers about their brands and to issue warnings. However, consumers can misinterpret these claims by incorrectly accepting as true pragmatic implications of claims, by making incorrect inferences from comparative statements with missing referents (Shimp 1978), and by changing how they evaluate brands after exposure to puffery claims (Cowley 2006). Older and younger adults tend to perform comparably on comprehension questions about claims that are present during the test phase and that require automatic or very simple inferential processing (Gaeth & Heath 1987). However, older adults may encounter problems with comprehension of claims and warnings that were recently heard or read but are no longer available and with claims that are potentially misleading due to the presence of a pragmatic implication or that require complex inferential reasoning (Gaeth & Heath 1987; Rousseau et al. 1998; Uekermann, Thoma, & Daum 2008).

Gaeth and Heath (1987) investigated whether there are differences between younger and older adults in abilities to judge truthfulness of claims with pragmatic implications in print advertising. A direct claim would state something such as, "Royalguard tires are safe tires on which to drive," but a claim with a pragmatic implication would read, "Have a safe winter. Drive on new Royalguard tires." Gaeth and Heath (1987) found no age differences in judgments about claims with pragmatic implications when consumers judged statement truthfulness from memory because everyone did poorly. However, younger adults were more likely than older adults to correctly judge the truthfulness of claims with pragmatic implications when the advertisements were available during assessment.

Uekermann et al. (2008) studied age differences in comprehension of proverbs. To understand a proverb, one must take the limited, very concrete information and infer a more general lesson or moral. Uekermann et al. compared 105 (ages 20–39, 40–59, and over 60) participants' ability to select the correct figurative nonliteral meaning of 32 proverbs (e.g., barking dogs seldom bite). The older participants selected significantly fewer correct interpretations, even though they reported more familiarity with each proverb. The authors speculated that older adults' relative impairments on a variety of cognitive mechanisms may have contributed to their proverb interpretation problems.

Taken together, these results suggest that age differences in comprehension of claims depend on the types of claims. Age differences may be small for simple explicit sentences, which limit the inferences the consumer must make. For example, "use in a well-ventilated room" is simple but not explicit because the user must infer what well ventilated means. In contrast, "use in a room with at least one window open" is simple and explicit (Rousseau et al. 1998). This leads to the following proposition (P3): Age differences in claim comprehension will be smaller for simple explicit claims and larger for complex implicit claims or for claims with pragmatic implications.

Emotional Content

Several studies suggested that comprehension of everyday interpersonal issues increases with age, so that older adults make more accurate, complex inferences about social situations than younger adults (Blanchard-Fields, Jahnke, & Camp 1995; Hess, Osowksi, & Leclerc 2005). Mares (2007) reported results consistent with the idea that age differences in comprehension are minimized for emotional content. In her study, three groups of adults (ages 19–30, 65–70, and 71–78) watched two TV dramas. After each program, she assessed memory for characters' emotions and relationships, recognition, recall, and chronology of main events and ability to make inferences about the content. In general, the size of age difference in comprehension varied by measure of comprehension, so that age differences were smaller for comprehension of socioemotional content but larger for chronological sequencing and inference measures.

In marketing and psychology, researchers have found similar results for recall, with older adults remembering emotionally relevant content or preferring emotional ads, perhaps because older adults devote more attentional resources toward affective than factual information (see Chapter 3 this book; Drolet, Williams, & Lau-Gesk 2007; Fung & Carstensen 2003; Williams & Drolet 2005). Thus, our next proposition (P4) relates to age differences in comprehension of factual versus emotional information: Age differences in comprehension of marketing communications material will be larger for factual than for emotional information.

Visual Information

Because much marketing communications and many warnings combine both verbal and visual information, it is important to consider whether age differences will emerge in the process of integrating and comprehending communications with both verbal and visual information (Wyer, Hung, & Jiang 2008). Wyer et al. presented evidence that incompatibility between visual and verbal information harms product evaluations, especially for people who are inherently visualizers. An interesting study suggested that older adults spontaneously generate visual images consistent with their situational model for text, while younger adults spontaneously generate visual images consistent with the surface form of the text (Dijkstra, Yaxley, Madden, & Zwaan 2004). From a communicator's perspective, these results suggest that older and younger visualizers may spontaneously generate different visual information after exposure to text, and that there may be age differences in judgments about the consistency of visual and verbal information.

Symbols are important not only in brand logos, but also as an alternative means of conveying warning information. Generally, symbols are easily understood by individuals with different backgrounds (Rousseau et al. 1998). But, the results are mixed about whether they will reduce age differences in warning comprehension because older and younger adults do not always comprehend symbols in the same way. For example, studies investigating age differences in comprehension of traffic signs have typically reported comparable levels of comprehension for signs across young and old age groups (e.g., Kline, Ghali, Kline, & Brown 1990). In contrast, one study compared younger adults' (ages 18–34), middle-aged adults' (ages 35–54), and older adults' (ages 55–64 and 65–91) comprehension of common safety symbols. This study reported that the older adults more poorly comprehended some, but not all, common safety symbols (e.g., Hancock, Rogers, & Fisk 2001). This leads to the proposition (P5) that there will be age differences in judgments about text/visual information consistency and in comprehension of symbols in warnings, especially when the visual information is unfamiliar.

Context

Clutter and Noise

Noise and clutter may increase age differences in comprehension. For example, age differences in performance on speech perception tests tend to be greater in noisy conditions than in less-noisy conditions (Hutchinson 1989). Hutchinson speculated that this may occur because background babble has a masking effect on acoustic cues that aid in understanding. Gorn, Goldberg, Chattopadhyay, and Litvack (1991) extended this research by predicting and finding that background music in television commercials impairs learning among older consumers. In their study, recall of product claims was lower for older adults exposed to the commercials with background music than when compared to older adults exposed to the same commercials without background music.

When printed information is very detailed with similar information mixed together, such as that found on a nutritional label, older and younger adults differ in their ability to correctly use the printed information. Cole and Gaeth (1990) examined how age differences in selective attention might affect older adults' ability to use the printed nutritional information contained on product labels and found that while both older and younger adults benefitted from the use of a perception aid that encouraged them to focus on the relevant information, older consumers were still less capable than younger consumers of using the information to make good nutritional choices. In a follow-up study, the relevant information was boxed and placed in a separate location on the label; older subjects who scored moderately well (but not those who scored poorly) on an Embedded Figures Test were helped. This test measures one's ability to detect simple objects embedded in larger, more elaborate figures. The Cole and Gaeth study indicated that the interplay between individual characteristics (disembedding ability) and copy characteristics (information complexity and placement) affect use of printed material.

In general, older adults who are poor inhibitors may be more susceptible to interference from distracting and irrelevant information than younger adults (Lustig, May, & Hasher 2001). The distractions may arise from external sources (e.g., from background noise) or from internal sources (e.g., personal concerns), and the inability to inhibit them might interfere with comprehension. The bottom line, which is summarized in the next proposition (P6), is that age differences in comprehension will be smaller when the information is clearly presented in a consistent location or without competing visual/auditory information, but age differences in comprehension will increase when the information is inconspicuous or surrounded with distracting information.

Repetition

Another characteristic that affects age differences in comprehension is the repetition of the information. Luna (2005) studied how consumers' comprehension at the level of the situation model evolves across multiple ads for a brand. He showed that advertisers can facilitate construction of the situation model if an ad series possesses referential continuity (each of the parts explicitly or implicitly refers to an entity introduced in the previous parts). Consequently, we expect that for ad series with high levels of referential continuity, age differences in comprehension of the situational model will be low, but for ad series with low levels of referential continuity, age differences in comprehension will be larger. This finding may generalize to warning literature such that multiple ads showing the proper use of a product may minimize age differences in comprehension if referential continuity is high across ads.

Older adults are more vulnerable to the truth effect (the tendency to believe repeated information more than new information) because older adults have relatively poor context or source memory but relatively intact familiarity with repeated claims (Law et al. 1998). Interestingly, Skurnik et al. (2005) found that repeatedly identifying a claim as false helped older adults remember it as false in the short term but made them more likely to remember it as true after a 3-day delay. In contrast, younger adults' memories for truth benefited from repeated warnings after both short and long delays. For the older adults, this unintended effect of repetition was due to increased familiarity with the claim itself but decreased recollection of the claim's original context.

These findings lead to Proposition 7, that the effects of repetition may depend on the level of comprehension assessed: Increased repetition of visual elements and story elements across an ad series will reduce age differences in comprehension of the situation model, but increased repetition of specific claims will make older adults more vulnerable to the truth effect than younger adults and will increase age differences in comprehension at the text base level.

Individual Differences

Knowledge

Research indicates that crystallized intelligence may remain stable or increase across the adult life span (Cattell 1987; Park & Gutchess 2006). Crystallized intelligence refers to individuals' knowledge bases, such as vocabulary, understanding about how people operate, and knowledge about media. Rich knowledge bases facilitate basic information processing (Harris, Durso, Mergler, & Jones 1990). Mares (2007) reported results consistent with knowledge mitigating age differences in comprehension. In her study, half the adults within each age group were familiar with the characters and typical story lines in a television program that they watched. In general, the size of age differences in comprehension was greater for unfamiliar than familiar programs.

Similarly, older consumers may protect themselves from marketing scams with persuasion knowledge, which is knowledge about persuasion tactics and methods of resisting persuasion attempts. However, when cognitive capacity is constrained, consumers are less likely to recruit persuasion knowledge to resist selling efforts. This suggests that older adults may encounter problems accessing their richer knowledge bases for comprehension tasks (Campbell & Kirmani 2000). This leads to our next proposition (P8): Age differences in comprehension will be smaller for familiar domains in which consumers possess knowledge and when consumers can easily access this knowledge, but larger for unfamiliar domains and when knowledge is harder to access (e.g., telephone solicitations).

Processing Strategies

Individual differences in processing strategies may also explain age differences in comprehension. Yoon (1997) initially examined schema-based versus detailed processing strategies between older and younger adults and found that although older adults exhibit greater use of schema-based processing in general, specific task conditions had a significant effect. Older adults were able to engage in levels of detailed processing when exposed to high-incongruity cues during their optimal time of day (morning), but during their nonoptimal time of day, the presence of any level of incongruity led to the use of schema-based processing. To explain an age-associated decrease in systematic processing, Hess, Rosenberg, and Waters (2001) proposed a resource allocation hypothesis, which states that, as people age, they learn to better allocate and conserve their mental energy so that they rely on heuristic processing unless explicitly motivated to use detailed processing. However, even given proper instructions or context, not all older adults are able to use systematic processing. Age-related changes in prefrontal brain regions may limit some, although not all, older adults' abilities to use detailed processing (Denburg, Tranel, & Bechara 2005; Hedden & Gabrieli 2004). This leads to our final proposition (P9): Age differences in comprehension will be smaller when all adults are able and motivated to use systematic processing.

General Discussion

On the one hand, some firms and organizations have straightforward global messages that they want understood by both older and younger consumers. Such messages—such as getting a flu shot or trying a new restaurant—will likely be readily comprehended by all age groups. As we have seen, there are minimal age differences in consumers' ability to construct situation models.

On the other hand, organizations concerned about comprehension of specific claims in a message or warnings need to take the target market's information-processing skills into account. For example, the health clinic staff may want consumers to know that they should come in before November 1 to get a flu shot. As a result, marketers may want to adapt the format, content, location, and timing of marketing communications, including warnings, to the comprehension abilities of the target market.

Marketers may initiate such adaptations by pilot testing comprehensibility of claims and warnings on older adults. They may want to experiment with providing information at the times it is needed (e.g., during product use), not just prior to purchase, or with making information easily accessible to consumers, either with product handouts or through online Web pages. Firms and industry associations may also develop internal sets of guidelines as a proactive way of preventing potential litigation and negative publicity as well as enhancing a firm's or industry's reputation for socially responsible behavior. Involving key individuals from influential groups such as AARP in company decision making in the area of marketing to older adults is another avenue to consider. In addition, industries and nonprofit organizations may introduce training programs to help increase and update older adults' knowledge about claims and symbols. Gaeth and Heath (1987), for example, developed an interactive training program to reduce susceptibility to misleading claims in advertising and found that the training reduced susceptibility to misleading statements among older adults.

Finally, given increased media attention to unfair advertising practices or lack of adequate warning signs and labels, lawmakers may be inclined to become more involved in preventing unfair or deceptive practices through increased legislation. For example, the Consumer Product Safety Commission and the U.S. Congress have been in an ongoing tug of war to set new labeling rules for toys (Trottman 2008). The Federal Trade Commission (FTC), which considers how advertising practices affect the targeted consumer in judging unfairness and deception, may order offending firms to produce corrective advertising. For example, the FTC ordered Novartis to spend $8 million on corrective advertisements regarding claims it made about Doan's back medication (Darke, Ashworth, & Ritchi 2008). In terms of public policy, simply making accurate information available will not necessarily ensure that older consumers will comprehend it; further empirical evidence needs to be provided for the propositions we have identified in Table 8.1.

References

Abernathy, L. Ty, & Carolyn E. Adams-Price (2006), Memory and Comprehension of Magazine-Based Prescription Drug Advertisements Among Young and Old Adults, *Journal of Current Issues & Research in Advertising, 28,* 1–13.

Adams, C., M. C. Smith, L. Nyquist, & M. Perlmutter (1997), Adults Age-Group Differences in Recall the Literal and Interpretive Meanings of Narrative Text, *Journal of Gerontology: Psychological Sciences, 52B,* 187–195.

Blanchard-Fields, F., H. C. Jahnke, & C. Camp (1995), Age Differences in Problem-Solving Style: The Role of Emotional Salience, *Psychology and Aging, 10,* 173–180.

Bonifield, C., & C. Cole (2007), Advertising to Vulnerable Segments, in *The Sage Handbook of Advertising,* Gerry J. Tellis & Tim Ambler (Eds.), London: Sage, 430–444.

Bradley, S., & R. Meeds (2004), The Effects of Sentence-Level Context, Prior Word Knowledge and Need for Cognition on Information Processing of Technical Language in Print Ads, *Journal of Consumer Psychology, 14,* 292–302.

Campbell, Margaret C., & Amna Kirmani (2000), Consumers' Use of Persuasion Knowledge: The Effects of Accessibility and Cognitive Capacity on Perceptions of an Influence Agent, *Journal of Consumer Research, 10,* 69–83.

Cattell, R. B. (1987), *Intelligence: Its Structure, Growth and Action,* New York: Elsevier.

Cole, Catherine A., & Gary J. Gaeth (1990), Cognitive and Age-Related Differences in the Ability to Use Nutritional Information in a Complex Environment, *Journal of Marketing Research, 27,* 175–184.

Cole, Catherine A., & Michael J. Houston (1987), Encoding and Media Effects on Consumer Learning Deficiencies in the Elderly, *Journal of Marketing Research, 24,* 55–63.

Cowley, Elizabeth (2006), Processing Exaggerated Advertising Claims, *Journal of Business Research, 59,* 728–734.

Craik, F., & M. Byrd (1982), Aging and Cognitive Deficits: The Role of Attentional Resources, in *Aging and Cognitive Processes: Advances in the Study of Communication and Affect,* F. Craik & S. Trehub (Eds.), New York: Plenum, 191–211.

Darke, Peter Laurence Ashworth, & Robin J. Ritchie (2008), Damage From Corrective Advertising: Causes and Cures, *Journal of Marketing, 72,* 81–97.

Denburg, N., L. D. Tranel, & A. Bechara (2005), The Ability to Decide Advantageously Declines Prematurely in Some Normal Older Persons, *Neuropsychologica, 43,* 1099–1106.

Dijkstra, Katinka, Richard H. Yaxley, Carol J. Madden, & Rolf A. Zwaan (2004), The Role of Age and Perceptual Symbols in Language Comprehension, *Psychology and Aging, 19,* 352–356.

Drolet, Aimee, P. Wiliams, & L. Lau-Gesk (2007), Age-Related Differences in Responses to Affective Versus Rational Ads for Hedonic Versus Utilitarian Products, *Marketing Letters, 18,* 211–221.

Fung, H. H., & L. Carstensen (2003), Sending Memorable Messages to the Old: Age Differences in Preferences and Memory for Advertisements, *Journal of Personality and Social Psychology, 85*, 163–178.

Gaeth, Gary J., & Timothy B. Heath (1987), The Cognitive Processing of Misleading Advertising in Young and Old Adults: Assessment and Training, *Journal of Consumer Research, 14*, 43–54.

Glader, Paul (2008, December 3), Home Appliances to Soothe the Aches of Aging Boomers, *Wall Street Journal*, D1.

Gorn, Gerald, Marvin Goldberg, A. Chattopadhyay, & D. Litvack (1991) Music and Information in Commercials: Their Effects With an Elderly Sample, *Journal of Advertising, 31*, 23–32.

Hancock, H., W. A. Rogers, & A. D. Fisk (2001), An Evaluation of Warning Habits and Beliefs Across the Adult Life Span, *Human Factors, 43*, 343–354.

Harris, J. F., F. T. Durso, N. L. Mergler, & S. K. Jones (1990), Knowledge Base Influences on Judgments of Frequency of Occurrence, *Cognitive Development, 5*, 223–233.

Hasher, L., Rose T. Zacks, & Cynthia P. May (1999), Inhibitory Control, Circadian Arousal, and Age, in *Attention and Performance, 17, Cognitive Regulation of Performance: Interaction of Theory and Application*, D. Gopher & A. Koriat (Eds.), Cambridge, MA: MIT Press, 653–657.

Hedden, Trey, & John D. E. Gabrieli (2004), Insights Into the Ageing Mind: A View From Cognitive Neuroscience, *Nature Reviews: Neuroscience, 5*, 87–96.

Hess, T. M., N. L. Osowski, & C. M. Leclerc (2005), Age and Experience Influences on the Complexity of Social Inferences, *Psychology and Aging, 20*, 447–510.

Hess, Thomas, Daniel C. Rosenberg, & Sandra J. Waters (2001), Motivation and Representational Processes in Adulthood: The Effects of Social Accountability and Information Relevance, *Psychology and Aging, 16*, 629–642.

Hutchinson, K. (1989), Influence of Sentence Context on Speech Perception in Young and Older Adults, *Journal of Gerontology: Psychological Sciences, 44*, 36–44.

Jacoby, Jacob, & Wayne D. Hoyer (1989), The Comprehension/Miscomprehension of Print Communication: Selected Findings, *Journal of Consumer Research, 15*, 434–443.

Kline, T. J., L. Ghali, D. Kline, & S. Brown (1990), Visibility Distance of Highway Signs Among Young, Middle Aged and Older Observers: Icons Are Better Than Text, *Human Factors, 32*, 609–619.

Law, Sharmistha, Scott A. Hawkins, & Fergus I. M. Craik (1998), Repetition-Induced Belief in the Elderly: Rehabilitating Age-Related Memory Deficits, *Journal of Consumer Research, 25*, 91–107.

Light, L., & J. Capps (1986), Comprehension of Pronouns in Young and Older Adults, *Developmental Psychology, 22*, 580–585.

Luna, David (2005), Integrating Ad Information: A Text Processing Perspective, *Journal of Consumer Psychology, 15*, 38–51.

Lustig, Cindy, Cynthia P. May, & Lynn Hasher (2001), Working Memory Span and the Role of Proactive Interference, *Journal of Experimental Psychology: General, 130*, 199–207.

Mares, Marie-Louise (2007), Developmental Changes in Adult Comprehension of a Television Program Are Modified by Being a Fan, *Communication Monographs*, 74, 55–77.

Naveh-Benjamin, M. (2000), Adult Age Differences in Memory Performance: Tests of an Associative Deficit Hypothesis, *Journal of Experimental Psychology: Learning, Memory, and Cognition*, 26, 1170–1187.

Park, D., & A. Gutchess (2006), The Cognitive Neuroscience of Aging and Culture, *Current Directions in Psychological Science*, 15, 105–108.

Radvansky, Gabriel, Rolf A. Zwaan, Jacqueline M. Curiel, & David E. Copeland (2001), Situation Models and Aging, *Psychology and Aging*, 16, 145–160.

Rogers, W. A., N. Lamson, & G. K. Rousseau (2000), Warning Research: An Integrative Perspective, *Human Factors*, 42, 102–139.

Rousseau, G., N. Lamson, & W. Rogers (1998), Designing Warnings to Compensate for Age-Related Changes in Perceptual and Cognitive Abilities, *Psychology and Marketing*, 15, 643–662.

Schechner, Sam, & Vishesh Kumar (2009, January 16), Retirement Living TV Gets Boost: Comcast Deal Will Expand Audience as More Marketers Pursue Older Crowd, *The Wall Street Journal*, B9.

Shimp, T. A. (1978), Do Incomplete Comparisons Mislead? *Journal of Advertising Research*, 18, 21–28.

Skurnik, Ian, Carolyn Yoon, Denise C. Park, & Norbert Schwarz (2005), How Warnings About False Claims Become Recommendations, *Journal of Consumer Research*, 31, 713–724.

Stine, E., & A. Wingfield (1987), Process and Strategy in Memory for Speech Among Younger and Older Adults, *Psychology and Aging*, 2, 272–279.

Stine-Morrow, E., M. Loveless, & L. M. Soederberg (1996), Resource Allocation in On-Line Reading by Younger and Older Adults, *Psychology and Aging*, 11, 475–486.

Stine-Morrow, E., L. Miller, & C. Hertzog (2006), Aging and Self-Regulated Language Processing, *Psychological Bulletin*, 132, 582–606.

Trottman, M. (2008, August 29) U.S. News: Consumer-Products Agency Faces Looming Deadlines on Rules, *The Wall Street Journal*, A4.

Uekermann, Jennifer, Patrizia Thoma, & Irene Daum (2008), Proverb Interpretation Changes in Aging, *Brain and Cognition*, 67, 51–57.

Was, Christopher, & Dan Woltz (2007), Reexamining the Relationship Between Working Memory and Comprehension: The Role of Available Long-Term Memory, *Journal of Memory and Language*, 56, 86–102.

Williams, Patti, & Aimee Drolet (2005), Age-Related Differences in Responses to Emotional Advertisements, *Journal of Consumer Research*, 32, 343–354.

Wyer, R. S. (2002) Language and Advertising Effectiveness: Mediating Influences on Comprehension and Cognitive Elaboration, *Psychology and Marketing*, 19, 693–712.

Wyer, Robert, Iris Hung, & Y. Jiang (2008) Visual and Verbal Processing Strategies in Comprehension and Judgment, *Journal of Consumer Psychology*, 18, 244–257.

Yoon, Carolyn (1997), Age Differences in Consumers' Processing Strategies: An Investigation of Moderating Influences, *Journal of Consumer Research*, 24, 329–342.

Yoon, Carolyn, Catherine Cole, & Michelle P. Lee (2009) Consumer Decision Making and Aging: Current Knowledge and Future Directions, *Journal of Consumer Psychology, 19,* 2–16.

Yoon, Carolyn, Michelle P. Lee, & Shai Danziger (2007), The Effects of Optimal Time of Day on Persuasion Processes in Older Adults, *Psychology & Marketing, 24,* 475–495.

9

Impact of Age on Brand Choice

Raphaëlle Lambert-Pandraud
ESCP Europe

and

Gilles Laurent
HEC Paris

Introduction

In terms of actual brand choice and brand choice processes, important differences characterize consumers of different age groups. Yet, interest in the impact of age on brand choice moves well beyond its managerial significance for marketing. In many categories, brand choice typifies the choices made among competing alternatives that have become known to decision makers at very different dates (e.g., one of the leading perfumes was introduced almost 90 years ago, while dozens of new perfumes are launched every year). Thus, a given consumer typically encounters different brands at different periods of life (e.g., one brand at age 15 years and another brand at age 60 years), and similarly, each given brand appears to different consumers at different periods of their lives (e.g., when they come of age or when they retire). Brand choice therefore offers a critical field of investigation that contrasts vividly with lab choices that provide only artificial material, for which all competing options are equally new to the respondents.

Several theoretical mechanisms attempt to explain how these differences in dates and ages may create observed differences in brand choice and brand choice processes. Some mechanisms rely on affective factors, whereas others pertain to changes in cognitive abilities. For example, a consumer may have developed an affective attachment to a specific car brand over several decades, perhaps since the consumer first started driving, but new car brands must start from scratch. Another consumer may have encoded a given car brand in long-term memory decades ago, when young, whereas numerous new car brands must struggle to be encoded.

In this chapter, we present some selected results regarding brand choice and brand choice processes, and we review a variety of mechanisms that might be evoked to explain those results. This analysis enables us to propose questions for further research.

Selected Results for Brand Choice and Choice Processes

Previous literature indicated that older consumers are more likely to prefer longer-established brands, maintain a smaller consideration set (and more generally, a shrinking purchase process), and repeat purchase the brands they have owned in the past. These tendencies create important market share differences across different consumer age ranges. (We follow Schaie's [1996] age categorization, distinguishing "young-old," 60–74 years, from the "old-old," 75 years and older, and comparing both groups with middle-aged, 40–59 years, and the young, 39 years and younger.)

Preference for Long-Established Brands

Older car buyers tend to favor longer-established brands (Furse, Punj, & Stewart, 1984; Lambert-Pandraud, Laurent, & Lapersonne, 2005). For example, older French buyers purchase one of the three leading, long-established, national brands of car (Peugeot, Renault, or Citroën) with increased frequency: 49% among buyers 39 years or younger, 56% for those aged 40–59, 69% for those aged 60–74, and 74% for those 75 years and older. Similarly, perfumes introduced before 1982 enjoy a 54% share among French consumers aged 60 years and older, compared with only 20% among those 30 years and younger, according to a 2002 survey; in the radio market, stations created before 1981 have a market share of 58% among the older audience versus 12% among the younger group according to 2007 data (Médiamétrie, 2007).

Smaller Consideration Set, Shrinking Purchase Process

Before making a purchase, older consumers tend to consider fewer brands (Cole & Balasubramanian, 1993; Johnson, 1990; Lambert-Pandraud et al., 2005; Lapersonne, Laurent, & Le Goff, 1995; Uncles & Ehrenberg,

1990; Uncles & Lee, 2006). Similarly, Deshpandé and Zaltman (1978) and Deshpandé and Krishnan (1981) found that older consumers tend to make fewer price comparisons and collect less information before they purchase. Uncles and Ehrenberg (1990) observed that, on average, households in which members are 55 years and older buy fewer brands of frequently purchased consumer goods, partly because of their lower purchase rates. Cole and Balasubramanian (1993) also found that older people consider fewer brands and varieties of cereals before a purchase. Similarly, Aurier and Jean (1996) reported that the number of drinks considered during specific purchase occasions decreases with age. In contrast, neither Gruca (1989) nor Campbell (1969) observed a significant relationship between consumer age and the size of the consideration set for coffee and grocery products, respectively.

Prior results converged more for new car purchases: Johnson (1990) and Srinivasan and Ratchford (1991) both observed that older consumers search for less information before they make a decision, and Maddox, Gronhaug, Homans, and May (1978) found that the increased age of consumers decreases the number of car brands they consider. From another perspective, Cattin and Punj (1983) revealed that car buyers who consider a single dealer are significantly older, a finding they attributed to the higher psychological cost of information search. Lapersonne and colleagues (1995, p. 55) indicated that being older than 60 years significantly increases the probability that the consumer will have a "consideration set of size one" before purchasing a new car, which in four of five cases involves a repeat purchase. Furthermore, Lambert-Pandraud and colleagues (2005) found that age significantly reduces the average number of car brands considered, from 2.24 for buyers 39 years and younger to 2.16 for those aged 40–59, 1.92 for the 60–74 age group, and only 1.77 for buyers 75 years and older. Older buyers of new cars also are much less likely to consider three or more brands (respectively 24%, 22%, 14%, and 7% for the same four age groups) and much more likely to consider only a single brand (respectively 11%, 15%, 26%, and 33% for the same age groups). Another way to simplify the purchase process is to consider a single dealer (respectively 47%, 53%, 66%, 79%) or a single model (respectively 6%, 11%, 20%, 28%).

Overall, these studies described the "shrinkage" of the decision process with age—fewer brands considered and bought, fewer price comparisons made, fewer drinks considered, less information sought, fewer dealers and fewer models considered—which means that older consumers consider fewer options on the basis of the more limited information they attain.

Higher Tendency to Repeat Purchase

Not surprisingly, smaller consideration sets lead older consumers to exhibit a higher tendency to repeat purchase the brand of their previous

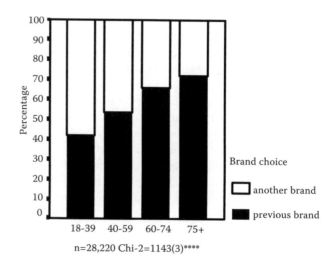

FIGURE 9.1
Older buyers more often repurchase the previous brand. Reprinted from Lambert-Pandraud et al., 2005.

car (Lambert-Pandraud et al., 2005), at levels of 42% among the group 39 years or younger, 54% among those aged 40–59, 66% among the group aged 60–74 years, and 72% among consumers 75 years and older (Figure 9.1).

Similarly, the frequency with which consumers purchase a new car from the same dealer increases (respectively for the same age categories 21%, 34%, 44%, and 49%). We observed comparable results in the context of intended votes during the 2007 presidential election in France: The older the person, the more likely he or she was to plan to vote for the same party as he or she had during the 2002 presidential election.

Market Shares Depend on Consumer Age and Brand Age

Perfumes launched around the same date tend to have similar profiles in terms of their consumers' ages. Consider two perfumes launched 6 years prior to a survey of French consumers; both perfumes experienced the same declining consumer age profiles: The older the consumers, the lower the perfume's success. Shares of choice equaled 5% (a high score for a perfume) for both perfumes among users around 20 years of age; these shares dropped to 3% among consumers aged 40 years, to 1% among consumers aged 60 years; finally, the two had shares of 0% and 1% among consumers aged 80 years. Two perfumes launched in the 1920s, more than 80 years before the survey, also possessed matching increasing age

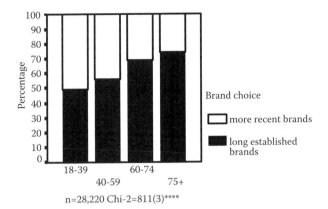

FIGURE 9.2
Older buyers more often buy long-established brands. Reprinted from Lambert-Pandraud et al., 2005.

profiles: The older the consumers, the greater their success. Finally, two mature perfumes launched about 30 years before the survey revealed the same inverted U-shaped consumer age profile: increasing between 20 and 40 years of age, reaching maximum share among consumers aged 40 years, then declining for those older than 40.

These results implied very strong differences in market shares across consumers from different age ranges. In the perfume survey, those scents launched in the preceding 10 years together earned a choice share of greater than 60% among consumers in the 20-year-old age group but of less than 20% among consumers older than 70. In contrast, the perfumes launched more than 70 years ago together achieved a share of approximately 10% among the younger consumers but more than 40% among the older consumers. Finally, the perfumes launched between 10 and 30 years prior to the survey attained their maximum share among mature consumers between 40 and 65 years of age (Lambert-Pandraud & Laurent, 2009). This finding replicated the results pertaining to both new car purchases (Figure 9.2) and radio audiences, as discussed in this chapter.

What explains older consumers' preference for long-established options, shrinking purchase process, and more frequent repeat purchase? Research suggested various mechanisms. Some of them are linked to aging itself (cognitive decline, biological aging, increased aversion to change, declining innovativeness). Some are linked to a reduced temporal horizon (socioemotional selectivity). Some mechanisms develop as time passes (attachment, expertise, habits). Some reflect the periods during which someone lived (nostalgia, cohort effects).

Possible Mechanisms

Cognitive Decline

A massive library of results from psychology research associated aging with spectacular declines in higher-order cognitive resources, such as memory (Salthouse & Ferrer-Caja, 2003). These declines seemed closely related and shared a high proportion of age-related variance, which suggests that a general, common factor may underlie the performance decrements associated with aging, as observed in studies conducted by different research teams using different material (Birren & Schaie, 2006). One of the most promising of these general factors is processing speed (Salthouse, 1996). Specifically, a central slowdown may reduce older people's processing speed (Bryan & Luszcz, 1996; Zelinsky & Burnight, 1997), which prompts consumers to simplify their purchase processes by considering fewer options or repeating their previous choice. The decrease of processing speed is highly correlated with performance in other resources, such as working memory (Chapter 1, this volume). Similarly, a declining capacity of working memory, associated with reduced processing speed, may lower a person's ability to encode information about new brands and retrieve previously stored information (Chapter 1, this volume; Park & Gutchess, 2004).

Biological Aging

The results from previous research also might reflect the decline of physical capacities that occurs because of biological aging or "the array of modifications happening in the organism with age and lowering its resistance and adaptability to the pressures of the environment" (Barrère, 1992, p. 16). For example, older persons with serious physical problems may have difficulty driving a car, or even walking, which could prevent them from visiting multiple car dealers or car dealers located far from their home. They also may suffer from hearing or eyesight losses, which make it difficult for older people to collect and absorb new information about brands.

Aversion to Change

An aversion to the risks linked to change, even if the present solution is far from ideal, is a well-documented phenomenon in gerontology research. Wallach and Kogan (1961) and Botwinick (1966) asked subjects to choose between two options: staying in a secure but mediocre occupation with limited prospects for a pay increase or changing to an occupation that will lead, with probability p, to a salary increase or, with probability $1 - p$, to financial disaster. Older subjects are markedly more likely to choose staying, whatever the value of p (Botwinick, 1978). Botwinick (1978) suggested two hypotheses to explain this resistance to change. First, due to their intellectual decline, older people may avoid making decisions. Second, older people may avoid the risk associated with a bad decision, especially one that may lead to financial risk. Thus, the purchase behavior of older persons could be the consequence of change aversion, which would lead them to repeat their previous choice; staying with the same brand and the same dealer provides a way to avoid the complexity of a new decision, as does considering a single model.

Innovativeness

Innovativeness refers to the "propensity of consumers to adopt novel products" (Hirschman, 1980, p. 283). Lesser and Kunkel (1991) described exploratory behavior as a main feature of younger respondents (18–39 years). Transposing this finding to consumer behavior, and specifically to brand choice, younger persons should be more likely to try new brands that may or may not prove satisfactory, whereas older people prefer to stick to well-known brands, even if they are not perfectly satisfying, because their available knowledge reduces risks. Unfortunately, relevant consumer behavior studies mostly attempted to find a relationship between age and the adoption of new product categories (rather than the adoption of new brands in an existing category), and they did not offer a consensus.

In an oft-quoted classical review, Rogers and Shoemaker (1971) mentioned 76 studies that found a positive correlation between age and time of adoption, 44 with negative correlations, and 108 studies in which no correlation existed. Thirty-two years later, Rogers (2003, p. 288) confirmed that, "Earlier adopters are no different from later adopters in age. There is inconsistent evidence about the relationship of age and innovativeness. About half of the many diffusion studies on this subject show no relationship, a few found that earlier adopters are younger, and some indicate they are older."

These variations also may reflect differences in the products under study. Hauser, Tellis, and Griffin (2006, p. 689) concluded that, "While some studies have shown that innovators are better educated, wealthier, more mobile, and younger, other studies have failed to validate these findings." In contrast, a negative relationship might exist between age and innovativeness, according to Tellis, Yin, and Bell (2005, p. 21), who claimed that innovativeness measured by "reluctance is best explained by age and income, closely followed by mobility, education and gender." Given these conflicting results, more empirical evidence needs to test whether younger consumers' proneness to exploration, variety, and change stimulate their choice of newer brands.

Socioemotional Selectivity

According to socioemotional selectivity theory (Carstensen, Isaacowitz, & Charles, 1999; Isaacowitz, Charles, & Carstensen, 2000), older adults perceive their temporal horizon as limited and therefore emphasize emotional goals over knowledge-related goals. This shift becomes progressive as persons "become increasingly aware that time is in some sense 'running out'" (Carstensen et al., 1999, p. 165). And more generally, persons of all ages feeling a limited time horizon seek "intimacy and affective gain in their social interactions" (Chapter 3, this volume). Older adults select more easily familiar social partners over new informative contacts (Fredrickson & Carstensen, 1990), which reduces their social network to their closest ties. Compared with younger respondents, they selectively remember more positive than negative attributes of the options they have chosen in the past (Mather & Johnson, 2000). These effects could lead older adults to prefer longer-established brands that they have known for a long time rather than new brands.

Attachment

Older consumers may develop strong bonds on the basis of their longer interactions with certain brands. These may form outside the "sensitive period" hypothesized by Holbrook and Schindler. Thomson, MacInnis, and Park (2005, p. 77) extended the parent–infant relationship (Bowlby, 1979) to their definition of attachment as "an emotion-laden target-specific bond between a person and a specific object." Kleine and Baker (2004) also found that attachments to objects mirror those to other people, such that continuous activities undertaken with the object (e.g., cleaning, displaying, discussing) imbue it with greater meaning. For Thomson and colleagues (2005), strong attachments required time, repeated interactions, and memories that pertained specifically to the object and thereby encouraged the person to invest the object with greater meaning. Price, Arnould, and Curasi (2000, p. 188), analyzing the "cherished possessions" of respondents aged 65 years and older, cited a verbatim: "It's almost like a history of our life." Attachment evolves according to self-meaning, such that brand choices made during the coming-of-age period may not satisfy the goals of a mature adult. This mature adult then may make new brand choices and initiate new attachments.

Expertise

Previous research often suggested expertise (Alba & Hutchinson, 1987) as the key reason older consumers consider fewer brands or may be more likely to make a repeat purchase. Through their longer experience, older consumers develop expertise, identify the brands that suit them best, and thus do not need to investigate other options any longer. This reasoning could explain the reduced consideration sets, higher repeat purchase rates, and preference for longer-established brands among older consumers. However, this rationale also assumes, in some sense, that the market and the available options remain identical over time, so that expertise, once acquired, remains valid (as it might for, say, chess or piano playing or knowledge of classical literature).

Consider the contrast between the automobile market and frequently purchased goods. Car purchases occur at long time intervals, during which the models offered change markedly, so even experienced purchasers cannot rely only on knowledge they have accumulated from past purchases to make a choice among current models. Many markets for durables change rapidly, such as high-tech consumer electronics. In contrast, in frequently purchased categories, the offerings change minimally, or not at all, between purchase occasions; thus, accumulated expertise is much less subject to obsolescence. Lambert-Pandraud and colleagues (2005) found that self-reported expertise with cars leads respondents to search for more, rather than less, information before purchasing a new car.

Habits

The repeat purchase of a brand could be driven by habit, developed through a history of repeatedly purchasing that brand, which then leads automatically to a propensity to repeat the behavior in an unconscious manner (Drolet, Suppes, & Bodapati, 2009). According to Drolet (2008, p. 21), "As people age, the relationships between associations and stimuli and those between associations and behaviors become increasingly reinforced. Therefore, the elderly are more likely to activate (through external stimuli) and rely on habits to make decisions." Hence, "the average stated likelihood of buying the same item on the next shopping occasion was higher for the elderly versus young" (Drolet, Suppes, et al., 2009, p. 23). This adaptation may be a useful way to compensate for age-related declines in cognitive and other abilities. However, there should be differences across product categories. For example, such routinization should be more likely for brands sold in supermarkets, where the frequency of purchases by definition is much higher, which creates more opportunities for developing associations in memory, especially if the available options remain identical across successive purchase occasions. However, routinization should be less likely for durable goods, whose infrequent purchase creates too few opportunities to develop associations, especially if the options change markedly between successive purchase occasions.

Nostalgia

Although the word *nostalgia* originally was coined to describe a long-ing for a native country, Holbrook and Schindler (1991, p. 330) defined it as "a preference ... toward objects (people, places, or things) that were more common (popular, fashionable, or widely circulated) when one was younger (in early adulthood, in adolescence, in childhood, or even before birth)." Psychologists explained that a person has an early critical period in terms of psychological development (Schindler & Holbrook, 2003, p. 277). Holbrook and Schindler (1994, p. 414) further explained that "consumers form enduring aesthetic preferences during a sensitive period," specifi-cally their "late adolescence or early adulthood" (Holbrook & Schindler, 1989, p. 119) or "late teens and early twenties" (Schindler & Holbrook, 1993, p. 551), and they suggested that consumers maintain these early imprinted preferences for the rest of their lives. Note that this claim is similar to the results of the famous Bennington study (Alwin, Cohen, & Newcomb, 1991) that noted the persistence of political preferences people acquire during their college years.

The specific limits of this formative period are somewhat uncertain, however. Consumers most like pop songs introduced when they were about 23 years of age (Holbrook & Schindler, 1989), fashion styles that emerged when they were 33 (Schindler & Holbrook, 1993), movies stars from when they were about 14 (Holbrook & Schindler, 1994), motion pic-tures awarded an Oscar when they were about 27 (Holbrook & Schindler, 1996), and automobiles from when they were about 26 (scored by male subjects; Schindler & Holbrook, 2003). This stream of research consid-ered salient but unbranded items, such as pop songs, movie stars, motion pictures, and car models, but its main hypothesis likely can be extended to predict nostalgic preferences for brands encountered in consumers' youth as well.

Cohort Effects

In the mechanisms described, consumers change their behavior as they age. As an alternative explanation, these differences may be due to a cohort effect: Consumers from different cohorts behave differently. In this con-text, a cohort is "the aggregate of individuals who experienced the same event within the same time interval" (Rentz, Reynolds, & Stout, 1983, p. 12; based on Ryder, 1965). For a focus on brand choice, the experiences to con-sider should not be major events that occurred when persons came of age, such as the Vietnam war (as in Meredith & Schewe, 2002), but rather the brand situation at a particular time. In the French car market, for example, why could we expect that older cohorts would have a higher rate of repeat purchases, favor longer-established brands, and consider fewer models?

This could be linked to the market structure that existed in France when each cohort came of age and became interested in cars. When older people came of age, the market belonged almost entirely to a few French brands, including the three that still remain the market leaders (Renault, Peugeot, and Citroën), and each of these offered only a few models. Breakdowns were frequent and largely regarded as normal. When younger cohorts came of age, dozens of foreign brands had appeared, the number of available models was massive, and breakdowns were rare, such that consumers who faced a breakdown might switch to another brand.

Thus, multiple mechanisms likely underlie the phenomena associated with brand choice. Some mechanisms predict only some of these phenomena. This gap leaves multiple research questions, as reviewed in the next section.

Questions for Further Research

Testing the Impact of Cognitive Variables

Previous marketing literature mostly offered affective mechanisms, mainly nostalgia, to explain preferences for long-known options. Thus, the impact of cognitive factors provides an alternative avenue for interesting research. As indicated, reduced cognitive resources may lead consumers to simplify their purchase processes by considering fewer options or repeating their previous choices. In turn, a first question pertains to whether cognitive factors can explain why older consumers focus more on longer-established brands, repeat purchase more, and so forth. If they do, which cognitive factor is primarily at play? Are the observed differences in brand choices due to memory problems, or do central slowdowns in processing speed and short-term memory capacity lead older consumers to resort to simplifying heuristics, such as repeat purchases? Cognitive factors also may influence specific stages of the choice process, such as information search or consideration, and additional research should attempt to identify these effects. Moreover, assume memory is important; then, is it that consumers encode brand information more easily when they are younger, so that longer-established brands, or information about them, are more likely to be encoded in long-term memory than more recent brands? Or, is it that all brands are equally well encoded, but that among older persons, retrieval is easier when it comes to information encoded at a younger age, which usually means information about longer-established brands? Finally, do cognitive factors play a role for products bought in a recognition context, such as fast-moving consumer goods displayed on a supermarket shelf?

Specific Measures of Affective and Cognitive Variables

Previous marketing literature mostly used age as the operational explanatory variable. For example, Holbrook and Schindler (1994) statistically analyzed the impact of age on option preferences to support their theory about nostalgia. This reliance on age may result from the operational constraints on using secondary data (e.g., panel data) about brand choice, which rarely include information about psychological variables, whether affective or cognitive. However, it would be interesting to develop specific measures of such variables in addition to measuring age itself. For example, to assess the possible impact of cognitive decline on brand choice, researchers need to measure cognitive ability, separately from age, to assess whether cognitive decline mediates, totally or partially, the impact of age on brand choice (i.e., preference for older brands, repeat purchase, reduced consideration sets).

Precise Specification of Age-Related Differences

Nostalgia, attachment, and socioemotional selectivity make different predictions about the shape of age-related effects. According to the nostalgia approach, a consumer maintains preferences acquired ("imprinted") early but does not develop new preferences after the end of that formative period. In contrast, the attachment approach suggests a consumer can initiate an emotional attachment at any age, even after the formative period ends. The effects of socioemotional selectivity reportedly occur when persons perceive their horizon as limited, typically because of old age, not when persons grow older but do not suffer from this feeling, such as moving from their 40s to their 50s or from 20s to 30s. These contrasting predictions suggest different specifications of the impact of age on brand choice; these specifications should be tested against one another.

Expertise

On average, expertise should increase with experience and therefore with age. However, these variables also require separate measures for any analysis of their relationships and to assess their impact on brand choice phenomena. Involvement in a product category and frequent usage may explain expertise better than age. Certain categories evolve very quickly, such as those that rely on technological innovations and the appearance of new models, in which case expertise may be uncorrelated or negatively correlated with experience. Brand choice also may offer a dynamic setting for the impact of expertise compared with the immutable setting of, say, chess. In addition, experts may be able to collect more complete information and analyze it with greater complexity and thereby exercise their judgment on a more informed basis. That is, expertise may lead to larger consideration sets or more complex choice processes.

Research Across Adulthood

Should we consider that changes occur after mature adulthood, when consumers turn, say, 60 or 70 years? Or, is the change process continuous, beginning as early perhaps as a person's 20s? In most brand choice studies, observed variables changed in a continuous and often linear manner over adulthood. This trend also emerged for fundamental psychological variables, such as processing speed and working memory capacity. Therefore, to answer the new research questions evoked by this chapter, researchers should go beyond a simple contrast between respondents of college age and respondents 65 years and older; they should study age-related changes in brand choice processes (and more generally, consumer behavior) more systematically across adulthood and over a broad range of ages.

Impact on Consumer Satisfaction in Daily Life

Research that shows older consumers have different choice processes, which lead to different brand choices, leaves open the question of the practical consequences of these differences on consumer satisfaction. For example, according to socioemotional selectivity theory, older persons give more weight to affective factors, which logically leads them to prefer long-known options that become the most satisfying solution for them. Equally, some difference certainly should exist between the level of satisfaction resulting from a brand choice that derives from a smaller consideration set, largely focused on the previously purchased brand, and a theoretically "optimal" brand choice based on a sophisticated analysis that takes into consideration all available information about all brands. Yet, this difference may have only marginal value, such that the buyer, at the end of the simplified purchase process, may be reasonably satisfied with the product chosen. As discussed, developing habits may be an efficient way for persons with reduced cognitive ability to make satisfying choices. Again, research therefore should distinguish among stable and mature markets and those that change rapidly, in which older buyers may routinely choose options that have grown obsolete.

Public Policy

Depending on the mechanisms at work, the public policy implications of this research are very different. If older buyers are handicapped mostly by cognitive declines, they may benefit from external guidance and support, which would give them easier, more complete access to all market opportunities, especially in fast-changing categories, such as consumer electronics. However, such public policy guidance and support must be carefully designed because source memory weakens in older consumers (Law, Hawkins, & Craik, 1998), which may create confusion between commercial and consumerist sources (Skurnik, Yoon, Park, & Schwarz, 2006). In addition, any adopted policies should be careful not to interfere with heuristics or habits that consumers may have developed to compensate for age-related declines in cognitive and other abilities. For an older car buyer, limiting the consideration set to a small number of well-known brands may be a useful process to avoid the consequences of reduced ability to encode and analyze complex data about many new brands.

Age–Cohort–Period

As discussed, differences in a cross-sectional data set between older and younger consumers might be due to an aging effect or to a cohort effect. To separate the two, as Rentz and colleagues (1983) demonstrated, researchers need to analyze similar data at different dates. However, with such data, a third effect may be at work, namely, a period effect: Consumers tend to behave similarly on the same date but differently on different dates. These potential effects create a major statistical problem because perfect collinearity exists among the three variables. That is, if a cohort depends on the person's birth year and the period equals the year of observation, by definition, Age = Period – Cohort. In a regression approach, the matrix of explanatory variables does not achieve full rank, and the ordinary least-squares estimate cannot be computed because the same predicted values (and errors) would be obtained by different combinations of the age, period, and cohort coefficients. Despite the proposals of several solutions to this difficulty, they all pose problems, and there remains room for the development of better statistical methods.

Other Data Issues

Age is obviously an exogenous variable and can be easily measured, but existing analyses often bear on underlying mechanisms and therefore the hypothesized roles of mediating variables influenced by age (or birth date) that reportedly influence the dependent variables related to brand choice. Some variables, although strongly influenced by age, are conceptually different and should be measured separately. A typical example includes measures of the current cognitive ability of each respondent (e.g., processing speed, working memory capacity). A more difficult case pertains to the value of the same variables at a particular point in the past, such as the cognitive ability that an 80-year-old person had when the specific brand launched 20 years prior. This variable seems impossible to measure. A third case entails past values of certain variables that may be measured by retrospective questions, such as the brand of a person's first car. The degree of reliability of the answer likely varies according to the topic: A respondent is more likely to remember the brand of his or her first car than the brand of an initial purchase in a frequently purchased category such as coffee. In addition, the quality of the retrospective data may be jeopardized by a respondent's level of cognitive decline.

Some of the mechanisms discussed attempted to predict differences across cohorts (e.g., Holbrook and Schindler's (1989) analysis of preferences for music styles as a function of birth year), whereas others predicted differences within cohorts (e.g., persons with different degrees of cognitive decline or different perceived time horizons may behave differently). The latter approach requires individual-level data, whereas the former can employ data aggregated at the cohort level. For analyses that cannot collect actual panel data (i.e., repeated observations of the same subjects), researchers might use pseudopanels (i.e., same cohorts observed repeatedly, using different individuals for each observation date).

Some brand choice phenomena appear difficult to reproduce or simulate in a lab through the use of new, artificial material and relatively young subjects, such as college students. In most categories, competing brands have been introduced at different dates, and a consumer therefore has multiple opportunities to encounter and encode them, including at different ages (a brand introduced when he or she was 15 years of age versus one introduced when the consumer was 60) and over different lengths of time (if the consumer is now 61, he or she had the opportunity to encounter the first brand for 46 years versus just 1 year for the second brand). Such differences in encoding opportunities may be a cause of the brand choice differences observed today.

References

Alba, J. W., & Hutchinson, J. W. (1987), Dimensions of consumer expertise, *Journal of Consumer Research*, 13, 411–455.

Alwin, D. F., Cohen, R. L., & Newcomb, T. M. (1991), *Political attitudes over the lifespan: The Bennington women after fifty years*, Madison: University of Wisconsin Press.

Aurier, P., & Jean, S. (1996), L'ensemble de considération du consommateur: une approche "personne*objet*situation," in J. M. Aurifeille (Ed.), *Actes du 12° Congrès Annuel de l'Association Française du Marketing* (pp. 599–614), ESCP Europe, Paris.

Barrère, Hélène (Ed.) (1992), *La relation psychosociale avec les personnes âgées*. Toulouse, France: Privat.

Birren, James E., & Schaie, K. Warner (2006), *Handbook of the psychology of aging* (6th ed.), Amsterdam: Elsevier.

Botwinick, Jack (1966), Cautiousness in advanced age, *Journal of Gerontology*, 21, 347–353.

Botwinick, Jack (1978), *Cautiousness in decision, aging and behavior*, New York: Springer, pp. 128–141.

Bowlby, John (1979), *The making and breaking of affectional bonds*, London: Tavistock.

Bryan, Janet, & Luszcz, Mary A. (1996), Speed of information processing as a mediator between age and free-recall performance, *Psychology and Aging*, 11, 3–9.

Campbell, Brian M. (1969), *The existence and determinants of evoked set in brand choice behavior*, doctoral dissertation, Columbia University, New York.

Carstensen, Laura L., Isaacowitz, Derek M., & Charles, Susan T. (1999), Taking time seriously. A theory of socioemotional selectivity, *American Psychologist*, 54, 165–181.

Cattin, Philippe, & Punj, Girish (1983), Identifying the characteristics of single retail (dealer) visit new automobile buyers, *Advances in Consumer Research*, 10, 383–388.

Cole, Catherine A., & Balasubramanian, Siva K. (1993), Age differences in consumers' search for information: Public policy implications, *Journal of Consumer Research*, 20, 157–169.

Deshpandé, Rohit, & Krishnan, S. (1981), Correlates of deficient consumer information environments: The case of the elderly, *Advances in Consumer Research*, 9, 515–519.

Deshpandé, Rohit, & Zaltman, G. (1978), The impact of elderly consumer dissatisfaction and buying experience on information search: A path-analytic approach, in R. L. Day & H. K. Hunt (Eds.), *Third annual conference on consumer satisfaction, dissatisfaction and complaining behavior* (pp. 145–152), Bloomington, IN: Indiana University.

Drolet, Aimee (2008), Aging and habit in decision making and brand choice by older consumers, HEC Paris; Cahiers de Recherche.

Drolet, Aimee, Suppes, Patrick, & Bodapati, A. V. (2009), *Habits and free associations: Free your mind and mind your habits* (Working Paper), Los Angeles: University of California.

Fredrickson, Barbara L., & Carstensen, L.L. (1990), Choosing social partners: How old age and anticipated endings make people more selective, *Psychology and Aging*, 5, 335–347.

Furse, David H., Punj, G. N., & Stewart, D. W. (1984), A typology of individual search strategies among purchasers of new automobiles, *Journal of Consumer Research*, 10, 417–431.

Gruca, Thomas S. (1989), Determinants of choice set size: An alternative method for measuring evoked sets, *Advances in Consumer Research*, 16, 515–521.

Hauser, John, Tellis, G. J., & Griffin, A. (2006), Research on innovation: A review and agenda for *Marketing Science*, *Marketing Science*, 25, 6, 687–717.

Hirschman, Elizabeth (1980), Innovativeness, novelty seeking and consumer creativity, *Journal of Consumer Research*, 7, 283–295.

Holbrook, Morris B., & Schindler, R. M. (1989), Some exploratory findings on the development of musical tastes, *Journal of Consumer Research*, 16, 119–124.

Holbrook, Morris B., & Schindler, R. M. (1991), Echoes of the dear past: Some work in progress on nostalgia, *Advances in Consumer Research*, 18, 330–333.

Holbrook, Morris B., & Schindler, R. M. (1994), Age, sex, and attitude towards the past as predictors of consumers' aesthetic tastes for cultural products, *Journal of Marketing Research*, 31, 412–422.

Holbrook, Morris B., & Schindler, R. M. (1996), Market segmentation based on age and attitude toward the past: Concepts, methods and findings concerning nostalgic influences on customer tastes, *Journal of Business Research*, 37, 27–39.

Isaacowitz, Derek M., Charles, S. T., & Carstensen, L. L. (2000), Emotion and cognition, in F. I. M. Craik & T. A. Salthouse (Eds.), *The handbook of aging and cognition* (2nd ed., pp. 593–631), London: Erlbaum.

Johnson, Mitzi M. S. (1990), Age differences in decision making: A process methodology for examining strategic information processing, *Journal of Gerontology: Psychological Sciences*, 45, 75–78.

Kleine, Susan Schultz, & Baker, S. M. (2004), An integrative review of material possession attachment, *Academy of Marketing Science Review* [Online], 1–36, http://www.amsreview.org/articles/kleine01–2004.pdf.

Lambert-Pandraud, Raphaëlle, Laurent, G., & Lapersonne, E. (2005), Repeat purchasing of new automobiles by older consumers: Empirical evidence and interpretations, *Journal of Marketing*, 69, 97–103.

Lambert-Pandraud, Raphaëlle, & Laurent, G. (2009), Why do older consumers buy older brands? The role of attachment and declining innovations. Working paper, Paris: ESCP Europe.

Lapersonne, Eric, Laurent, G., & Le Goff, J.-J. (1995), Consideration sets of size one: An empirical investigation of automobile purchases, *International Journal of Research in Marketing*, 12, 55–66.

Law, Sharmistha, Hawkins, S. A., & Craik, F. I. M. (1998), Repetition induced belief in the elderly: Rehabilitating age-related memory deficits, *Journal of Consumer Research*, 25, 91–107.

Lesser, Jack A., & Kunkel, S. R. (1991), Exploratory and problem-solving consumer behavior across the life span, *Journal of Gerontology: Psychological Sciences*, 46, 259–269.

Maddox, Neil R., Gronhaug, K., Homans, R. E., & May, F. E. (1978), Correlates of information gathering and evoked set size for new automobile purchasers in Norway and in the U.S., *Advances in Consumer Research*, 5, 167–170.

Mather, Mara, & Johnson, M. K. (2000), Choice-supportive source monitoring: Do our decisions seem better to us as we age? *Psychology and Aging*, 15, 596–606.

Meredith, Geoffrey, & Schewe, C. D. (2002), *Defining markets, defining moments: America's 7 generational cohorts, their shared experiences and why business should care*, New York: Wiley.

Park, D. C., & Gutchess, A. H. (2004), Long-term memory and aging: A cognitive neuroscience perspective, in R. Cabeza, L. Nyberg, & D. C. Park (Eds.), *Cognitive neuroscience of aging: Linking cognitive and cerebral aging* (pp. 218–245), New York: Oxford University Press.

Price, Linda L., Arnould, E. J., & Curasi, C. F. (2000), Older consumers' disposition of special possessions, *Journal of Consumer Research*, 27, 179–201.

Rentz, O. Joseph, Reynolds, F. D., & Stout, R. G. (1983), Analyzing changing consumption patterns with cohort analysis, *Journal of Marketing Research*, 20, 12–20.

Rogers, E. M. (2003), *Diffusion of innovations* (5th ed.), New York: Free Press.

Rogers, E. M., & Shoemaker, F. F. (1971), *Communication of innovations*, New York: Free Press.

Ryder, Norman B. (1965), The cohort as a concept in the study of social change, *American Sociological Review*, 30, 843–861.

Salthouse, Timothy A. (1996), The processing-speed theory of adult age differences in cognition, *Psychological Review*, 103, 403–428.

Salthouse, Timothy A., & Ferrer-Caja, E. (2003), What needs to be explained to account for age-related effects on multiple cognitive variables? *Psychology and Aging*, 18, 91–110.

Schaie, K. Warner (1996), Intellectual development in adulthood, in J. E. Birren & K. W. Schaie (Eds.), *Handbook of the psychology of aging* (pp. 266–281), San Diego: Academic Press.

Schindler, Robert M., & Holbrook, M. B. (1993), Critical periods in the development of men's and women's tastes in personal appearance, *Psychology & Marketing*, 10, 549–564.

Schindler, Robert M., & Holbrook, M. B. (2003), Nostalgia for early experience as a determinant of consumer preferences, *Psychology & Marketing*, 20, 275–302.

Skurnik, Ian, Yoon, C., Park, D., & Schwarz, N. (2006), How warnings become recommendations: Paradoxical effects of warnings on beliefs of older consumers, *Journal of Consumer Research*, 31, 713–724.

Srinivasan, Narasimhan, & Ratchford, B. T. (1991), An empirical test of a model of external search for automobiles, *Journal of Consumer Research*, 18, 233–242.

Tellis, Gerard J., Yin, E., & Bell, S. (2005), *Global consumer innovativeness: Country differences and individual commonalities* (Working Paper), Los Angeles: University of Southern California.

Thomson, Matthew, MacInnis, D. J., & Park, C. W. (2005), The ties that bind: Measuring the strength of consumers' emotional attachments to brands, *Journal of Consumer Psychology*, 15, 77–91.

Uncles, Mark D., & Ehrenberg, A. S. C. (1990), Brand choice among older consumers, *Journal of Advertising Research*, 30, 19–22.

Uncles, Mark D., & Lee, D. (2006), Brand purchasing by older consumers: An investigation using the Juster scale and the Dirichlet model, *Marketing Letters*, 17, 17–29.

Wallach, M. A., & Kogan, N. (1961), Aspects of judgment and decision making: Interrelationships and changes with age, *Behavioral Science*, 6, 23–36.

Zelinski, Elizabeth M., & Burnight, K. P. (1997), Sixteen-year longitudinal and time lag changes in memory and cognition in older adults, *Psychology and Aging*, 12, 503–513.

10

Why Do Older Consumers Tell Us They Are More Satisfied?

Carolyn Yoon, Fred Feinberg, and Norbert Schwarz
University of Michigan

Introduction

A common consumer complaint is that "they don't make things the way they used to" (e.g., Moore, 2005). From appliances to furniture and cars, products presumably were sturdier and more reliable in the past. Combined with older people's general tendency to reminisce about the "good old days" (Bohlmeijer, Roemer, Cuijpers, & Smit, 2007), this complaint might lead one to believe that older consumers are less satisfied with what the marketplace has to offer than younger consumers, who presumably do not know any better. Nothing could be more misleading. Empirically, older consumers reliably report higher customer satisfaction levels than younger consumers, irrespective of demographic characteristics or business sector (Fornell et al., 2005). Moreover, this finding is robust and holds across different countries and cultures (e.g., United States, Sweden, China) and different response modes (e.g., self-report questionnaire, telephone interviewing).

The first section of this chapter illustrates this "older-and-more-satisfied" effect with cross-sectional data, drawing on the American Customer Satisfaction Index (ACSI). The general phenomenon of older consumers' higher customer satisfaction has received little attention, and viable explanations are missing. The bulk of the chapter begins to fill this gap by reviewing a host of different processes that may plausibly contribute to the older-and-more-satisfied effect. Few of these processes are mutually exclusive, and the available data do not allow us to evaluate their empirical merit and relative contribution. Accordingly, we focus on offering plausible hypotheses and discuss what would be needed to test them. We hope that our conjectures will set the stage for the systematic investigation of a fascinating question: Why do older consumers report higher customer satisfaction? On the theoretical side, addressing this question promises new insights into core issues of consumer behavior, from consumers' perception of changes in the marketplace to changes in customers' expectations over time, and from the role of accumulating expertise in the consumption domain to the role of age-related changes in the judgment process. On the applied side, the sheer fact that one of every five Americans will be age 65 or older by 2030 renders an understanding of age and cohort differences in customer satisfaction of utmost importance for marketers.

Older and More Satisfied: Findings From the American Customer Satisfaction Index

The ACSI, established in 1994, consists of cross-sectional data representing customer satisfaction with products and services of over 200 companies in 45 industries, as well as government agencies (see Fornell, Johnson, Anderson, Cha, & Bryant, 1996, for a detailed description of the ACSI). ACSI data are collected every year from individual customers via telephone. Potential customer respondents are selected from probability samples by screening for a randomly chosen adult (age 18 and over) in each telephone household. Respondents are asked questions about the purchase and use of specific products and services, and those who qualify as respondents are then asked specific questions related to customer satisfaction, expectations of overall quality, and complaint behavior, among other variables, for a specific company. The ASCI is based on interviews with more than 75,000 customers annually.

Analysis of 15 years (1994 to 2008) of cross-sectional ACSI data, across all industries, show an overall positive relationship between age and satisfaction for a broad variety of products and services: As consumers age, they report, as a cohort, being more satisfied. Figure 10.1a shows mean ASCI ratings (based on a response scale of 1 to 10) as a function of customers' age in 2008. Overall, satisfaction scores were higher by 0.8 points, or almost 10%, from the youngest (18–49) to the oldest (over 79) cohort. Figure 10.1b shows the mean ASCI ratings in 2008 as a function of customers' age for three selected industries—automobiles, hospitals, and electric service utilities—with satisfaction scores following a similar increasing trend with age.

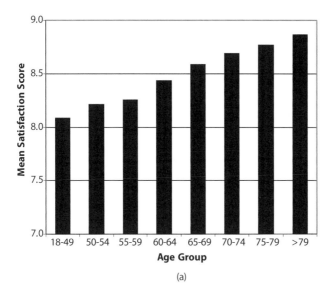

(a)

FIGURE 10.1

(a) Mean customer satisfaction scores averaged over 45 industries, by age group, in 2008.

Assessing the degree to which age ties into satisfaction is complicated by the noisiness of individual-level satisfaction data. This can be largely overcome by examining the *average* satisfaction score for each age level represented in the sample, from 18 to 97, that is, 80 ages in all. Correlation can then be assessed by performing a weighted least-squares regression, with weights proportional to group size (e.g., there were 930 thirty-year-olds, 2,244 sixty-year-olds, but only 86 ninety-year-olds in the year 2008 data set used). The overall (group-size weighted) correlation between age and average satisfaction score was .90, suggesting a very strong positive association. The coefficient on age was 0.0153, meaning each 10-year increase in age roughly translated—when all other variable effects were averaged out—into a 0.15 increase in mean satisfaction score, a nontrivial difference given the "grand mean" satisfaction score of 8.31.

Further analyses of the ACSI data were conducted, testing the relationship between age and satisfaction scores for 45 industries, while controlling for education, income, and gender. The strength of the relationship between age and customer satisfaction across different industries is reported in Table 10.1. The rightmost column of the table indicates the percentage of years (for all the years for which data are available for a given industry) for which there was a significant positive effect of age on customer satisfaction (at $p < .10$). "Strong" effects of age were indicated in 33 of 45 (73%) industries (using a cutoff of 2/3 of all the years showing significance), and more moderate effects (at least 25% of the years showing

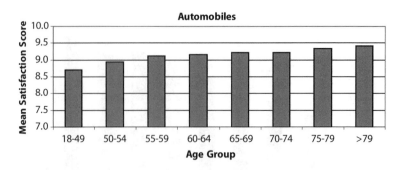

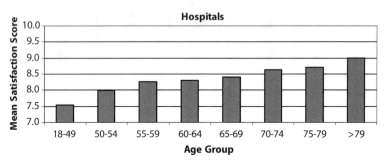

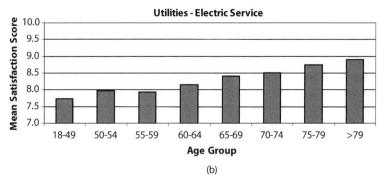

(b)

FIGURE 10.1 (continued)
(b) Mean customer satisfaction scores, by age group, for three specific industries in 2008.

significance) were observed in an additional 9 of 45 (20%) industries. Interestingly, satisfaction did not appear to increase with age in three industries, all related to the media: newspaper publishing, TV broadcasting, and motion pictures.

As shown in Figure 10.2, the overall trend primarily seemed to be driven by an age-related increase in the likelihood of endorsing a value of 10, indicative of very high satisfaction: The older the age group, the greater the proportion of ACSI respondents within that group reporting very high satisfaction scores. This effect held uniformly at the aggregate level

TABLE 10.1

Number of Years With Significant Effects of Age on Customer Satisfaction
Scores Across ACSI Industries, Controlling for Education, Income, and Gender
(Sorted Alphabetically by Industries, Within Each Set of Industries With
Strong, Moderate, or Weak Effects)

Industry	Number of Years of ACSI Data (1994–2008)	Percentage of Years With Significant Effects of Age (at $p < .10$)
Strong Effects		
Airlines, scheduled	15	100
Apparel	15	67
Automobiles	15	93
Banks	15	93
Beverages, beer	15	73
Cellular phone manufacturers	6	100
Cellular phone service providers	5	100
Department and discount stores	15	100
E-business travel service	6	83
Electronic auction	5	100
Electronic financial services	6	83
Electronic retail services	6	83
Food processing	15	93
Garbage pickup, city	11	100
Garbage pickup, suburban	9	89
Gas service stations	15	93
Health care insurance	6	83
Hospitals	15	100
Hotels	15	67
Life insurance	15	80
Parcel delivery, express mail	15	67
Personal care products	15	93
Personal computers	15	87
Personal property insurance	15	87
Police, city	11	91
Police, suburban	9	100
Restaurants, limited service	14	100
Specialty stores	8	100
Supermarkets	15	100
Telecommunications, cable television	7	71
Telecommunications, local	15	100
Telecommunications, long distance	14	100
Utilities, electric service	12	100

continued

TABLE 10.1 (continued)
Number of Years With Significant Effects of Age on Customer Satisfaction
Scores Across ACSI Industries, Controlling for Education, Income, and Gender
(Sorted Alphabetically by Industries, Within Each Set of Industries With
Strong, Moderate, or Weak Effects)

Industry	Number of Years of ACSI Data (1994–2008)	Percentage of Years With Significant Effects of Age (at $p < .10$)
Moderate Effects		
Athletic shoes	14	29
Beverages, soft drinks	15	60
Consumer electronics, TV/VCR/DVD player	15	60
E-business news and information	5	40
Health and personal care stores	7	57
Household appliances	15	33
Pet foods	12	42
Tobacco, cigarettes	15	33
U.S. Postal Service	15	27
Weak Effects		
Motion pictures	15	13
Newspaper publishing	15	0
TV broadcasting	15	0

Note: For expository purposes, the cutoff for "strong" was set at 2/3 of the years for which data were available, while that for "moderate" was 25%.

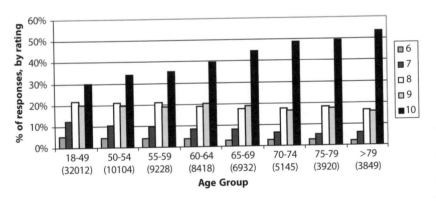

FIGURE 10.2
Percentage of responses, by rating, for each age group. *Note:* Total sample size for each age group appears in parentheses. Ratings of 1 through 5 were roughly equivalent across age groups and are not shown in this figure.

for each of the 15 years. A noteworthy exception occurred in the same three media industries (newspaper publishing, TV broadcasting, motion pictures), which did not reveal a positive relationship between age and satisfaction scores; the tendency to report customer satisfaction ratings of 10 did not hold in any of the 15 years.

A parallel age trend has been observed in the literature on general life satisfaction (e.g., Diener, Suh, Lucas, & Smith, 1999; Ehrlich & Isaacowitz, 2002; Yang, 2008). As is the case for customer satisfaction, life satisfaction increased with age, except for the final years of terminal decline. While these parallel trends may reflect similar processes, they also suggest a conceptual distinction: whether a specific individual is more satisfied overall or is more *easily* satisfied by a specific experience. The former could well refer to an "omnibus test" of life (or consumer) satisfaction: Do things seem better in one's life now, perhaps compared with how they used to be? The latter refers instead to one's "reservation level," that is, one's expectations for *new* things and situations encountered, even if those things are familiar (e.g., how well one expects to be treated by salespeople or to like a product one has bought many times before). The latter is what most closely aligns with standard definitions of customer satisfaction and with our focus in the present chapter.

Studies of customer complaint behavior appear to accord with greater customer satisfaction as people age. Lee and Soberon-Ferrer (1999), in a survey using telephone interviews conducted on a national sample, found lower reports of dissatisfying experiences among older consumers (age 65 and over) compared to their younger counterparts (age 18–64). Analysis of the ACSI data appeared to support these prior findings; to the extent there was a significant effect of age on complaint behavior, older consumers complained less than younger consumers. Also consistent with the older-and-more-satisfied phenomenon are findings regarding brand preference and choice by older consumers. For example, older buyers of cars tend to favor longer-established brands (Furse, Punj, & Stewart, 1984; Lambert-Pandraud, Laurent, & Lapersonne, 2005). Accordingly, older consumers are more likely to exhibit repeat purchase behavior, buying the same car brand as their previous one (Lambert-Pandraud et al., 2005).

Importantly, the nature of the ASCI dictates that all findings are based on cross-sectional data, which imposes limits on the feasible comparisons and interpretations. What the data show is merely that, at a given point in time, older consumers report higher satisfaction than younger consumers. This may reflect an effect of individual aging or a cohort difference. On the one hand, satisfaction may increase with age, such that a given person becomes more satisfied over the life course; if so, the currently young can also be expected to be increasingly satisfied as they age. On the other hand, older cohorts differ from younger cohorts in their lifetime of consumption experiences and expectations. These historic differences may give rise

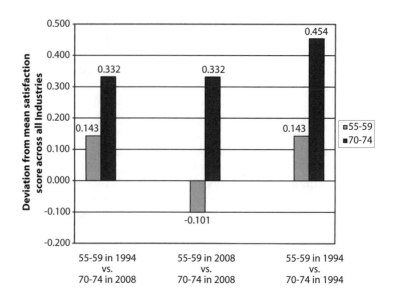

FIGURE 10.3

Comparisons of mean customer satisfaction scores across all industries for (left to right) same birth cohorts across time (1994 vs. 2008); different age cohorts in 2008; and different age cohorts in 1994. *Note*: All differences within comparison pairs are significant at $p < .0001$.

to differential satisfaction with current consumption, suggesting that the currently young may not become more satisfied as they age. While our data did not lend themselves to a conclusive test of these possibilities, we gauged their likely plausibility by comparing the satisfaction levels of the same birth cohort at different ages. Figure 10.3 (leftmost set of bars) does so for respondents born 1938 to 1944, who were aged 55 to 59 in 1994 and aged 70 to 74 in 2008 (Comparison 1). The middle set of bars compares groups aged 55–59 and 70–74 in 2008 (Comparison 2), and the rightmost set of bars compares groups aged 55–59 and 70–74 in 1994 (Comparison 3). As shown, the same birth cohort provided higher satisfaction scores in 2008 than in 1994; further, the other comparisons showed that the older cohort (aged 70 to 74) was more satisfied in both 1994 and 2008. This pattern of findings across comparisons thus favors an aging account, rather than a cohort account, of age differences in customer satisfaction.

Next, we turn to possible explanations for the older-and-more-satisfied phenomenon. They can be broadly classified into explanations based on (a) historical changes in the economy or society over time (i.e., external factors) and individual changes of consumers over the life course that affect either (b) consumers' behavior, decision making, and judgment or (c) the process of answering satisfaction questions. Moreover, (d) the available findings are open to methodological accounts in terms of heterogeneity among consumers, covariate effects, and various interactions. We discuss these explanations, delineate possible underlying processes, and note the types of studies needed to test them. We hope that our discussion stimulates researchers in economics, marketing, psychology, and sociology to take interest in the phenomenon of higher satisfaction among the elderly and to consider how the expertise and data of their disciplines can be brought to bear on its explanation.

Explanations Based on Changes in External Factors

Long-Term Differences in Product Quality and Need Satisfaction

One possible explanation of the older-and-more-satisfied effect is illustrated by a variant of the complaint that "they don't make things they way they used to": "They don't, thank goodness. They make them so much better!" (Graphically Speaking, 2009). From this perspective, older consumers have experienced many improvements in the way in which products satisfy basic consumer needs. For example, the advent of antibiotics, plastics, transistor-based electronics, and consumer aviation provided, respectively, relief from bacterial infections, durable packaging, compact/portable entertainment, and practical long-distance transportation. In many cases, the specific products and technologies are new, but the consumer needs for which they provide solutions are not (Levitt, 1960), allowing for meaningful comparisons of need satisfaction over time. This account treats the observed cross-sectional differences as a cohort effect. Identifying such cohort effects in the domain of subjective well-being, Elder (1974) reported that the "children of the great depression" were more likely to report high life satisfaction the more they had to suffer under adverse economic conditions when they were adolescents. The accumulation of early negative experiences presumably established a baseline against which subsequent events could only be seen as an improvement.

From this perspective, the older-and-more-satisfied effect is a function of actual improvements in the extent to which consumers' needs are met. Hence, the size of the older-and-more-satisfied effect should be predicted by objective improvements in a consumption domain. Conversely, older consumers should be less satisfied than younger consumers in domains in which need satisfaction has deteriorated over time, although our data do not include any domain in which older consumers reported significantly lower satisfaction. Assuming that suitable indicators of changes in objective product quality over time can be identified, these issues lend themselves to statistical modeling and provide a promising avenue for systematic testing.

However, in stark contrast to the optimistic assumption that the marketplace offers ever-higher need satisfaction, older consumers often lament what they perceive as declines when comparing specific products. Anecdotes suggest that perhaps the most common such complaint involves durability since few products other than housing are built to last decades any longer (e.g., furniture, electronics) (Bayus, 1998; Cooper, 2004). Technology- and labor-driven market forces are progressively pushing "high-quality" items and "high-service" firms to the periphery of a cost-driven global market, reducing the number of repairable items and service people capable of repairing them (Nevius, 2005). Balancing the contrasting effects of increases in certain aspects of quality (e.g., new features on phones) and decreases in other aspects (e.g., durability) can be particularly subtle for older consumers. Research teasing out and assessing these effects could take many forms. Among these is having older consumers compare various dimensions of "quality" and "satisfaction" with a representative sample of products currently on the market versus matched samples (e.g., telephones) of those available from their young adulthood. This would provide the critical benefit of covarying out temporal and cohort effects, provided there was suitable age variation *within* the older sample. For example, if perceptions of quality and satisfaction were primarily effects of *aging*, per se—as opposed to unique "shocks" based on rapid progress in certain consumer goods categories over a period of decades—this would manifest as differences in levels of satisfaction in comparisons of older and younger demographically matched samples.

Long-Term Differences in Variety

As production, transportation and other technological costs have diminished, product *variety* has increased. Just between 1980 and 1999, the average number of products (i.e., universal product codes, UPCs) carried by U.S. supermarkets increased by nearly 250%, from 14,145 to 49,225 (Food Marketing Institute, 2004). It is therefore more likely that today, compared with the past, there is something precisely suited to one's needs. However, the likely contribution of increased variety to need satisfaction is to some extent counterbalanced by the burden of increased choice, which can impair satisfaction (Botti & Iyengar, 2006; Iyengar & Lepper, 2000). Moreover, this "paradox of choice" (Schwartz, 2004) may be exacerbated by older consumers' relatively diminished memory and cognitive resources, which increase the burden involved in the choice process. Complicating things further, the relative inability of older consumers to inhibit information and their susceptibility to memory interference (Hasher & Zacks, 1988) could also lead to their dwelling more on foregone choices. Finally, it is possible that, even with ever-greater product variety, the specific brands recalled—and explicitly preferred—by older consumers are increasingly phased out of the market due to obsolescence or the disappearance of their core buyer base. Each of these effects would, ceteris paribus, lead to *lower* satisfaction among older consumers, despite the seemingly increased presence and benefits of "variety." However, the simple main effect of there being more product variants to choose from (relative to the past) may overwhelm these potential moderators, such that older consumers report higher levels of satisfaction. By contrast, younger consumers, lacking this long-past basis for comparison, would be, all else equal, less satisfied overall.

Intensification of Consumer Marketing

Over the past several decades, consumer marketing has intensified dramatically. For example, the U.S. Census Bureau's "Service Annual Surveys" show that, over a 25-year period, advertising expenditure increased from $27.9 billion (1.7% of gross domestic product [GDP]) in 1975 to $247.5 billion (2.5% of GDP) in 2000, a nearly 10-fold increase (and over 3-fold, inflation adjusted). As mentioned, the number of products available in the typical supermarket increased at approximately the same threefold clip. Consequently, younger consumers *expect* to have companies cater to their needs and will differentially notice when they are not being met. Older consumers were brought up at a time when product choice was limited, markets were more mass oriented, one-to-one marketing literally did not exist, and needs-based segmentation was relatively primitive. They may also be more willing to accept products and services that do not precisely mesh with their needs because the bulk of modern products and services were designed for younger consumers, who are perceived by marketers to be a more lucrative segment. Marketing has trained younger consumers to expect that their desires will generate products to match; older consumers may not have learned marketers' lessons to the same degree. When a product does match their needs, older consumers may feel lucky or especially satisfied, while younger people may not see this as particularly noteworthy.

Implications

These diverse considerations converge on suggesting profound cohort differences in the standards against which older and younger consumers evaluate consumption experiences. Whereas younger consumers may expect that their needs are met by a large variety of products tailored to their desires, older consumers may be less likely to take this for granted. Moreover, older consumers may compare the current offerings to previous versions that younger consumers never experienced. Accordingly, the size of the older-and-more-satisfied effect should vary as a function of actual improvements in the quality and variety of products offered in a specific consumption domain, and the effect should reverse for domains in which need satisfaction deteriorated.

Explanations Based on Age-Related Changes in the Evaluation Process

The preceding discussion treated the older-and-more-satisfied phenomenon primarily as a cohort effect that reflects changes in the marketplace over time and corresponding changes in consumers' expectations and the extent to which they are met. Next, we turn to possible explanations that treat the phenomenon as a function of individual aging. Normal human aging is associated with an increasing accumulation of expertise in many domains of life as well as with profound changes in cognitive functioning and social behavior (for reviews, see Park & Schwarz, 2000; Chapter 1, this volume; Chapter 4, this volume). Both of these types of changes can affect consumers' consumption decisions and satisfaction judgments.

Wiser Choices?

Simply by dint of having lived longer, an older consumer will have accumulated considerable expertise with many classes of products and services as well as with their own habits and preferences. Hence, older consumers may know themselves better, may have a better grasp of budgets, and may be less likely to try new and "unproven" products that could lead to bitter disappointment. This possibility is consistent with the general observation that older adults have greater self-knowledge (Lachman, Röcke, Rosnick, & Ryff, 2008). If so, older consumers may make wiser consumption choices, selecting familiar products that are more likely to meet their (better understood) needs. Older consumers' preference for familiar products is further enhanced by their increased cost of information search in light of declining cognitive resources. Empirically, older consumers have been found to search for less information than younger consumers in many domains, from frequently purchased, nondurable goods like packaged cereal (Cole & Balasubramanian, 1993) to high-cost and high-involvement goods and services like automobiles (e.g., Lambert-Pandraud et al., 2005), financial investments (e.g., Lin & Lee, 2004), and medical services (e.g., Ende, Kazis, Ash, & Moskowitz, 1989). The observed age differences are robust and hold even when brand loyalty (Cole & Balasubramanian, 1993) or satisfaction with the last purchase (Lambert-Pandraud et al., 2005) is controlled. Hence, older consumers' increased reliance on familiar choices may reflect both increased self-knowledge and experience as well as increased cost of information search.

Both of these factors are also likely to contribute to a tendency to choose products that are "good enough" instead of chasing the best possible option. As experimental research demonstrated (Schwartz, 2004), attempts to maximize utility by finding the best possible product are often associated with lower satisfaction than attempts to "satisfice" by finding a product that simply meets one's needs. To explore this possibility, we administered the Maximization Scale (Schwartz et al., 2002) to 35 younger (mean age = 18.5) and 31 older (mean age = 71.8) adults at the University of Michigan. As expected, younger adults showed a preference for maximizing (mean $[M]$ = 4.54, standard deviation $[SD]$ = .81), whereas older adults were more likely to satisfice (M = 3.68, SD = .84; $F(1, 62)$ = 16.21, $p < .0001$). No gender effects were observed. Note, however, that age-related changes as well as cohort differences may contribute to this finding. On the one hand, older adults' higher experience and lower cognitive resources may limit their need or ability to chase a better option; on the other hand, older cohorts grew up at a time when information was dramatically more costly (in terms of time, energy, and actual funds) to gather and hence may be more accustomed to terminating search when a suitable option has been identified. Future experiments may fruitfully address this question and may explore to which extent age-related differences in satisficing contribute to the older-and-more-satisfied phenomenon.

Accessibility of Comparison Products

Younger and older consumers may further differ in the comparison standards that come to mind when they evaluate a product. As numerous studies in the domain of life satisfaction demonstrated, people can draw on a wide variety of different standards in evaluating their current situation, from what they expected to what they previously had or what others have. Which one they use depends on which one is most accessible at the time of judgment (for a review, see Schwarz & Strack, 1999). In some consumer domains, such as high-tech products, younger consumers may know more about the "latest and greatest," or currently standard, offerings available, compared with older consumers, and may also have speedier replacement cycles. For example, older consumers may choose to replace their computers infrequently (e.g., because they place fewer demands on them or do not require state-of-the-art capabilities) and so compare their present computer to an old and strongly superseded one, resulting in differential satisfaction; younger consumers, by contrast, may compare their own computer to the best of what their friends have or to what is readily available online. If so, satisfaction should depend on one's type of expertise: The more one knows about the *current* offerings in the product class, the less one is satisfied with a given, slightly outdated exemplar, but the more experience one has with *previous* offerings in the product class, the more satisfied one is with the same exemplar. This possibility lends itself to experimental investigation.

In actual field data, however, the assumed dynamics may be confounded with the differentially greater ability of older consumers to afford superior goods: An older consumer with substantial income and savings may be able to *achieve* satisfaction more easily than a younger consumer on a tight budget. But, it may also be confounded by a lower *willingness* to pay for advanced technology. These sorts of "endogeneity" issues are now being examined in detail by empirical modelers in marketing, but dedicated experiments would seem more expedient in separating out satisfaction, choice effects, knowledge, and both ability and willingness to pay across multiple product and service classes.

Explanations Based on Age-Related Changes in the Response Process

We now turn to explanations that trace the older-and-more-satisfied phenomenon to age-related changes in cognitive functioning and social behavior that may affect the survey response process (for a review, see Schwarz & Knäuper, 2000). From this perspective, the phenomenon may, at least in part, reflect artifacts of the measurement process rather than actual age or cohort differences in customer satisfaction.

Scale Use

A smattering of evidence suggests that older respondents use ratings scales in surveys in a less-granular way: Targets are broadly classified as good, bad, or neutral, resulting in less-differentiated ratings (e.g., Knäuper & Seibt, 1999; Schwarz & Knäuper, 2000). Given that most consumers are reasonably satisfied, this lack of differentiation would lead older consumers' responses to cluster near the highest scale point. This effect is most pronounced for the oldest old (Knäuper & Seibt, 1999), and the data shown in Figure 10.2 are compatible with this possibility (as with many others). If so, the obtained pattern may simply reflect that younger consumers report more fine-grained differentiations of customer satisfaction, whereas older consumers tend to report very high satisfaction once a threshold is passed. However, an inspection of the distribution of satisfaction ratings for the three media industries in which we did not observe a relationship between the ratings and age (newspaper publishing, TV broadcasting, motion pictures) casts some doubt on this account: Ratings of these industries showed no increased endorsement of 10 by the oldest age groups. Moreover, the parallels between survey reports of customer satisfaction and complaint behavior (Lee and Soberon-Ferrer, 1999) suggest that the older-and-more-satisfied phenomenon goes beyond an artifact of scale use. This issue can be further addressed through systematic experimentation and formal modeling.

Specifically, models of scale usage heterogeneity (Rossi, Gilula, & Allenby, 2001) could be used to determine which covariates—including age itself—drive what sorts of changes in how respondents use scales, over and above any product attribute effects. Three a priori hypotheses present themselves about older consumers' use of rating scales: (a) "lumping" toward the midpoint (or away from it); (b) "compression" to the midpoint (either of the scale itself or of the product's mean satisfaction level, the latter being a "variance reduction," and not a mean shifting, effect); and (c) a simple right skew, as suggested by the raw ACSI data. In principle, any of these could lead to higher *means* among older consumers, but they would each entail a different *distribution*. Experiments could help determine whether these potential distributional artifacts might be reduced via detailed directions on scale usage, practice using the scale, and variations in scale format.

Social Desirability and Self-Presentation

Previous research also indicates that older people score higher on social desirability scales (e.g., Gove & Geerken, 1977; Lewinsohn, Rohde, Seeley, & Fischer, 1993), suggesting that socially desirable response behavior may increase with age. If so, older respondents may be more hesitant than younger respondents to express negative evaluations of a product or service, a difference that may be exacerbated when the product or service is perceived as popular. However, two observations suggest that socially desirable responding is not a major driver of the older-and-more-satisfied effect. First, socially desirable responding primarily predicts an avoidance of undesirable answers in the form of dissatisfaction reports; it does not necessarily entail a need to report very high, instead of merely high, satisfaction. Empirically, however, it is older consumers' tendency to report very high satisfaction that drives the effect, whereas reports of dissatisfaction show no age differences. Unfortunately, such reports are rare in all age groups, primarily because dissatisfied customers tend not to make repeat purchases and hence would more likely fall out of the sample of current customers that forms the basis of the ASCI ratings. Second, socially desir-able responding decreases with increasing anonymity of the research sit-uation; it is more pronounced in face-to-face interviews than in telephone interviews and least pronounced under self-administered questionnaire conditions (DeMaio, 1984). However, the older-and-more-satisfied effect has been observed with different modes of administration—telephone interviews and online surveys (*ACSI Methodology Report*, 2008) as well as mail surveys (Chow, Lau, Lo, & Yun, 2007)—although comparisons of the relative effect size are fraught with uncertainty, due to sample differ-ences. Finally, social desirability effects are context sensitive: It is more acceptable to express negative opinions in some domains than in others. In contrast, the older-and-more-satisfied effect is relatively robust across consumption domains, and the observed domain differences (shown in Table 10.1) do not easily lend themselves to an interpretation in terms of differential social desirability; why, for example, would media industries be the only ones for which an enthusiastic response is not called for?

Differential Self-Selection

Research indicated that happy people enjoy higher health and lon-gevity and may outlive their less-happy cohort mates by 8 to 10 years (for a meta-analysis, see Veenhoven, 2008). It is therefore conceivable that general happiness and an upbeat temperament (which is a major predictor of happiness; see Diener & Lucas, 1999) contribute to older consumers' likelihood of entering the ASCI database because they are more able and willing to participate in research, to try new products, and to seek out products that meet their needs well. Such differential self-selection and survivor effects may contribute to the observation that the oldest consumers are particularly likely to report very high customer satisfaction.

Interactions, Heterogeneity, Person and Product Covariates

Unfortunately, the various possibilities discussed in the preceding sec-tions are not mutually exclusive. Instead, many of them may operate in concert, reinforcing or attenuating one another and giving rise to complex interaction effects. Moreover, the variables involved in all possible influ-ences discussed are themselves subject to change over time: Over a period of decades, the consumer environment changed, individuals aged and amassed more consumer experience, and so on. Hence, despite *conceptual* independence, the types of explanations we discussed are necessarily (temporally) *correlated,* which raises serious methodological challenges for isolating their relative influence.

Moreover, we have discussed "satisfaction" as if it were a univariate construct—ranging from very low to very high—but an increasing body of research suggests a more nuanced view (Bearden & Teel, 1983; Spreng, MacKenzie, & Olshavsky, 1996; Westbrook & Oliver, 1991). Satisfaction can comprise multiple dimensions, and consumers can be *heterogeneous* in terms of what they especially value. Simply put, some older consumers may be more satisfied for one reason ("The product lasted longer than I expected") and some for another ("It was inexpensive for how good it was"). This heterogeneity is partly explicable by individual difference variables, like demographics or behavior. For example, consumers who were gadget enthusiasts or ham radio devotees 50 years ago would be delighted in today's digital playground; other older consumers may find the high-tech product world an incomprehensible nightmare, yet be glad that modern anti-inflammatory drugs ease arthritis. Both groups might report high satisfaction with "technology" but grossly different aspects of it. Researchers will need to take note of the fact that various product classes offer multiple, differential benefits, and moreover that different older consumers may express high satisfaction with a specific class or product within it for substantively distinct reasons. Marketers have become highly adept at deploying hierarchical Bayes models for this purpose (Rossi & Allenby, 2003), but even the most sophisticated model will fail in the absence of appropriate covariate data, in this case pertaining to product classes, to specific products within them, and to individuals.

We have also not addressed within-group demographic variation and how it might play into differences in self-reported satisfaction. To take one extreme example, data from the 2000 U.S. Census suggested that boys outnumber girls through early adulthood, but that among those 85 and over, there were approximately 2.5 women for every man. So, if women reported higher satisfaction than men in general, much or all of the older-and-more-satisfied phenomenon might be attributable to between-age-group *gender* differences. Fortunately, many data collection efforts, including the ACSI, avoid this obvious confound by appropriate stratification and oversampling. But, it is notoriously difficult to "correct" for other such differences, especially so across age groups. Younger consumers today are, in general, more educated, taller and heavier, far more adept at technology, media savvy, and ecologically conscious, among dozens of other differences. Ostensive between-age-group comparisons will therefore invariably involve systematic differences in other characteristics, on average, as well.

Finally, the quest for a unified account of what drives the older-and-more-satisfied phenomenon may be overly ambitious. Different explanations may hold in different categories and situations. Decades of research in marketing have documented profound differences in evaluation and choice processes among durables, frequently purchased goods, and services, not to mention similarly vast differences in how they are advertised, promoted, distributed, stored, and featured by retailers. It may be that a final resolution of the older-and-more-satisfied phenomenon may arise only from the isolated studies of various effects and interactions, many of which we propose in this chapter. Based on these studies, researchers may then be able to determine the conditions in which different explanations most reliably hold. In any case, systematic explorations of the processes underlying the older-and-more-satisfied phenomenon will illuminate the influence of age- and cohort-related variables on consumer judgment and may provide managerially useful information about a rapidly aging population.

References

ACSI methodology report. (2008). National Quality Research Center, Ann Arbor, MI: Stephen M. Ross School of Business at the University of Michigan.

Bayus, B. L. (1998). An analysis of product lifetimes in a technologically dynamic industry. *Management Science, 44*, 763–775.

Bearden, W. O., & Teel, J. E. (1983). Selected determinants of consumer satisfaction and complaint reports. *Journal of Marketing Research, 20*, 21–28.

Bohlmeijer, E., Roemer, M., Cuijpers, P., & Smit, F. (2007). The effects of reminiscence on psychological well-being in older adults: A meta-analysis. *Aging and Mental Health, 11*, 291–300.

Botti, S., & Iyengar, S. S. (2006). The dark side of choice: When choice impairs social welfare. *Journal of Public Policy & Marketing, 25*, 24–38.

Chow, I. H., Lau, V. P., Lo, T. W., & Yun H. (2007). Service quality in restaurant operations in China: Decision- and experiential-oriented perspectives. *International Journal of Hospitality Management, 26*, 698–710.

Cole, C. A., & Balasubramanian, S. K. (1993). Age differences in consumers' search for information: Public policy implications. *The Journal of Consumer Research, 20*(1), 157–169.

Cooper, T. (2004). Inadequate life? Evidence of consumer attitudes to product obsolescence. *Journal of Consumer Policy, 27*, 421–449.

DeMaio, T. J. (1984). Social desirability and survey measurement: A review. In C. F. Turner & E. Martin (Eds.), *Surveying subjective phenomena* (Vol. 2, pp. 257–281). New York: Sage.

Diener, E., & Lucas, R. E. (1999). Personality and subjective well-being. In D. Kahnemann, E. Diener, & N. Schwarz (Eds.), *Well-being: The foundations of hedonic psychology* (pp. 213–229). New York: Sage.

Diener, E., Suh, E. M., Lucas, R. E., & Smith, H. L. (1999). Subjective well-being: Three decades of progress. *Psychological Bulleting, 125*(2), 276–302.

Ehrlich, B. S., & Derek, M. I. (2002). Does subjective well-being increase with age? *Perspectives in Psychology, 5*, 20–26.

Elder, G. H. (1974). *Children of the great depression.* Chicago: University Press.

Ende, J., Kazis, L., Ash, A., & Moskowitz, M. A. (1989). Measuring patients' desire for autonomy. *Journal of General Internal Medicine, 4*(1), 23–30.

Food Marketing Institute. (2004). *Trends in the United States: Consumer attitudes and the supermarket, 2004.* Washington, DC: Research Department.

Fornell, C., Johnson, M. D., Anderson, E. W., Cha, J., & Bryant, B. E. (1996). The American Customer Satisfaction Index: Nature, purpose, and findings. *Journal of Marketing, 60*, 7–18.

Fornell, C., VanAmburg, D., Morgeson, F., Anderson, E. W., Bryant, B. E., & Johnson, M. D. (2005). *The American Customer Satisfaction Index at ten years: ACSI 1994–2004.* Ann Arbor, MI: National Quality Resource Center at the University of Michigan.

Furse, D. H., Punj, G. N., & Stewart, D. W. (1984). A typology of individual search strategies among purchasers of new automobiles. *Journal of Consumer Research, 10*, 417–431.

Gove, W. R., & Geerken, M. R. (1977). Response bias in surveys of mental health: An empirical investigation. *American Journal of Sociology, 82*, 1289–1317.

Graphically Speaking. (2009). Not just brick and mortar. Retrieved July 24, 2009, from http://www.graphicallyspeaking.net/home3.htm

Hasher, L., & Zacks, R. T. (1988). Working memory, comprehension, and aging: A review and a new view. In G. Bower (Ed.), *The psychology of learning and motivation* (Vol. 22, pp. 193–225). New York: Academic Press.

Iyengar, S. S., & Lepper M. R. (2000). When choice is demotivating: Can one desire too much of a good thing? *Journal of Personality and Social Psychology, 79*, 995–1006.

Knäuper, B., & Seibt, B. (1999, May). *Rating scale use among the oldest old: Limited discrimination between categories.* Paper presented at the annual conference of the American Association for Public Opinion Research (AAPOR), St. Pete Beach, FL.

Lachman, M. E., Röcke, C., Rosnick, C., & Ryff, C. D. (2008), Realism and illusion in Americans' temporal views of their life satisfaction: Age differences in reconstructing the past and anticipating the future. *Psychological Science, 19*, 889–897.

Lambert-Pandraud, R., Laurent, G., & Lapersonne, E. (2005). Repeat purchasing of new automobiles by older consumers: Empirical evidence and interpretations. *Journal of Marketing, 69*, 97–113.

Lee, J., & Soberon-Ferrer, H. (1999). An empirical analysis of elderly consumers' complaining behavior. *Family and Consumer Sciences Research Journal, 27*, 341–371.

Levitt, T. (1960, July–August). Marketing myopia. *Harvard Business Review, 38*, 45–56.

Lewinsohn, P. M., Rohde, P., Seeley, J. R., & Fischer, S. A. (1993). Age-cohort changes in the lifetime occurrence of depression and other mental disorders. *Journal of Abnormal Psychology, 102*, 110–120.

Lin, Q. C., & Lee, J. (2004). Consumer information search when making investment decisions. *Financial Services Review, 13*(4), 319–332.

Moore, S. (2005). They sure don't make things like they used to. Retrieved July 24, 2009, from http://www.consumeraffairs.com/news04/2005/appliances.html

Nevius, C. W. (2005, July 16). Disposing with the fix-it guys. *San Francisco Chronicle*, p. B-1.

Park, D. C., & Schwarz, N. (Eds.). (2000). *Cognitive aging: A primer*. Philadelphia: Psychology Press.

Rossi, P. E., & Allenby, G. M. (2003). Bayesian statistics and marketing. *Marketing Science, 22*, 304–328.

Rossi, P. E., Gilula, Z., & Allenby, G. M. (2001). Overcoming scale usage heterogeneity: A Bayesian hierarchical approach. *Journal of the American Statistical Association, 96*, 20–31.

Schwartz, B. (2004). *The paradox of choice*. New York: Ecco.

Schwartz, B., Ward, A., Monterosso, J., Lyubomirsky, S., White, K., & Lehman, D. R. (2002). Maximizing versus satisficing: Happiness is a matter of choice. *Journal of Personality and Social Psychology, 83*(5), 1178–1197.

Schwarz, N., & Knäuper, B. (2000). Cognition, aging, and self-reports. In D. Park & N. Schwarz (Eds.), *Cognitive aging: A primer* (pp. 233–252). Philadelphia: Psychology Press.

Schwarz, N., & Strack, F. (1999). Reports of subjective well-being: Judgmental processes and their methodological implications. In D. Kahneman, E. Diener, & N. Schwarz (Eds.), *Well-being: The foundations of hedonic psychology* (pp. 61–84). New York: Sage.

Spreng, R. A., MacKenzie, S. B., & Olshavsky, R. W. (1996). A reexamination of the determinants of consumer satisfaction. *Journal of Marketing, 16*, 15–32.

U.S. Census Bureau. Service Annual Surveys, Available at http://www.census.gov/services

Veenhoven, R. (2008). Healthy happiness: Effects of happiness on physical health and the consequences for preventive health care. *Journal of Happiness Studies, 9*, 449–464.

Westbrook, R. L., & Oliver, R. L. (1991). The dimensionality of consumption emotion patterns and consumer satisfaction. *Journal of Consumer Research, 18*, 84–91.

Yang, Y. (2008), Social inequalities in happiness in the United States, 1972 to 2004: An age-period-cohort analysis. *American Sociological Review, 73*, 204–226.

11

Age Branding

Harry R. Moody
AARP

and

Sanjay Sood
UCLA Anderson School of Management

Introduction

Age branding is the creation of brands that are targeted to older consumers, such as AARP or Sun City. Given the demographic shifts taking place in the United States, age branding is a strategy that will continue to grow in importance. In 2000, there were 35 million Americans age 65 or above, approximately 13% of the U.S. population. That number is expected to rise to 50 million by 2010 and 70 million in 2030, or 20% of the U.S. population (Federal Interagency Forum on Aging-Related Statistics, 2000). The trend is not limited to the United States but is evident in advanced industrialized countries of Europe and in Japan. Older people control 70% of the net worth of U.S. households at a level equal to $7 trillion. Moreover, market research suggests that the 55 to 65+ age group has twice the discretionary spending of the younger market, that young age group (18 to 49) that commands so much attention from advertisers (De Asis, 2006). Creating brands specifically designed with the older demographic in mind, what we will call *age branding*, will be a key to reaching this huge marketplace.

In this chapter, we identify four different "families" of age brands that represent distinctive cultures of aging. Age brands can be successful in different ways because each brand family meets a specific need that is relevant to the older consumer segment. This does not imply that age branding involves a new marketing strategy. Rather, traditional techniques must be designed with the older consumer as the target market from the outset. The four families are (a) age-denial brands ("I don't have to get old"); (b) age-adaptive brands ("Age presents problems, but I can deal with them"); (c) age-irrelevant brands ("Mind over matter; if you don't mind, it doesn't matter"); and (d) age-affirmative brands ("The best is yet to be"). We also consider troubled age brands. In what follows, we describe each brand strategy, identify related academic research, and provide some best practice examples from the marketplace.

Age-Denial Brands

An old vaudeville joke has it that "Denial is not just the name of a river in Egypt." But, age-denial branding is no joke. It is a big business and likely to grow even bigger as the baby boomers move toward Golden Pond. Every age-denial brand, explicitly or not, appeals to the illusion of Peter Pan, to the fantasy of never growing up and never becoming old. Denying one's age involves seeking out brands such as Botox that help older consumers look young. Importantly, successful age-denial brands have recognized that the purchase of these age-denial brands may also be accompanied by information-processing strategies that help older consumers also *feel* young.

One such processing strategy is *self-enhancement*, or the need to perceive oneself favorably (Greenwald, 1980; Greenwald, Bellezza, & Banaji, 1988). *Self-enhancers* have been defined as people who think about themselves more positively than they think about others. For example, people state that positive traits are much more descriptive and characteristic of self than of the average person, and negative traits are less descriptive of the self than of the average person (Alicke, 1985; Messick, Bloom, Boldizar, & Samuelson, 1985). According to past research, self-enhancement can be achieved by a social comparison process by which people make downward comparisons to maintain a positive self-image. In other words, people may actively seek out comparisons with other seniors who do not look as young in order to help themselves feel better about aging.

An interesting comparison regarding the potential effectiveness of age-denial branding can be made between the success of Botox and the failure of Geritol. Since its introduction, Botox has become a widely known brand, even a household name (Kane, 2002). Increasingly, cosmetic surgery and Botox are becoming part of mainstream American life, and age-denial branding has grown along the way. For example, today there are more physicians who are members of the American Academy of Anti-Aging Medicine than there are board certified geriatricians in the United States.

One of the success factors of branding Botox is in the use of personal and social comparisons that help make Botox the brand it is today. Typical of other medical brands, Botox emphasizes a before-and-after comparison of wrinkles to demonstrate product performance. The branding of Botox, however, also includes social comparisons by which users of the product compare themselves to other consumers in the same age range. These social comparisons help Botox users boost self-esteem by reaffirming how much younger they look with Botox as the hero.

The failure of Geritol shows what can happen if social comparisons are not managed effectively. Geritol achieved fame briefly in the late 1950s as sponsor for the fabled quiz show *Twenty One* but could not sustain its market share over time. As a brand, Geritol found itself linked to negative social comparisons that stereotyped seniors as a group. In the public mind, there were jokes and sneers of all kinds about "the Geritol crowd." For example, American country music singer George Jones recorded a song whose lyrics were "I don't need your rockin' chair, your Geritol or your Medicare." Advertising sponsorship only helped legitimize these comparisons. For years, Geritol was promoted on TV shows like *Hee Haw, The Lawrence Welk Show,* and *Ted Mack's Original Amateur Hour,* all programs beloved by the senior citizen market. Geritol continually battled these negative associations, and ultimately the brand paid a price in the marketplace.

Age-Adaptive Brands

A second category of brands, age-adaptive brands, are brands that are more functional in nature and help seniors to recognize age-related issues and proactively adjust to the effects of aging. It is worth noting that individual factors can lead a person to be more or less open to age-adaptive brands. One classic example would be eyeglasses or hearing aids to compensate for sensory deficits that can accompany age. Because these deficits typically come on slowly, with insidious onset, it is possible to deny for a long time that any deficit has occurred. Everyone can recognize examples of family, friends, or colleagues whose eyesight or hearing has deteriorated with age but who insist that their capacity is "as good as it's ever been." Such answers amount to a kind of therapeutic nihilism ("What's the use?") that keeps prospects from responding to age-adaptive brands.

Refusal to buy age-adaptive products has a different psychological dynamic than what we see in age-denial products. Indeed, denial is what fuels the purchase of cosmetics, plastic surgery, or antiaging medicine. As long as denial persists, people will be unwilling to consider age-adaptive products such as hearing aids, home monitoring technology, long-term care insurance, or continuing care retirement communities. In all cases, the answer from consumers is likely to be, "I'm not ready for that yet." This delicate dance between denial and adaptation will be visible in our subsequent discussion of age-adaptive branding.

Age-adaptive brands are products that acknowledge the negative elements of aging but seek to compensate for decline through goods or services that make life better—in short, the essential definition of "successful aging" defined as "decrement with compensation" (Rowe & Kahn, 1997). Instead of denial, age-adaptive brands appeal to consumers by recognizing a problem and taking realistic steps to address the problem. Instead of self-enhancement, age-adaptive brands appeal to mature problem solving with brands that meet a functional need.

One success factor for age-adaptive branding is to highlight a point of reference that creates a favorable frame of mind in the consumer. The psychological construct of habituation can provide some insight toward understanding how to craft effective age-adaptive branding strategies. *Habituation* refers to the fact that people adapt to whatever stimuli exist in their environment (Helson, 1964). For example, a person who moves into a house next to a busy highway may at first be disturbed by the noise, but in time the person will likely adapt to the new environment almost to the point at which the person does not notice the noise at all. Thus, habituation to a stimulus reflects a type of neutral point at which an individual is at equilibrium with the environment.

Habituation is important because the adapted state will determine the decision frame and the reference point from which consumers base decisions. The concepts of decision frames and reference points are central to research on judgment and decision making. Most importantly, Kahneman and Tversky (1984) specified that decisions can be drastically different when outcomes are framed in terms of gains and losses relative to a reference point. One famous example that illustrates this point is known as the Asian disease problem. Respondents are told to imagine that there is an outbreak of an Asian disease that is expected to kill 600 people. They are then asked to choose between two possible solutions. In one version, the gain frame, one option would result in 200 people saved and the other option had a one-third probability that 600 people would be saved and a two-thirds probability that no people would be saved. In another version, the loss frame, in the first option 400 people would die, and in the second option there was a one-third probability that no one would die and a two-thirds probability that 600 people would die. Although the two versions are equivalent, in the gain frame 72% of the respondents chose the first option, whereas in the loss frame only 22% favored this option. Hence, the decision critically depended on whether the outcome was framed in terms of lives saved or lives lost.

These results have direct implications for age-adaptive branding because aging naturally involves a type of habituation; we get used to changes that come with growing old. Thus, effective age-adaptive branding recognizes that decisions may be quite different depending on the reference point. If consumers are satisfied with their current state, then they may not appropriately recognize problems and/or seek out solutions in the form of age-adaptive brands. On the other hand, if a consumer's decision frame can be shifted to consider alternative reference points, then they may prefer age-adaptive brands. For example, consider public health campaigns and health promotion. The effectiveness of health campaigns may depend on how consumers think about their current state of health versus their future state of health. Chronic health problems of later life are typically the result of lifestyle choices made many years before (e.g., poor diet and lack of exercise). Diabetes, cardiovascular disease, chronic obstructive pulmonary disease, and many forms of cancer can be directly attributed to poor health behavior many decades earlier. If a consumer thinks that these diseases are a natural part of aging, habituation may lead to decision inertia, and consumers may not seek out treatment.

The campaign may become more effective by changing the reference point from current health to future health. Thinking about the future may invoke a loss frame that prompts consumers to respond differently from when they think about current health. Prevention, then, becomes the strategy for age-adaptive branding in public health campaigns as well as consumer marketing. To reach consumers in this way, it becomes important to convey the message "It's not too late" for better health. Age-adaptive brands, such as hypertension drugs, can position themselves to convey that message, but the message will only be heard to the extent that the reference point is shifted. Age-adaptive branding, therefore, needs to be linked to age-affirmative images that lodge in the minds of consumers. An age-adaptive strategy need not frighten people about the risk of stroke for untreated hypertension. Instead, the age-adaptive message could be packaged in terms of "the good life" in the later years, without dwelling on age or disability at all. As long as consumers recognize a better outcome is possible, the brand can be the hero that saves the day.

Ultimately, age-adaptive brands are problem-solving brands. Skillful marketers such as Viagra find ways to embed age-adaptive messages in ways that the frame of reference becomes positive as opposed to negative for aging consumers. Viagra is the commonly recognized name of a drug for erectile dysfunction sold by Pfizer Corporation. The drug was initially patented in 1996 and first sold in the United States in 1998. It quickly became a huge success for Pfizer. By 2000, Viagra accounted for more than 90% of the market for erectile dysfunction drugs (Keith, 2000), but by 2007 Pfizer's global share of the market had dropped to around 50% as competitors, such as Levitra and Cialis, entered the marketplace (McGuire, 2007).

Erectile dysfunction, like hearing loss, is not limited to older people, but the problem is definitely age associated. Therefore, it was not surprising that Pfizer enlisted former Senator Robert Dole as a celebrity endorser for the drug. Dole was 75 years of age the year that Viagra was introduced, and he soon became a household name linked to the drug in the public mind. Dole himself, as a well-known personal age brand, became a natural vehicle to promote acceptance of Viagra as an age-adaptive brand.

The success of branding Viagra did not depend on Bob Dole or his age. In fact, aging itself was never explicitly mentioned in the advertising, although it was there in the background. One factor that may have helped Viagra appeal to a younger target as well was that Pfizer explicitly used the term erectile dysfunction rather than impotence. Using erectile dysfunction rather than impotence changed the frame of reference from being exclusively about aging to about how it can occur at any age. Doing so helped Viagra achieve significant market share with seniors and younger consumers.

The effectiveness of creating an appropriate frame of reference can also be contrasted in the branding of home monitoring products made by Intel and QuietCare. Home monitoring technologies are electronic devices that keep track of people at home, collecting health data or providing interventions on an emergency basis (Sixsmith et al., 2007). The potential U.S. market for home monitoring technologies is vast and growing. By some estimates, the market for home monitoring technologies could reach $2.5 billion by 2012, and in that year only a small portion of baby boomers will have passed age 65. In 2008, technology giant Intel entered the home monitoring marketplace with its own care management system permitting health care professionals to monitor patients with chronic conditions while the patients are still at home (R. J. Moody, 2008). Intel expects to launch many more such products in the future. "It's a big area of focus and a growth opportunity for Intel" (p. 1), Mariah Scott, director of sales and marketing for Intel's Digital Health Group, said of Intel's 3-year-old health division.

The new Intel product is called Intel Health Guide and offers a touchscreen computer with videoconferencing capabilities and a multimedia health education library for patients. This initial device is focused on specific disabilities, namely, congestive heart failure and chronic obstructive pulmonary disease. The device is not passive but can actually initiate previously scheduled checkups several times a day, collecting vital signs and sending information digitally to health care professionals. In building its brand, Intel faces some distinctive challenges common to age-adaptive brands. As with hearing aids, people may "need" a product by some objective standard, but they resist it because of stigma associated with the product: "I'm not ready for that yet." In the case of Intel Health Guide, there could be reluctance to accept a product that is distinctively disease oriented (e.g., for congestive heart failure) until a patient reaches a point at which symptoms become acute or life threatening. People already confined to their homes may resist an age-adaptive brand that does nothing to overcome their isolation, even if it delivers benefits of safety, low cost, and accurate medical data collection. Conventional "features and benefits" of a product, even an age-adaptive brand, may not be enough to close the sale.

The QuietCare brand creates an alternative reference point, calling the product an embedded-in-the-environment device (Larson, 2007). The name *QuietCare* conveys the essence of the brand and does not strictly focus on the life stage of the customer. QuietCare is similar to an alarm system, but instead of responding to an emergency event, like a fall, QuietCare instead silently monitors movement and uses a form of artificial intelligence to learn about individual behavior patterns. For example, the QuietCare system can indicate a possible bathroom fall by analyzing data from the activity sensors. If a client remains in the bathroom for more than 1 hour, the family caregiver or a monitoring office will receive a signal advising about the possibility of a fall.

QuietCare, like Intel, has promoted its product as a means of detecting potential risks and preventing adverse outcomes. However, it also aims to promote the idea of independence plus security, a combined message not always easy to maintain. QuietCare claims to protect privacy and dignity because it does not use cameras or microphones but rather uses artificial intelligence to identify potential health risks. These differing reference points and multiple values underscore the complexity of age-adaptive branding.

Age-Irrelevant Brands

If the older consumer market is growing, what would be more natural than to pitch products directly to older people as such? In fact, explicit appeals linked to age can be a disaster, as many examples confirm. For instance, the venerable food giant H. J. Heinz stumbled when it tried to promote a new, easily digestible brand under the label of Senior Foods. Even marketing powerhouse Johnson & Johnson lived to regret its effort to introduce its new Affinity shampoo as just right for "older hair." Johnson & Johnson managed to recover from its poisoned Tylenol episode, but it did not recover from trying to pitch shampoo for older hair. The product was quietly abandoned. Similarly, Southwestern Bell dialed a wrong number when it published its separate Silver Pages telephone directory filled with ads aimed at older people. Even Ken Dychtwald, famed guru of senior marketing, failed in an attempt to create a nationwide chain of stores catering to senior adults and their needs. The list goes on, and these failures raise a natural question: How could so many marketing experts and blue-chip companies fail to understand this lucrative aging marketplace?

David Wolfe's (personal communication) answer is that they blundered by making age itself the centerpiece of their marketing appeal. These campaigns all focused on seniors as the target segment, and yet they flopped in the marketplace, perhaps because the explicit focus on seniors made the product less appealing. That is, if a product becomes associated too closely with one consumer segment, then there may be a backlash such that consumers actively avoid that product. Prior to focusing on the target consumer, previous research had shown that effective branding often involves an understanding of the brand concept first (Park, Jaworski, & MacInnis, 1986). Park et al. defined three types of brand concepts that reflect different types of consumer needs: functional, symbolic, and experiential. For example, a functional brand solves a specific problem, such as a shampoo that eliminates dandruff; a symbolic brand meets internal consumer needs, such as a car fulfills a desire for status; and an experiential brand provides sensory pleasures, such as a perfume with a pleasant smell.

Keller (1993) suggests that these brand concepts can be represented as knowledge structures in memory. That is, consumers have a web of associations related to a brand that include thoughts about attributes, benefits, and image associations. When a consumer thinks about Pepsi, for example, the consumer may think about attributes such as sweet taste, benefits such as thirst quenching, or image associations related to celebrity spokespeople such as Britney Spears. The takeaway is that brands live in consumer memory, so it is imperative that the brand be linked with positive associations that stay consistent over time. As was the case with Geritol, often the positive associations do not highlight seniors as the exclusive target market. In fact, for many age-irrelevant brands, age is not highlighted at all. Instead, the brand is marketed as an image or an experience that anyone can enjoy.

Holland America Line is an example of a company that has prospered by focusing on the mature market but not by doing so in an explicit or overt way. Age branding remains critical for the travel industry because of its customer base. Americans over age 50 (the threshold for AARP membership) already account for 45% of all leisure trips in the United States, and people over age 65 account for nearly a third (31%) of those trips. According to the Consumer Expenditure Survey, spending on cruises does not hit its peak until ages 65 to 74, and people over 50 account for 70% of all cruise passengers. Among household groups in this category, spending on hotels and airlines also remains above average. But, do not look for leisure travel companies like Holland America any time soon to advertise a "granny cruise." They would not get many customers if they did. The indirect approach works better. We can also speculate that senior discounts of the past are likely to be scarcer for a variety of reasons. One factor is the rising educational levels of successive cohorts of older people. Boomers, as noted, have higher levels of college attendance than generations before them, and vacation spending rises linearly with the number of years of education. But, explicit age appeals are likely to fail.

Rising educational levels are an important factor because the higher the level of education, the less likely it is that people will identify with age-based programs of any kind. Research on so-called age identification has repeatedly confirmed this point. Overt or explicit age identification, in other words, is a risky strategy for reaching the aging marketplace. As Wolfe, Schewe, Stroud, and others have argued (Meredith & Schewe, 2002; Stroud, 2005; Wolfe & Snyder, 2003), age-irrelevant branding becomes the way to go.

Wolfe suggested that New Balance athletic shoes also represent effective age-irrelevant branding (Wolfe & Snyder, 2003). The brand positioning for New Balance does not ignore age completely, but rather it targets specific age groups by indirect means such as media selection or managing the content and channeling of messages. This strategy of age-targeted, but age-irrelevant, messaging has shown remarkable success. The proof of the pudding, claimed Wolfe, is the fact that New Balance has outperformed its major competition (e.g., Nike) in annual sales growth since the mid-1990s. The case of New Balance is intriguing. After all, athletic shoes are not something we immediately associate with older people. But, the growth of New Balance has cut across generations, and it has been enjoying impressive growth among younger markets. As Wolfe pointed out, the values promoted by New Balance connect strongly with those in the second half of life, the group Wolfe calls the "new customer majority."

The branding strategy of New Balance contrasts sharply with that of competitor Nike, with its famous slogan, "Just Do It." These two brands are polar opposites. Consider their names. *Nike* conjures up a Greek god promising victory over competitors. By contrast, the name *New Balance* appeals to values better appreciated in the second half of life, such as steadiness and wisdom, rather than impulsiveness in action. The very name New Balance might suggest a brand of yoga retreats more than success in a running competition. To make this point, Wolfe gave an example of an ad by New Balance (Wolfe & Snyder, 2003). The ad showed a single man running along a road set against a scenic mountainside above a beautiful sea. There is no reference here to a social group or a running race; in fact, there is no competition at all. Instead, the figure running is isolated, and there is, implicitly, an appeal to self-actualization and the inner self. Another New Balance ad showed a woman jogging down a remote country lane, seemingly ageless from the distance as we view her. The copy below the ad reads:

> One more woman chasing a sunset
> One more woman going a little farther
> One more woman simply feeling alive
> One less woman relying on someone else.

This New Balance ad offered a message attuned to what Carl Jung called *individuation,* fulfilling the true self in the second half of life. In addition, there may also be an appeal here to female achievement and self-reliance, not so far from that old Virginia Slims tagline, "You've come a long way, baby." But, achievement has given place to individuation. Yes, you have come a long way. But now, in the second half of life, where are you going next? Of course, aging is never mentioned, and the messaging is age irrelevant. Wolfe's point (Wolfe & Snyder, 2003) was that the New Balance ads like these are cross generational in their appeal, proving that it is possible to market to older people without ignoring younger people.

Age-Affirmative Brands

Age-affirmative brands are brands that promise us a positive benefit linked to age. Age-affirmative brands do not ignore or deny age but instead focus on elements we can celebrate and affirm. Age-affirmative branding conveys a message of hope and positive aging. Some marketers are beginning to see this as an opportunity in a time of demographic change. For example, long-time advertising leader John Zweig has noted that the marketing environment today offers a chance to support "values of meaning and contribution that are appropriate for older people to embrace as their material lives wind down. This should not be a fact that we ignore or deny, as it is one of the real opportunities of aging that we can become less concerned with the superficial and more focused on core values" (Ageism Taskforce, n.d.). The key success factor is to embrace the benefits of aging without stereotyping seniors. In other words, the branding program needs to understand and perhaps even celebrate the lifestyle of the older consumer (John Zweig, personal communication).

One way to accomplish this goal is to carefully construct the brand's personality to make certain that it reflects the personality of the consumer. Research has shown that consumers often personify brands, imbuing brands with personality traits similar to humans. Aaker (1997) conducted a large study that measured 37 brands on 114 personality traits. The end result was a brand personality scale that included five personality dimensions: sincerity, excitement, competence, sophistication, and ruggedness. Although a brand may overindex on multiple dimensions, often there is a single personality that represents the brand to the majority of consumers. For example, in Aaker's study Porsche represented excitement while Levi's represented ruggedness.

If people often choose brands that reflect their own personality, the question then becomes how to create brand personality. Advertising plays an important role in determining brand personality. The look and feel of the ad, the content and tone of the message, and the emphasis or lack of user imagery all help to create brand personality. For example, Michael Jordan defines a brand personality for Nike in general and Air Jordans in particular. When brand personality emotionally connects with a consumer segment, the brand is sought out by consumers because it reflects the self. Keller (1998) described this stage as a type of resonance between the brand and the consumer; consumers want to have a relationship with the brand. Fournier (1998) defined brand personality in specific relationship terms. She identified 15 types of relationships that consumers have with brands. For example, a committed partnership involves a long-term relationship between consumer and brand that involves rules much like a marriage. On the other hand, consumers can also have a fling relationship with brands that are more short term in nature.

To create a long-lasting relationship with aging consumers, then, age-affirmative brands need to highlight the positive facets of aging and speak to older consumers in a tone that is credible. In our contemporary world, is it possible to imagine that products could be branded and marketed with a *positive* image of age? The answer is "yes" because age-affirmative branding has already proved successful, at least in certain cases. Analyzing those successful cases can give us clues about how marketing and branding can become a more positive force in our aging society in the future.

One example of effective age-affirmative branding is embodied by Sun City Retirement Communities. The very first modern retirement community was Sun City, Arizona, launched on New Year's Day in 1960. It remains the most successful retirement community network of all time and offers many lessons for age-affirmative branding. The first Sun City at the time it opened included five models, a shopping center, recreation center, and golf course. At opening weekend, it drew an unexpected 100,000 people, 10 times the number expected. Traffic jams mounted for miles, and Sun City founder Del Webb found himself on the cover of *Time* magazine. Sun City quickly became a well-established age brand and clearly an age-affirmative brand. It appealed to a market niche that regarded retirement as a good thing and aging into retirement as something positive. Sun City was marketed as the leisure destination of a lifetime, and the public bought the idea. In the years since then, Sun City has been replicated many times and has proved to be a resilient and powerful brand, always with an age-affirmative orientation.

Sun City founder Del Webb was always a visionary entrepreneur. During a long and colorful career, he built government housing during World War II, then later became the owner of the New York Yankees. Sun City was in its time a new and untested idea. When bankers doubted whether to risk a 30-year mortgage on a 60-year-old home buyer, Del Webb believed in the future, and he gambled on it. He won the bet, and his company prospered. But, no brand endures unchanged with time. By the time Del Webb died in 1974, Sun City mangers had begun to sell off some of the company's assets. As the marketplace changed, the Del Webb Company found that it needed to alter its marketing approach. Its approach to age-affirmative branding itself began to change. For example, it began to include more attention to continued employment instead of leisure alone as the defining feature of retirement living.

Despite the success of Sun City, selling retirement communities presents a challenge for branding and marketing. The reason goes back to deeply ambivalent attitudes toward aging. The consumer marketplace remains divided on retirement communities: Some people love them, and some people hate them. The brand category itself can become polarizing. For example, it is not unusual for people to say, "I couldn't stand living only with people my own age," or "I wouldn't want to live with all those old people." Yet, a market niche for age-segregated retirement living clearly exists today just as much as when Sun City opened its doors. Retirement communities, from the beginning, were age-segregated communities. Such a lifestyle appeals to some and repulses others. So, we wonder: Why the outright hostility from some segments of the marketplace, including some gerontologists, to the very idea of age-segregated housing?

David Wolfe (personal communication) believes the answer is that a retirement community can itself become a symbol of stigmatized old age. His answer to the polarity problem is to blur the marketing message, for example, to show intergenerational scenes. This approach may work for some prospects, but this answer may also miss a larger point. There are, and always have been, significant numbers of people for whom an age-segregated community is exactly what they want, not intergenerational living. That is the reason why many age-segregated communities maintain strict age limits, even going to the point of enforcing age restrictions that would evict, for instance, older families whose grandchildren are living with them. Clearly, this distinctive segment of the market is not going to respond well to scenes of intergenerational living.

So, how should one pitch retirement communities to a consumer marketplace that harbors strong suspicion about age-linked brands? Specifically, how will Sun City, and other retirement communities, market themselves to aging boomers? One answer from the senior living industry has been to rebrand retirement communities as "active adult communities," keeping age limits but in the background if at all possible. The strategy of an active adult image is precisely the age-irrelevant branding strategy recommended by Wolfe, and again, it has proven its power for a certain segment of the marketplace.

One of the most remarkable examples of age-affirmative branding was the Dove campaign calling itself "Pro-Age" and focusing on a line of personal care products. In 2007, Dove launched its "Beauty Comes of Age" Global Research Study of attitudes toward physical appearance and age. The research was conducted in nine countries (Brazil, Canada, Germany, Italy, Japan, Mexico, France, the United Kingdom, and the United States) and surveyed 1,450 women ages 50–64. As part of the campaign, a global advertising initiative was launched questioning whether ideal attributes of youthful beauty are still relevant. The ad campaign included images of women whose appearances differed from the conventional ideal. One of the most striking of these featured Irene Sinclair, age 95, with a wrinkled face, asking: "Will society ever accept old can be beautiful?" Her question might remind us of the comment by aging Italian movie actress Anna Magnani to her makeup man when he tried to smooth over her wrinkles: "Don't take a single one. I paid for them" (Hillman, 1999).

In short, Pro-Age was an entirely different kind of ad campaign, a bold and risky one, based on age-affirmative branding (Milner, 2007). Instead of the negative and fear-driven thrust of typical "antiaging" ads, Dove stressed affirmation and hope. One of the pictures even contained the label "Too old to be in an anti-aging ad." The models used in print advertising were all women over 50 shown in natural postures. The message of the campaign was that no matter how old a woman is, she could reveal "real beauty" that transcends limits of age. The Dove campaign, in short, was much more than an effort to sell personal care products. More broadly, it was a vehicle for age resistance, a challenge to prevailing ageist attitudes in society, and an effort to replace denial and avoidance with age-affirmative branding.

Age-affirmative advertising still has a long way to go. Furlong (2007) cited the case of Dayle Haddon, a top model from decades past. Haddon was fired, at age 38, for being "too old." She later spent years trying to educate beauty industry executives about why older women feel left out of society and ignored by ads aimed at them. Dayle Haddon now develops ads herself for L'Oreal and writes about "ageless living." In her words, "What I'm doing is shifting the balance. ... A lot of people reach out to me because they want to look younger. But they walk away with other things that are more important. What I bring is inspiration about the spiritual side of life. It's about deep value and how we find meaning" (Furlong, 2007, p. 108). Haddon's campaign for ageless living is actually closely related to age-irrelevant branding. But, the Dove campaign aimed at something more with its undeniable personality. It remains a milestone in the creation of age-affirmative branding in the world of advertising.

Elderhostel, now known as "Exploritas," is perhaps a paradigm case of age-affirmative branding. When one of the authors served as chairman of the national board of directors, younger people would often comment, "I can't wait to be old enough to be eligible for Elderhostel!" Elderhostel is a program offering liberal education and travel for people above age 55 (Mills, 1993). Indeed, it is now the world's largest educational travel organization, attracting nearly 200,000 participants each year. Elderhostel currently offers 10,000 programs annually in all 50 U.S. states and in over 90 countries around the world. Elderhostel sometimes describes itself as "the way college was supposed to be." It is very far from being just a Club Med for the old folks. Elderhostel maintains its appeal not only through academic offerings but also by the informal socialization it provides for Elderhostelers in each program. In fact, its distinctive style blends travel with learning, offering noncredit courses that are guided by the drive for self-actualization, noted by Wolfe as dominant in the second half of life (David Wolfe, personal communication).

Elderhostel's age-affirmative brand offers interesting lessons for marketers. For one thing, its appeal springs from the way it evokes the "Explorer" archetype described by Mark and Pearson (2001) in *The Hero and the Outlaw*. We think of young people as explorers and adventurers. But, Elderhostel breaks that mold and appeals to the love of adventure at any age. Therefore, the Elderhostel brand personality closely matches the target consumer personality.

Troubled Age Brands

Any account of age branding would not be complete without attention to age brands that have run into problems. These are what are here dubbed "troubled age-brands." In some cases, the trouble has been fatal: The brand is now extinct. In other cases, the brand has been challenged, sold, renamed, or lingers on without any reality to match its name. In every case, there are important lessons to be learned from troubled age brands.

Senior centers are a widely recognized age brand and initially were a successful social program but now are very troubled. The first senior center, the William Hodson Community Center, opened in the Bronx in 1943. In time, the model began to spread. From the beginning, senior centers were created because social workers and planners believed that elderly people lived in isolation and vulnerability. Their needs, it was said, could be met in congregate settings.

Eventually, the senior center model was reinforced by public policy. Since 1965, the Older Americans Act has provided support to more than 6,000 senior centers, offering service contracts for program activities. In 1972, the act was amended to make senior centers the centerpiece of a national aging network. Today, it is estimated that there are 15,000 senior centers in the United States that reach up to 10 million older Americans each year.

But, senior centers have also become a troubled brand. The reason lies in the very idea of age-targeted services. Increasingly, older people feel that a local facility limited to "old people" is the last place they want to be. Such a negative response to the senior center brand is not limited to the United States (Lund & Engelsrud, 2008). And, even senior centers located in areas with high numbers of potential "customers" are finding it hard to attract people. For example, Pennsylvania has one of the highest proportions of older people in the United States. From 2001 to 2005, the number of Pennsylvanians 55 or older living in their own homes increased 6.4%, from about 2.92 million to more than 3.11 million. But, senior center membership numbers were falling, down more than 6% during the same period.

Why are older people reluctant to go to senior centers? In a 2005 poll, more than two thirds of center directors surveyed by the National Institute for Senior Centers believed that boomers and those just a few years older would simply not relate to being called "seniors" (Reitz, 2008). "With the number of baby boomers poised to swell to nearly 40 million people within the next few years, senior centers are scrambling to refurbish and redefine their facilities and programs," said Prof. James McCabe of Arizona State University ("Senior Center Research," 2007). McCabe was part of a research group assembled by the National Institute of Senior Centers to focus on the age-branding problem. "To better serve the needs of this emerging population, we recommended, among other things, that senior centers establish a new 'identity' or 'brand' beyond their senior service focus. Today's senior centers offer many sedentary programs, such as bingo, which simply will not appeal to boomers."

How will senior centers reposition themselves to new generations of older people? One strategy is to look for new ways to "rebrand" the senior center itself, changing the social comparison by putting less emphasis on the word *senior*. For example, one Pennsylvania senior center actually changed its name to PEAK, People Experiencing Activity, Arts, and Knowledge. "We listened to our people and … found that they didn't like our name," the center director said. "People don't want to be associated with a name that has now developed negative connotations." In California, the Palo Alto Senior Center changed its name to "Avenidas." A state Department on Aging official said, "The current participants are getting older and there's just not that newer group to replace them."

As part of their rebranding effort, senior centers are rushing to offer everything from exercise programs and computer classes to fall prevention and environmental monitoring. It remains to be seen if rebranding will work. Part of the challenge is to move away from a deficit-oriented approach to aging, which had been the original inspiration for senior centers and the basis for public funding. But today, potential senior center members prefer health and wellness programs instead of low-cost lunches. Responding to the challenge, Phoenix, Arizona, has reconfigured its 17 senior centers to move away from cafeteria-style meals and card-playing groups, replacing them with a more "hip" design that blends fitness centers, coffee shops, and computer terminals. The senior center of the future may have to base itself on a strategy of "successful aging" (Beisgen & Kraitchman, 2003).

Another troubled brand that struggled for a market was a magazine called *My Generation*. In the spring of 2001, AARP, the world's largest aging organization, announced the single largest launch in magazine publishing history. Its flagship magazine, *Modern Maturity*, would now be supplemented by a new publication targeted at the leading edge of aging baby boomers. The magazine would be called, appropriately, *My Generation*. The publishers were enthusiastic about the launch, but this story has an unhappy ending: Two years later, the new magazine folded.

There are many lessons from this episode. *My Generation* was inspired by a persistent and appealing idea, namely, that boomers "constitute a unique club, one whose members feel a special affinity toward one another based on a shared history and culture," as one analyst put it (Bercovici, 2003). The other bright idea was that *My Generation* as a magazine would age along with its readers, in effect consolidating cohort membership and identity over time. But bright ideas do not always work. By 2003, it was evident that the new boomer magazine had failed to attract enough attention from readers and advertisers to support the expense of producing a separate publication for boomers. So, AARP went back to the drawing board and came up with another approach: rebranding the familiar *Modern Maturity* with the sponsoring organization's core brand name, namely, *AARP The Magazine*.

The new strategy deployed age targeting but with a subtle difference. Each issue of the AARP magazine is published in three separate editions, invisible to the reader: for those in their 50s, 60s, and above age 70. The new branding strategy seemed to make sense. It was based on brand loyalty combined by narrowing of age focus, but in a subtle way.

The *My Generation* episode reflects the tendency to think of seniors as one homogeneous group. However, seniors are a multidimensional segment that requires multidimensional branding strategies. Rather than speak to seniors as one group, it may have been better to create separate brands with distinct personalities that could appeal to each group separately. Wolfe suggested that age is more important than cohort, or at least that "cohort-altry," the mindless celebration of cohort identity, has its limits (H. R. Moody, 2008).

The personality of a brand that appeals to 70-year-olds should be different from the personality of a brand that appeals to 50-year-olds.

Conclusion: The Future of Age Branding

We have identified four types of age-branding strategies that have been used successfully by various brands. Age-denial branding involves enhancing consumer self-esteem by positioning the brands around a youth theme. Age-adaptive branding involves a focus of consumer reference points on the possibilities of what could be, providing an opportunity for solution-oriented products. Age-irrelevant branding involves the development of brand concepts that create an appropriate image that may not focus on age at all. In contrast, age-affirmative branding celebrates age and uses it as a central theme in developing a brand personality.

As these examples illustrate, one key to successful age branding lies in "positioning" of brands in the minds of consumers. There are important lessons for the future of age branding to be learned from the history of successful service innovation companies, such as companies that pioneered with service innovation, for example, overnight package delivery (Federal Express), retail stock brokerage (Charles Schwab), storefront tax services (H & R Block), drive-in fast food (McDonald's), automated teller machines (Citibank), and selling over the Internet (eBay). Our aging society is unprecedented in historical terms, and age branding will be a key area for marketing innovation in the future.

References

Aaker, J. L. (1997). Dimensions of brand personality. *Journal of Marketing Research, 34*, 347–356.

Ageism Taskforce. (n.d.). Combating ageism in media and marketing. *International Longevity Center.* Retrieved from http://www.aging.org/

Alicke, M. D. (1985). Global self-evaluation as determined by the desirability and controllability of trait adjectives. *Journal of Personality and Social Psychology, 49*, 1621–1630.

Beauty comes of age. (2007). DOVE Campaign for Real Beauty. Retrieved from http://www.dove.us/#/cfrb/

Beisgen, B. A., & Kraitchman, M. C. (2003). *Senior centers: Opportunities for successful aging.* New York: Springer.

Bercovici, J. (2003, January). From *My Generation* to AARP *The Magazine*: Org's new plan to capitalize on huge membership. *Media Life Magazine*. Retrieved from http://www.medialifemagazine.com/

De Asis, K. V. (2006, July). Tapping the gray market. *Brand Channel*. Retrieved from http://brandchannel.com/

Federal Interagency Forum on Aging-Related Statistics. (2000). Retrieved Feb. 12, 2010 from http://www.agingstats.gov/

Fournier, S. (1998). Consumers and their brands: Developing relationship theory in consumer research. *Journal of Consumer Research, 24*, 343–373.

Furlong, M. (2007). *Turning silver into gold: How to profit in the new boomer marketplace*. Upper Saddle River, NJ: FT Press.

Greenwald, A. G. (1980). The totalitarian ego: Fabrication and revision of personal history. *American Psychologist, 35*, 603–618.

Greenwald, A. G., Bellezza, F. S., & Banaji, M. R. (1988). Is self-esteem a central ingredient of the self-concept? *Personality and Social Psychology Bulletin, 14*, 34–45.

Helson, H. (1964). Current trends and issues in adaptation-level theory. *American Psychologist, 19*, 26–38.

Hillman, J. (1999). *The force of character: And the lasting life*. New York: Random House.

Kahneman, D., & Tversky, A. (1984). Choices, values, and frames. *American Psychologist, 39*, 341–350.

Kane, M. (2002). *The Botox book*. New York: St. Martin's Press.

Keith, A. (2000). The economics of Viagra. *Health Affairs, 19*, 147–157.

Keller, K. L. (1993). Memory retrieval factors and advertising effectiveness. In A. A. Mitchell (Ed.), *Advertising exposure, memory, and choice* (pp. 11–48). Hillsdale, NJ: Erlbaum.

Keller, K. L. (1998). Brand equity. In R. Dorf (Ed.), *Handbook of technology management* (pp. 12:59–12:65). Boca Raton, FL: CRC Press.

Larson, C. (2007, February 4). In elder care, signing on becomes a way to drop by. *The New York Times*. Retrieved from http://www.nytimes.com/

Lund, A., & Engelsrud, G. (2008). I am not that old: Inter-personal experiences of thriving and threats at a senior centre. *Ageing and Society, 28*, 675–692.

Mark, M., & Pearson, C. (2001). *The hero and the outlaw: Building extraordinary brands through the power of archetypes*. New York: McGraw-Hill.

McGuire, S. (2007). Cialis gaining market share worldwide. *Medical Marketing & Media, 42*, 9.

Meredith, G., & Schewe, C. D. (2002). *Defining markets, defining moments: America's 7 generational cohorts, their shared experiences, and why businesses should care*. New York: Wiley.

Messick, D. M., Bloom, S., Boldizar, J. P., & Samuelson, C. D. (1985). Why we are fairer than others. *Journal of Experimental Social Psychology, 21*, 480–500.

Mills, E. S. (1993). *The story of Elderhostel*. Hanover, NH: University of New Hampshire Press.

Milner, C. (2007). Marketing effectively to baby boomers. *Journal on Active Aging, 6*(2), 46–47.

Moody, H. R. (2008). Aging America and the boomer wars. *Gerontologist, 48*, 839–844.

Moody, R. J. (2008, August). Intel launches first medical device. *Portland Business Journal*. Retrieved from http://portland.bizjournals.com/portland/

Park, C. W., Jaworski, B. J., & MacInnis, D. J. (1986). Strategic brand concept-image management. *Journal of Marketing, 50*(4), 135–145.

Reitz, S. (2008, September 27). U.S. senior centers plan for boom of "boomers." *The Associated Press.*

Rowe, J. W., & Kahn, R. L. (1997). Successful aging. *Gerontologist, 37,* 433–440.

Senior center research earns recognition. (2007, April 12). *ASU News.* Retrieved from http://asunews.asu.edu/

Sixsmith, A., Hine, N., Neild, I., Clarke, N., Brown, S., and Garner, P. (2007). Monitoring the well-being of older people. *Topics in Geriatric Rehabilitation, 23,* 9–23.

Stroud, D. (2005). *The 50-plus market: Why the future is age neutral when it comes to marketing and branding strategies.* London: Kogan Page.

Wolfe, D. B., & Snyder, R. E. (2003). *Ageless marketing: Strategies for reaching the hearts and minds of the new consumer majority.* Chicago: Dearborn Trade.

12

Designing Products for Older Consumers: A Human Factors Perspective

Neil Charness, Michael Champion, and Ryan Yordon

Psychology Department, Florida State University

Introduction

Our goals in this chapter are to provide a brief introduction to human factors and to the Center for Research and Education on Aging and Technology Enhancement (CREATE) approach for ensuring adequate person–environment fit, as well as to provide an overview of normative changes in perception, cognition, and psychomotor functioning with age that should influence product design considerations. We look at some example products and outline how modeling can provide a useful alternative to traditional usability testing when trying to decide on the relative merits of alternative designs.

Human factors is the discipline concerned with "the role of humans in complex systems, the design of equipment and facilities for human use, and the development of environments for comfort and safety" (Salvendy, 1997, p. xxi). Human factors practitioners typically attempt to optimize product design from the perspective of three criteria: productivity/efficiency, safety, and comfort/enjoyment. The first two criteria are often the primary focus, particularly when the products are deployed in work settings. However, the last criterion, comfort/enjoyment (are the products easy and enjoyable to use), is possibly more important when we consider older consumers using products at home. Designers also have to juggle other criteria that manufacturers hold dear, such as product quality, cost, and ease of manufacturing. As the old engineering joke goes: "You can have your product be of good quality, inexpensive, quick to get to market: good, cheap, quick. Pick any two."

There are a huge number of products available to the consuming public. For convenience, we categorize them into those used primarily in work settings, home settings, and public places.

Other chapters provide the backdrop for why older consumers, the so-called silver market, are perceived as a growing and important market for products. Although we are all aging, it is convenient to segment that amorphous "age 65+" group into three subgroups: the young-old group, typically age 65–74; the middle-old group, typically age 75–84; and the old-old group, those 85+. These groups often have different needs (and wants) in products. However, for the most part, we contrast data from younger and older adults when it comes to looking at normative, age-related changes in functional status.

Although there are well-defined normative changes in function with age, it is not clear that self-perceptions of older adults map very well to their own physical aging. That is, older adults do not necessarily see themselves as old (Guiot, 2001), although objective measures may indicate otherwise. The senior author, when helping an older gentleman walk down a street in Squirrel Hill in Pittsburgh a decade ago, vividly remembers hearing the man's sister complain: "Milton, you are walking like an old man!" Milton was around 90 years old at the time. Neither he nor his sister probably defined themselves as older adults. Thus, older consumers may not be attracted to products advertised as for "older adults." Rather, products aimed at improving functional abilities may be attractive, particularly ones that improve comfort and enjoyment.

Human Factors Framework for Product Use

Although focused primarily on technology products, CREATE (http://www.create-center.org) provided a useful framework for conceptualizing the human–technology relationship structure. An example appears in Figure 12.1.

Users, particularly older consumers, bring a set of capabilities to performing a task with a product or system. These include cognitive, psychomotor, and perceptual capabilities. These capabilities are a product of a person's genetic endowment and their developmental and sociocultural history (cf. Baltes, Rösler, & Reuter-Lorenz, 2006). Example factors that influence such capabilities include a person's age, education level, and specific experiences with the product class. The product or system with which users interact makes a set of demands on these capabilities (e.g., for technology products, via their software, hardware, and instructional

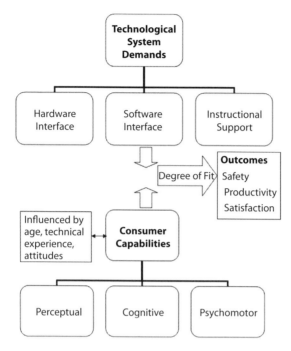

FIGURE 12.1
CREATE framework for understanding person–system interaction.

support components). To the extent that product demands are met by user capabilities, the product or system is usable and enhances performance. When the demands exceed capabilities, then the system becomes difficult to use and may not help the user achieve his or her goals. This can have an impact not only on usage but also on product acceptance, attitudes toward the product, and personal feelings of competence (self-efficacy). CREATE research has shown that cognitive capabilities, attitudes, and self-efficacy were important predictors of technology use in a large, diverse American sample (Czaja et al., 2006).

Efficiency/productivity and safety are the usual outcomes that this demand–capability fit framework addresses. But, we need to pay attention to comfort/enjoyment dimensions as well. If the controls for a product are too difficult to manipulate (think of miniaturization in electronics products such as mobile phones) or to perceive (think too small font sizes for instruction booklets or product packaging), older consumers may never purchase the product. We now focus on outlining some of the normative changes in user capabilities with increased age. There are predictable changes with age in perception, cognition, and psychomotor performance that are very likely to have an impact on successful use of a product (Charness & Jastrzembski, 2009; Fisk, Rogers, Charness, Czaja, & Sharit, 2009).

Functional Capabilities and Aging

It is worth keeping in mind that older adults comprise a very diverse group of individuals. Young-old adults are much less impaired than middle-old adults, who are beginning to show some problems with instrumental activities of daily living (IADLs) such as shopping and cleaning, whereas old-old adults are likely to suffer from multiple disabilities that lead to problems with basic activities of daily living (ADLs) such as mobility, bathing, toileting. It is also worth remembering that although normative changes describe the general population well, not every older adult will be presbyopic or have hearing impairment. Older adults, as a group, are more variable than younger adults for functional capabilities (show greater interindividual variability). They are more variable as individuals across time as well (greater intraindividual variability: Hultsch, Macdonald, & Dixon, 2002). One way of capturing the last distinction is to consider aging as a process that degrades the reliability of the information-processing system. Aging processes can be conceptualized as adding unwanted noise to the system (Welford, 1981).

Vision

Despite their diversity, older adults generally do experience changes in vision that affect their ability to see as clearly as they did when they were younger. As we age, we can expect to experience one or more of the following: loss of acuity, particularly for near, but also for distance vision; a reduction in the field of vision; less sensitivity to light; and a reduction in the ability to distinguish colors (particularly within the short wavelengths, such as blue, green, and violet) and judge depth and distances. Although these visual impairments may occur for many reasons, typically they are due to the normal changes in structures (lens, pupil, cornea, and vitreous humor) of the eye.

One of the most common impairments, the inability to focus effectively on nearby objects, *presbyopia* or *farsightedness*, results from changes in the lens and usually occurs by the mid-40s. Over time, our lenses gradually become thicker, denser, and less flexible (Kline & Scialfa, 1996) as the width of the lens increases by as much as 50% between the ages of 20 and 80 years (Saxon & Etten, 2002). This thickening is often accompanied by changes in the lens that make it yellow, which limits the amount of light that can pass though the lens, impairs the refractive ability of the lens, and distorts colors.

In addition to the lens, the pupil can also limit the amount of light that enters the eye and stimulates photoreceptors as we age. Sensitivity to light declines due to age-related changes in the smooth muscles of the iris (also known as *senile miosis)* that cause the pupil to shrink in diameter. By the age of 80, our ability to adapt to changes in light under dark or dim conditions could be up to 40% less than it was when we were 20 (Margrain & Boulton, 2005).

Another common visual impairment, *floaters* or *myodesopia*, are loose cells that cast shadows on the retina. These cells often appear as brief flashes of light or opacities within the visual field and are able to "float" within our visual field due to changes in the consistency (less jelly-like) of the vitreous humor (Saxon & Etten, 2002). In addition to becoming liquid-like, the vitreous humor also becomes less transparent as we age, which can cause the light to be scattered throughout the posterior chamber of the eye rather than being focused on the fovea, where it is converted by photoreceptors into nerve activity. Changes in the refraction of light can result in blurred vision and an increased sensitivity to glare.

For designers who are trying to accommodate these changes, as well as other age-related changes not discussed here that typically result in decreased acuity in vision, there are three basic guidelines: increase illumination, minimize glare (i.e., by using matte surfaces instead of glossy ones), and use larger font sizes for text and symbols. A good guideline for adequate size is to ensure that the visual angle of subtense for a character be at least 0.6 degrees. Your thumb held at arm's length subtends about 2 degrees of visual angle for its width.

Hearing

We typically begin to notice subtle changes in our ability to hear high-frequency tones in our 40s, and those losses usually progress as we age. Hearing impairments are classified in three ways: conductive (interference with the transmission of sound through the outer or middle ear that affects its ability to reach the inner ear), sensorineural (disorders of the inner ear that affect transmission of sounds through auditory pathways), or mixed (both conductive and sensorineural) (Saxon & Etten, 2002). The most common form of sensorineural hearing loss, presbycusis, is due to degenerative changes in the cochlea or auditory nerve fibers that lead from the cochlea to the brain (Nelson & Hinojosa, 2006). These normal age-related changes in the ear result in a higher percentage loss in hearing across high frequencies (pitches) for older adults (Agrawal, Platz, & Niparko, 2008).

In addition, after the age of 60 hearing loss is approximately 1 dB per year (Lee, Matthews, Dubno, & Mills, 2005). This not only presents a problem for daily living and conversation, but also could present problems in product use. A variety of disorders can arise, such as the perception of muddled speech (consonants such as "s", "t", and "p" are hard to differentiate and perceive; Wallhagen, Pettengill, & Whiteside, 2006) and tinnitus (ringing in the ears; Noell & Meyerhoff, 2003) that causes interference with the perception of sound.

Auditory signals (e.g., beeps) are a popular form of feedback in many products. These products range from cellular phones and digital cameras to microwave ovens. However, such feedback might be lost on older adults depending on the intensity (decibel level) or pitch (frequency) of such a signal. Choosing pitches in the range of 500–1,000 Hz with an intensity of at least 60 dB should help keep signals audible for older consumers.

A further difficulty for older adults is background noise. Discerning audible signals within background noise is increasingly difficult for the older user compared to younger users, with intended signals needing to be of greater intensity. However, simply boosting the volume of all sounds (e.g., with a standard hearing aid) may not improve the signal-to-noise ratio and may even result in greater masking of the signal by noise sources.

Motor Performance

Among the changes for the older user is a loss in fine motor control. This could be viewed as being caused by having a noisier motor control system. Thus, we can expect an older adult to have increased difficulty in tasks that would require selecting small targets (e.g., on a computer screen) based on Fitts's law (e.g., Welford, 1977). Fitts's law states that movement time MT is determined by the amplitude A or distance of the movement and the width W of the target, which jointly comprise the index of difficulty ID for the movement. This is otherwise represented (Fitts, 1954; Jagacinski & Flach, 2003) as

$$MT = a + b\,ID$$

where

$$ID = \log_2\left(2A/W\right)$$

This equation indicates the need for larger targets or smaller distances between targets to lessen the index of difficulty. The constant b increases (approximately linearly) with age. That is, any given movement task can be expected to take longer for older than younger adults. Because of the push for miniaturization, particularly in electronic products, often buttons become very small (width W is diminished), posing a special problem for older users.

Anthropometrics and Physical Fitness

In addition to these changes, changes in body dimensions and capabilities may occur with increased age (e.g., Kroemer, 2005; Steenbekkers & van Beijsterveldt, 1998). *Sarcopenia* is a term used to refer to the age-related loss of muscle (Rosenberg, 1989), which can lead to disability and functional impairment (e.g., Doherty, 2003; Visser et al., 2002). This not only may result in decreased capabilities for IADLs, but also can affect ADLs and compromise performance with products requiring any physical exertion. It has been documented that even with preventive measures such as exercise, maintaining or even adding muscle mass will still result in overall loss of strength (Goodpaster et al., 2006), although exercise can clearly improve both physical and mental fitness (Kramer et al., 1999).

Sarcopenia is also sometimes accompanied by osteoporosis, which can diminish height due to the combination of bone loss and shrinking of the disks in the spine, although this affects women more than men. Many of these changes will show an onset in middle age or later and can result in reduced work ability or complete loss of certain abilities (Ilmarinen & Louhevaara, 1994; National Research Council, 2004). With this in mind, any device requiring physical exertion should aim to minimize physical effort (with the notable exception of exercise equipment).

Cognitive

Similar to the perceptual and psychomotor systems discussed, the cognitive system also changes as we grow older. However, unlike the other systems, these normal age-related changes in cognitive functioning can be both positive and negative. On the positive side, older adults benefit from their ability to draw on larger stores of previously acquired skills, knowledge, and experiences than younger adults. This accumulation of knowledge, or "crystallized intelligence," increases from the 20s and remains relatively stable throughout most of adulthood and may decline in the mid-60s (Horn, 1982). Conversely, "fluid abilities," abstract problem-solving capability, tend to decline from the 20s onward. Other more specific cognitive functions, such as working memory capacity (Maylor, 2005) and visual attention (Rogers, 2000), also show consistent decline functions from early adulthood and can be the source of challenges for older adults when interacting with technology artifacts. Age-related differences in divided attention tasks depend heavily on working memory capacity and functioning (Salthouse, Rogan, & Prill, 1984).

Selective attention is defined as the ability to process one stream of information while disregarding other, concurrent streams, whereas *divided attention* (sometimes referred to as *task switching*) requires the ability to process, maintain, and schedule two or more tasks simultaneously (Verhaeghen & Cerella, 2002). Research investigating age-related differences in divided attention indicated that the emergence of performance declines in older adults depends heavily on the complexity of the task, and that given sufficient practice, the severity of these declines will diminish (Rogers, 2000).

The term *working memory* describes a system of mental resources that must work together to hold and manipulate information (Baddeley, 1998). Working memory plays an important part in many cognitive tasks, such as learning and understanding. Empirical evidence suggests that normal age-related cognitive changes reduce working memory capacity, and that this reduction leads to an inability to inhibit irrelevant information and difficulty integrating newly acquired information (otherwise known as *executive control*) with already existing knowledge (Conway & Engle, 1994; Engle, 2002; Hasher & Zacks, 1988).

The most robust change with age is slowing in the general rate of information processing (Salthouse, 1996). Some processes slow more than others, as Jastrzembski and Charness (2007) pointed out in their analyses of cognitive, perceptual, and motor slowing. For processes like the average fixation time of the eye during reading, slowing is minor (about 15%). For other perceptual, cognitive, and motor processes, older adults take from 70% to 100% longer. Thus, one cannot expect older product users to respond rapidly to warnings in the middle of complex procedures. One should avoid short "time-out" intervals on devices, as in the case of repeatedly pressing the same key to input new characters on a mobile phone keypad.

As a general rule, given the decreased reliability of the human performance system with age, products should be designed to minimize the number of cognitive, perceptual, and psychomotor operations that are needed to accomplish a goal. That should not only minimize the time to carry out an activity with the product but also, more importantly, minimize the probability of error across that chain of steps.

Application of Knowledge About Aging

Given the changes outlined, there are relatively straightforward recommendations that can be given to designers to avoid overtaxing older adult capabilities. For specific guidelines see the work of Fisk et al. (2009). We can illustrate some of these guidelines by examining products and discussing their various pros and cons.

Examples of Products in the Office: Computer Systems

A ubiquitous tool in the office is the computer and its peripheral devices, such as the mouse, monitor, keyboard, printer, scanner, and other attachments. These devices can pose challenges for the older user. If, for example, a monitor was of a smaller size (e.g., 15 inches diagonal) and the typical settings of the computer's operating system presented everything with small icons and fonts, users could have difficulty reading from the monitor as they enter their presbyopic years. Corrections to this situation would be to increase the size of icons and fonts through software or to use a larger monitor (or to wear computer reading glasses). Generally, font sizes of 12 or larger are recommended for print for older adults. We can also recommend that LCD (liquid crystal digital) monitors should be preferred over CRT (cathode-ray tube) monitors due to their higher contrast ratios for text on background (Charness & Jastrzembski, 2009; Fisk et al., 2009).

Another important component for computer use is the pointing device, usually a mouse. To operate a mouse, a user must make hand or arm movements to position the cursor on the screen. For an older user who may have limited movements due to arthritis, a trackball could be a superior device to help minimize physical exertion when controlling a cursor, particularly for extended time periods with repetitive tasks (Chaparro, Bohan, Fernandez, Kattel, & Choi, 1999). For those with less control over movement, perhaps due to stroke or tremor, and who merely need to select items on a screen rather than enter data, a direct positioning device, such as a light pen or touch screen would be the most efficient (Charness, Holley, Feddon, & Jastrzembski, 2004).

The keyboard could also present problems. With newer laptop and notebook computers becoming smaller than their predecessors, some have keyboards with less-than-standard interkey spacing, making it difficult to touch type for those with larger hands. This miniaturization could also have a negative impact on older users. A smaller target (recall Fitts's law) could result in overshooting, causing errors or discomfort in typing. Thus, old and young alike should consider adding a standard keyboard to a notebook computer setup (e.g., by plugging one into a USB [universal serial bus] port). Notebooks and smaller netbooks pose additional problems, such as having relatively small screens that might result in added scrolling to read lines of text, and may have difficult-to-read characters when set at standard resolutions. Office users of notebooks should consider adding a docking station that would enable them to use a standard keyboard, mouse (or trackball), and monitor. Older adults might consider acquiring computer reading glasses that provide sharp intermediate-distance focusing (as opposed to typical bifocals that stress near distance) to improve vision. But, product designers should not assume that everyone will have access to those aids.

Examples of Products in the Home and for Personal Use

In our daily lives, we may rely on technologies big and small to help us throughout our day. These products can range from watches and phones to televisions and cable boxes. Some of these devices are relatively simple in function (i.e., the standard watch), while others can be complex (i.e., remote controls with many functions).

Our first example is the mobile phone. Older users will typically avoid features that are not key to the operation of device. Chattratichart and Brodie (2003) found that mobile phone functions were perceived to be too difficult to use (i.e., displays are too hard to read, multifunctional buttons are difficult to learn to use). Jastrzembski and Charness (2007) examined younger and older adult performance with two differently designed mobile phones. The phone with the keypad having closely positioned keys, although slightly small, produced quicker dialing times. Conversely, the phone that was slower in dialing was faster in a text messaging task by virtue of having fewer steps due to the more efficient menu structure. Menu structure can be an important issue when concerned with timing and usability. It was found that if a device contained a menu tree instead of changing menu screens it would reduce errors (Ziefle & Bay, 2006).

A good example of increasing complexity is the menu structure of television set-top boxes. Similar to the case of mobile phones, using a menu tree function instead of changing screens could enhance usability. As functions are added, the temptation is to increase the number of buttons on a remote control. Increasing the number of buttons may necessitate decreasing overall button size if remotes must fit in one's hand, and this will increase the index of difficulty for moving to a button per Fitts's law.

Examples of Products in Public Places

In our public lives, we interact with more technology with the aim to improve and facilitate services. Some of these devices are automated teller machines (ATMs), self-service kiosks, and even the credit and debit card pay stations at registers in nearly every store. These machines can often be confusing and even daunting to those with little to no experience with them, as may be the case with older adults. One way to improve usability would be to provide a help function on ATMs to allow help to be accessed at any point to assist with any transaction (Coley, Wright, Park, & Ntuen, 1997).

Another important publicly available system is the credit/debit card self-swipe machines at cash registers in stores. These devices are designed to improve the efficiency of sales transactions, particularly by eliminating the slow exchange of paper money and change and the writing and verification of paper checks. While these devices are convenient, improperly designed devices can increase difficulty and frustration for users. Information about how to position the card to swipe it should be clearly displayed. Buttons should be of adequate size, have adequate spacing, and be clearly marked. These are some of the same principles used in mobile phone designs and are transferable to any keypad design.

Ways to Design

Good design usually involves a feedback cycle by which a prototype is generated in accord with accepted design guidelines, it is tested with the targeted user population, flaws are identified, the product is redesigned, the revised product is resubmitted to testing, and so on. The cycle continues until the manufacturer is satisfied that it is marketable. The two main techniques available to designers to test product designs include usability testing and modeling. Modeling can often be used to help guide initial design choices. Usability testing, although often somewhat expensive, should be used to catch flaws that might not have been predicted through modeling or if modeling is infeasible.

Usability Testing

More and more products are formally evaluated for usability before entering the marketplace. Usability of a product is typically assessed on five dimensions: learnability, efficiency, memorability, error, satisfaction, which form the acronym LEMES. (One can cue that acronym from the phrase "Let every mature elder succeed.") *Learnability* refers to ease of learning to use the product. For older adults, who acquire new information at half the speed of younger adults (e.g., Charness, Kelley, Bosman, & Mottram, 2001), learnability of a product can be a significant factor in adoption. Testers need to consider typical uses of the product and then assess how long it takes for a user to reach a target proficiency level for these tasks. Proficiency would include both the time to complete the task and how long it may take to perform the task without committing any errors. The latter dimension becomes most important for medical devices.

Efficiency, the second dimension, is often assessed in comparison with competitor products. It includes similar testing criteria to learnability but also often assesses whether speed of performance can be achieved while minimizing frustration or fatigue. *Memorability*, the third dimension, refers to how easily the product can be used after initial learning but following a delay. Many products are only used occasionally, so products with good memorability characteristics can be picked up after a period of disuse and used efficiently with minimal forgetting about their functionality. Good design will often build in "affordances," product features that guide the user into the right actions. For instance, many hotel door cards include an arrow symbol that shows which of the four different vertical insertion orientations works for opening the door. (The size of the opening slot on the door helps eliminate trying the four horizontal possibilities. Superior but more costly designs can allow someone to place a card close to a sensor panel that unlocks the door.)

Error, the fourth dimension, refers to the goal of minimizing errors in product use, with particular attention to catastrophic errors that could harm the user. Testing focuses on establishing when, where, and why errors occur. Various classification schemes have evolved to describe types of errors (e.g., Sharit, 2006), with common types being slips (unintended actions such as pressing the wrong button inadvertently), mistakes (intentionally selecting an incorrect action believed to be the correct one), and mode errors (selecting an incorrect action due to misperceiving the current state of the environment).

The final dimension, *satisfaction*, refers to user perceptions about how much they enjoy using the product. Questionnaires and rating scales are typically employed to evaluate satisfaction, although some care is needed to probe for different aspects of a product rather than to elicit a global rating.

Usability testing draws on many different techniques. They can range from coding video recording of users who are interacting with prototypes to eliciting think-aloud protocols (Ericsson, 2006) during product use, to postuse questionnaires and interviews. Usability often begins with focus groups (Fisk et al., 2009) being asked to comment on potential product design features. Based on user perceptions, a prototype might be produced and submitted to more intensive testing (LEMES) and then feedback from testing used to modify the product to improve its performance. This process may iterate a number of times until the decision is made to manufacture and market the product.

Modeling

Because usability testing often involves fairly long time frames, it may be possible to shortcut product design through the use of simulations and models. Modeling involves abstracting human performance characteristics

by deriving parameters for typical cognitive, perceptual, and motor operations and detailing how people assemble sequences of operators to perform
tasks with a product. Alternative designs will make different demands on
information-processing capabilities and the model or simulation should
be able to predict which version results in better performance.

Card, Moran, and Newell (1983), in their book *The Psychology of Human-
Computer Interaction*, described an idealized model of a person, the model
human processor, and outlined a first approximation modeling technique,
GOMS (goals, operators, methods, selection rules). The model human processor perspective together with GOMS offers researchers and designers
a means of predicting the impact of different design decisions on user
performance, usually for predicting completion times for tasks with the
product. This modeling approach has also been extended to other formal
models of human information processing, such as Anderson's Adaptive
Control of Thought-Rational (ACT-R) architecture (Anderson, 1996), via
Bonnie John's CogTool (http://www.cs.cmu.edu/~bej/cogtool/).

Model Human Processor

The model human processor is a multifaceted approach to making predictions about users. If we were to consider a user as a complex system,
then this model breaks the user down further into subsystems consisting
of the perceptual, motor, and cognitive components. The overall system
and subsystems are comprised of sets of memories, processors, and principles (known as "principles of operation") working together. The perceptual system, as implied by its name, perceives the world through touch,
visual, and auditory pathways by encoding the signals into a format that
the cognitive system can understand. After the cognitive system receives
the recoded signals, its job is to determine a course of action based on previous knowledge. The course of action decided on is then carried out by
the motor system. Within each of these systems, system-specific memory
buffers and processors are utilized.

The usefulness of this approach is in the detailed path taken. Estimates
for the duration of each process are culled from experiments and literature in psychology. For example, to read a sentence, you typically fixate on
one word at a time and move on. The duration of one fixation after an eye
movement for older users is estimated to be about 267 ms (Jastrzembski &
Charness, 2007), while a younger user's fixation duration is estimated to
be about 230 ms (Card et al., 1983). While the slowing of only 37 ms may
seem insignificant, when repeated 100 times when reading a text passage,
older adults are already 3.7 s behind a younger user. Such age-related
changes in parameters are important to consider when designing for
such items as a mobile phone's text messaging system. Does the system
allow enough time for an older user to make desired character selections

when repeatedly striking a key before timing out and moving on to the next character?

GOMS Model

The GOMS model is a scalable model for predicting aspects, particularly the time, for user interaction with a system. A GOMS model explicitly represents goals (a main goal such as turning on the TV) and subgoals (such as finding the remote), operators (unit task operations such as pressing the power button on either the TV or remote), methods (sequences of operators to accomplish a goal), and selection rules for choosing methods (e.g., if a remote is not found, go to the TV). A more detailed example is presented next. A limitation for GOMS modeling is that it best characterizes routine cognitive tasks. Unless modified, it cannot easily account for user knowledge or for errors and error recovery processes. Despite such limitations, the GOMS model is a useful tool not only for testing existing systems but also for creating and testing imagined systems.

GOMS Example

Remote controls are growing in complexity every day. Modern functions of a remote can range from the standard changing of the channel and volume to complex features such as activating digital video recorder (DVR) functions and providing program guide listings.

For our example of GOMS modeling and Fitts's law, we use the program guide button. Shown in Figure 12.2, a mock-up of a remote for a popular cable/DVR device, is the "home" location, the area in which the user is likely to rest the thumb, the current guide button (Guide 1), and last a proposed location for the guide button (Guide 2).

By applying Fitts's law to assess the location of the guide buttons in relation to home, we would see a significant difference predicted for the *ID*. We can calculate this if home from Guide 1 and Guide 2 is 1 inch and 4 inches apart, respectively, as follows:

Guide 1:

$$\text{Log}_2(2A_1/W_1) = 2.415$$

$$A_1 = 1 \text{ inch} \qquad W_1 = 0.375 \text{ inch}$$

Guide 2:

$$\text{Log}_2(2A_1/W_1) = 4.415 \qquad A_2 = 4 \text{ inches} \qquad W_1 = 0.375 \text{ inch}$$

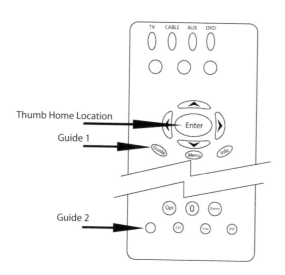

FIGURE 12.2

Example remote control indicating two potential positions for the guide button.

These equations show that for Guide 1 the *ID* is only 2.425, while Guide 2 is 4.425 if it were the same size button as Guide 1. However, in Figure 12.2, we notice that the button is much smaller; thus, the equation is as follows:

Guide 2:

$$\text{Log}_2(2A_1/W_1) = 5$$

$$A_2 = 4 \text{ inches} \qquad W_1 = 0.25 \text{ inch}$$

From this, we can see that the decreased size of the proposed guide button is not preferred due to the increase in the *ID* to 5. We can determine that, due to the increase in the *ID*, moving the button is not preferable.

Even though we have information for *ID* ratings of the proposed change, we have not evaluated time for task completion. The GOMS model lays out the steps needed to be taken to locate and press the guide (either 1 or 2) button (Table 12.1). What we should calculate is the time for each step based on parameters given by Jastrzembski and Charness (2007).

The following calculations are based on the usage of the remote by an older experienced user. By simply fixating on the remote in hand, the older user is expected to spend 267 ms. A cognitive process (118 ms) might then decide the area of interest from a memorized cognitive map of the remote. Next, we choose to fixate on the guide button within the area of interest (267 ms). The next step is the motor function of moving toward

TABLE 12.1

A GOMS Example on Accessing the Program Guide Through the
Remote Control With Mean Time Parameters in Milliseconds for
Younger and Older Users

GOMS Example	Process[a]	Younger (ms)	Older (ms)
Goal: Access guide function			
Goal: Locate guide button			
Fixate on remote	F	230	267
Decision of area of interest	C	70	118
Fixation on button	F	230	267
Verification	C	70	118
Fitts's law on time to move to button	Guide 1	312	569
	Guide 2	570	1021
Goal: Press button	M	70	146
Total: Given no errors in selection	*Guide 1:*	982	1485
	Guide 2:	1240	1937

Operator times taken from Jastrzembski and Charness (2007).
[a] Process is the process used during each task; C, cognitive process; F, eye
  fixation; M, motor process.

and then pressing the guide button. To calculate movement, we use the
model human processor's version of Fitts's law as follows:

$$\text{Movement time} = b * \text{Index of difficulty} + \text{Motor process cycle time}^*$$

where

$$b = \text{Slope of line with 100 for younger adults and 175 for older adults}$$

Motor process cycle = 70 ms for younger adults and 146 ms for older adults

As we complete the task, assuming no errors, an older user will take nearly
1.5 s to use Guide 1 and approximately 1.9 s to use Guide 2.

It may seem that when applied to a remote the time difference of 452 ms
does not seem significant. However, if this was applied to a work environment with a repetitive task, the time savings of knowing adequate placement would be worthwhile, result in significantly increased efficiency,
and might also increase worker comfort (Table 12.1).

Thus, GOMS modeling can provide an estimate of the time cost for positioning a button in an array of buttons, sparing the designer from the
necessity of doing costly usability testing.

---

* For our example, 175 * 2.415 + 146 = MT 569 ms; 175 * 5 + 146 = 1021 ms.

Summary

Aging reduces human capabilities in predictable ways, although there will always be broad individual differences within older samples. Because of these normative changes in perceptual, cognitive, and psychomotor abilities as a function of increased chronological age, products should be carefully designed to fit older consumers' waning capabilities. The human factors field provides useful methods, such as usability testing and modeling, as well as sound guidelines (Fisk et al., 2009) for improving product design. Better-designed products hold considerable promise for improving both the quality of life of older consumers and the bottom line for companies. An added bonus is that good design for older adults can usually be expected to improve product functioning for other consumers.

References

Agrawal, Y., Platz, E. A., & Niparko, J. (2008). Prevalence of hearing loss and differences by demographic characteristics among U.S. adults: Data from the National Health and Nutrition Examination Survey, 1999–2004. *Archives of Internal Medicine, 168,* 1522–1530.

Anderson, J. R. (1996). ACT: A simple theory of complex cognition. *American Psychologist, 51,* 355–365.

Baddeley, A. (1998). *Human memory: Theory and practice* (rev. ed.). Boston: Allyn and Bacon.

Baltes, P. B., Rösler, F., & Reuter-Lorenz, P. (Eds.). (2006). *Lifespan development and the brain: The perspective of biocultural co-constructivism.* New York: Cambridge University Press.

Card, S. K., Moran, T. P., & Newell, A. (1983). *The psychology of the human-computer interaction.* Hillsdale, NJ: Erlbaum.

Chaparro, A., Bohan, M., Fernandez, J., Kattel, B., & Choi, S. (1999). Is the trackball a better input device for the older computer user? *Journal of Occupational Rehabilitation, 9,* 33–43.

Charness, N., & Jastrzembski, T. S. (2009). Gerontechnology. In P. Saariluoma & H. Isomäki (Eds.), *Future interaction design II* (pp. 1–29). London: Springer-Verlag.

Charness, N., Holley, P., Feddon, J., & Jastrzembski, T. (2004). Light pen use and practice minimize age and hand performance differences in pointing tasks. *Human Factors, 46,* 373–384.

Charness, N., Kelley, C. L., Bosman, E. A., & Mottram, M. (2001). Word processing training and retraining: Effects of adult age, experience, and interface. *Psychology and Aging, 16,* 110–127.

Chattratichart, J., & Brodie, J. (2003, June 23–27). The age factor in the design equation of cell phones. *Proceedings of the 12th Annual Usability Professionals' Association Conference*, Scottsdale, Arizona.

Coley, K., Wright, S., Park, E., & Ntuen, C. (1997). Optimizing the usability of automated teller machines for older adults. [Proceedings Paper]. *Computers & Industrial Engineering, 33*(1–2), 209–212.

Conway, A. R., & Engle, R. W. (1994). Working memory and retrieval: A resource-dependent inhibition model. *Journal of Experimental Psychology: General, 123,* 354–373.

Czaja, S. J., Charness, N., Fisk, A. D., Hertzog, C., Nair, S. N., Rogers, W. A., et al. (2006). Factors predicting the use of technology: Findings from the Center for Research and Education on Aging and Technology Enhancement (CREATE). *Psychology and Aging, 21,* 333–352.

Doherty, T. J. (2003). Invited review: Aging and sarcopenia. *Journal of Applied Physiology, 95,* 1717–1727.

Engle, R. W. (2002). Working memory capacity as executive attention. *Current Directions in Psychological Science, 11,* 19–23.

Ericsson, K. A. (2006). Protocol analysis and expert thought: Concurrent verbalizations of thinking during experts' performance on representative tasks. In K. A. Ericsson, N. Charness, P. Feltovich, & R. Hoffman (Eds.), *Cambridge handbook of expertise and expert performance* (pp. 223–242). Cambridge, UK: Cambridge Press.

Fisk, A. D., Rogers, W. A., Charness, N., Czaja, S. J., & Sharit, J. (2009). *Designing for older adults: Principles and creative human factors approaches* (2nd Ed.). Boca Raton, FL: CRC Press.

Fitts, P. M. (1954). The information capacity of the human motor system in controlling the amplitude of movement. *Journal of Experimental Psychology, 47,* 381–391.

Goodpaster, B. H., Park, S. W., Harris, T. B., Kritchevsky, S. B., Nevitt, M., Schwartz, A. V., et al. (2006). The loss of skeletal muscle strength, mass, and quality in older adults: The health, aging and body composition study. *Journal of Gerontology: Medical Sciences, 61A,* 1059–1064.

Guiot, D. (2001). Antecedents of subjective age biases among senior women. *Psychology and Marketing, 18,* 1049–1071.

Hasher, L., & Zacks, R. T. (1988). Working memory, comprehension, and aging: A review and a new view. In G. H. Bower (Ed.), *The Psychology of Learning and Motivation* (Vol. 22, pp. 193–225). New York: Academic Press.

Horn, J. L. (1982). The theory of fluid and crystallized intelligence in relations to concepts of cognitive psychology and aging in adulthood. In F. I. M. Craik & S. Trelub (Eds.), *Aging and cognitive processes* (pp. 237–278). New York: Plenum Press.

Hultsch, D. F., MacDonald, S. W. S., & Dixon, R. A. (2002). Variability in reaction time performance of younger and older adults. *Journal of Gerontology: Psychological Sciences, 57B,* P101–P115.

Ilmarinen, J., & Louhevaara, V. (1994). Preserving the capacity to work. *Aging International, 21,* 34–36.

Jagacinski, R. J., & Flach, J. M. (2003). *Control theory for humans.* Mahwah, NJ: Erlbaum.

Jastrzembski, T., & Charness, N. (2007). The model human processor and the older adult: Parameter estimation and validation within a mobile phone task. *Journal of Experimental Psychology: Applied, 13,* 224–248.

Kline, D. W., & Scialfa, C. T. (1996). Visual and auditory aging. In J. E. Birren & K. W. Schaie (Eds.), *Handbook of the psychology of aging* (4th ed., pp. 181–203). San Diego, CA: Academic Press.

Kramer, A. F., Hahn, S., Cohen, N., Banich, M., McAuley, E., Harrison, C., et al. (1999). Aging, fitness, and neurocognitive function. *Nature, 400,* 418–419.

Kroemer, K.H.E. (2005). *"Extra-ordinary" ergonomics: How to accommodate small and big persons, the disabled and elderly, expectant mothers, and children.* Boca Raton, FL: CRC Press.

Lee, F. S., Matthews, L. J., Dubno, J. R., & Mills, J. H. (2005). Longitudinal study of pure-tone thresholds in older persons. *Ear and Hearing, 26*(1), 1–11.

Margrain, T. H., & Boulton, M. (2005). Sensory impairment. In M. L. Johnson (Ed.), *The Cambridge handbook of age and aging* (pp. 121–130). New York: Cambridge University Press.

Maylor, E. A. (2005). Age-related changes in memory. In M. L. Johnson (Ed.), *The Cambridge handbook of age and aging* (pp. 200–208). New York: Cambridge University Press.

National Research Council & Committee on the Health and Safety Needs of Older Workers. (2004). *Health and safety needs of older workers* (D. H. Wegman & J. P. McGee, Eds.). Washington, DC: National Academies Press, Division of Behavioral and Social Sciences and Education.

Nelson, E. G., & Hinojosa, R., (2006). Presbycusis: A human temporal bone study of individuals with downward sloping audiometric patterns of hearing loss and review of the literature. *Laryngoscope, 116*(9), 1–12.

Noell, C. A., & Meyerhoff, W. L. (2003). Tinnitus: Diagnosis and treatment of this elusive symptom. *Geriatrics, 58,* 28–34.

Rosenberg, I. H. (1989). Summary comments. *American Journal of Clinical Nutrition, 50,* 1231–1233.

Rogers, W. A. (2000). Aging and attention. In D. C. Park & N. Schwarz (Eds.), *Cognitive aging: A primer* (pp. 57–73). New York: Taylor & Francis.

Salthouse, T. A. (1996). The processing-speed theory of adult age differences in cognition. *Psychological Review, 103,* 403–428.

Salthouse, T. A., Rogan, J. D., & Prill, K. A. (1984). Division of attention: Age differences on a visually presented memory task. *Memory and Cognition, 12,* 613–620.

Salvendy, G. (Ed.). (1997). *Handbook of human factors and ergonomics.* New York: Wiley.

Saxon, S. V., & Etten, M. J. (2002). *Physical change and aging* (4th ed.). New York: Springer.

Sharit, J. (2006). Human error. In G. Salvendy (Ed.), *Handbook of human factors and ergonomics* (3rd ed., pp. 708–760). Hoboken, NJ: Wiley.

Steenbekkers, L. P. A., & van Beijsterveldt, C. E. M. (Eds.). (1998). *Design-relevant characteristics of ageing users.* Delft, The Netherlands: Delft University Press.

Verhaeghen, P., & Cerella, J. (2002). Aging, executive control, and attention: A review of meta-analyses. *Neuroscience and Biobehavioral Reviews, 26,* 849–857.

Visser, M., Kritchevsky, S. B., Goodpaster, B. H., Newman, A. B., Nevitt, M., Stamm, E., et al. (2002). Leg muscle mass and composition in relation to lower extremity performance in men and women aged 70 to 79: The Health, Aging and Body Composition Study. *Journal of the American Geriatrics Society, 50*, 897–904.

Wallhagen, M. I., Pettengill, E., & Whiteside, M. (2006). Sensory impairment in older adults: Part 1: Hearing loss. *American Journal of Nursing, 106*, 40–48.

Welford, A. T. (1977). Motor performance. In J. E. Birren & K. W. Schaie (Eds.), *Handbook of the psychology of aging* (pp. 450–496). New York: Van Nostrand Reinhold.

Welford, A. T. (1981). Signal, noise, performance, and age. *Human Factors, 23*, 97–109.

Ziefle, M., & Bay, S. (2006). How to overcome disorientation in mobile phone menus: A comparison of two different types of navigation aids. *Human-Computer Interaction, 32*, 393–433.

Author Index

M

MacGregor, D.G., 52, 86
MacInnis, D.J., 198, 236
MacKenzie, S.B., 225
MacPherson, S.E., 88
Macrae, C.N., 10
Madden, C.J., 180
Maddox, N.R., 193
Madrian, B.C., 121, 122, 124, 127, 132
Maguire, E.A., 14
Mankiw, N.G., 122
Mannetti, L., 78
Mano, H., 93
Marcus, G.E., 151
Mares, M.L., 180, 183
Margrain, T.H., 253
Maril, A., 10
Mark, M., 242
Markman, A.B., 136
Markus, H.R., 16, 66
Marquine, M.J., 10, 11
Marsiske, M., 14
Marson, D.C., 133
Martin-Hryniewicz, M., 80
Mason, J., 150, 151
Masuda, T., 13
Mather, M., 7, 9, 10, 16, 52, 57, 77, 87, 89, 198
Mather, N., 81
Matthews, L.J., 254
May, C.P., 8, 177, 182
May, F.E., 193
Maylor, E.A., 255
Mazzocco, K., 80
McAuley, E., 255
McAvoy, M., 11
McCracken, G., 151, 159, 164
McDowd, J.M., 5, 8
McFadden, D., 140
McFall, J., 89
McGill, A.L., 131
McGlone, F., 150
McGrew, K.S., 81
McGuire, S., 233
McInnes, M.M., 140, 141, 142
McIntosh, A.R., 6, 11

McIntyre, J.S., 134, 142
Meade, J.L., 14
Medford, N., 88
Médiamétrie, 192
Meeds, R., 176, 177
Meghir, C., 26
Mehta, C., 89
Meredith, G., 200, 237
Mergler, N.L., 183
Mertz, C.K., 79, 80, 92, 132
Messick, D.M., 230
Metrick, A., 122
Meyer, B.D., 110, 119
Meyer, B.J.F., 85
Meyerhoff, W.L., 254
Mikels, J.A., 7, 57
Miller, D., 150
Miller, E.L., 176
Mills, E.S., 242
Mills, J.H., 254
Milner, C., 241
Minear, J., 6
Miniussi, C., 6
Mitchell, O.S., 104, 110, 116
Miyake, N., 137
Modigliani, F., 26
Monterosso, J., 221
Moody, H.R., 244
Moody, R.J., 234
Moore, J., 104, 116
Moore, S., 209
Moorthy, S., 138
Moran, J.M., 10
Moran, T.P., 261
Moreau, C.P., 136
Morgan, D.H.J., 150
Morgeson, F., 209
Moroz, T.M., 10
Morrell, R.W., 92
Morris, J.C., 6
Morrow, D., 92
Moschis, G.P., 169
Moscovitch, M., 10
Moskowitz, M.A., 220
Mottram, M., 259
Moumjid, N., 133
Moye, J., 133

Subject Index